Issues of Information Communication Technology (ICT) in Education

Issues of Information Communication Technology (ICT) in Education

Editors

Dr. Shobana Nelasco
Dr. Meenu Agrawal
Dr. Austin Njiribeako Nosike

KANISHKA PUBLISHERS, DISTRIBUTORS
NEW DELHI-110 002

KANISHKA PUBLISHERS, DISTRIBUTORS
4697/5-21A, Ansari Road, Daryaganj
New Delhi-110 002
Phones : 2327 0497, 2328 8285
Fax : 011-2328 8285
E-mail : kanishka_publishing@yahoo.co.in

First Published 2009

ISBN 978-81-8457-118-9

PRINTED IN INDIA

Published by Madan Sachdeva for Kanishka Publishers, Distributors, 4697/5-21A, Ansari Road, Daryaganj, New Delhi-110 002. Typeset by Sunshine Graphics, Delhi, and Printed at Rajdhani Printers, Delhi.

Preface

"Nothing is permanent except change." In a world where change is the only constant there is a need for tools and techniques to help institutions become more effective. In a competitive world of business there is a need for ways to stay ahead or to go up before it is too late. And in a complex world there is need for mechanisms that can make apparently complicated things simpler.

This situation of continuous change, driven by informational capitalism and the neoliberal practices of privileging private interests, is also present in the educational sector. The Information Technology revolution has brought new challenges to higher education. The responsibility of institutions of higher education in the above changing scenario is not only confined to imparting education for this changing economy, but also to forecasting the future needs of this economy. The knowledge industry serving business is driven by innovation and that innovation is incubated in institutions of higher learning and research of developed countries, often marginalizing the developing world through the uneven distribution in penetration of information technology.

However, unlike in most businesses, the product of education is that of multi-skilled individuals and cohorts of students with a variety of disciplinary skills, a number of study skills, and a number of life-skills–typically formed over about twelve years of schooling and some more years of post-school education. This is a slow and complex process, and while the resources of current technologies clearly have something to offer education, these resources need to be woven into the complex web of, for example, physical, emotional and cognitive maturation; the generative authority of teachers; the need for peer interaction, cooperation and play; the need for critical thinking; and the need to give students desirable prospects in their context. So technology offers no magic wand.

At the same time, new resources of communication and information processing cannot but have implications for education: stored knowledge resources can be made much more available; there are new modes of peer and teacher-pupil communication and review; and while the core of educational learning has traditionally been focused around a classroom setting, with the advent of e-learning there is no need for physical meetings or a centralized location for the classes; and software packages with varying degrees of smartness may replace or enhance the teacher in some parts of the teaching job.

It is widely believed that the status of an education process and system in a country is an index of its future well-being. It is important to get education right, and to adapt it to the needs of our context.

This volume is a collection of contributions on Technology Enabled Education. How do various efforts to achieve this 'fit' into the prolonged and many-dimensional process of education? And how does this happen in different countries in an unequal world? And how do these approaches take account of the fact that the new technology enabled education of today often becomes outdated before its application in the field, if one accepts that every skill become outdated every three years?

This book is an adventure to provide a sharing platform of discussion for different country experts. Not only do the contributing scholars come from a wide variety of countries-most of them in the global South; the contributors address the issue of technology-enabled education from the perspective of school pupils, university students, professionals, teachers and education managers. If one had to name a focus to this set of contributions, it is perhaps on the reception of the new methods and technologies by the users, and their effectiveness. This focus of many of the contributors is important, in that it is of no use to idealize any particular technology-enabled educational tool if it does not both address human needs and fir well with other needful processes.

Contents

1

Students' Perception of Computer-Managed Package on Records Management in Nigerian Universities

Adebanjo, Adetayo Adekunle, Nigeria

Introduction

In an information-generation society such as ours, information in various for mats is being created on a daily basis by individuals and corporate bodies. These formats can be appropriately termed "records." Records and information are a corporate resource. It enables an organization to operate smoothly and achieve its goals. According to Michael (1993), record may be defined as recorded information in any form, regardless of media or characteristics. In other words, records are information resource management is a management tool, which cannot be dispensed within any organization, owing to the important role it plays in administration. Effective record keeping is sine qua non to administrative effectiveness in organizations or institution. It assures adequate documentation to make possible, rapid retrieval of information contained therein, whenever needed; secure maintenance, and lastly, the regular retirement procedures that simultaneously remove from active file the costly and confusing cluster of obsolete records and make provision for the preservation in the archives, of the small fraction of which has continuing value (Iwhiwhu, 2005).

He further revealed that for an organization or institution to operate smoothly and achieve its goal; records play an immeasurable role in administration, because managers and administrators employ it on a routine basis as an aid in carrying out diverse administrative duties especially in decision-making. The information received helps to enlighten and educate them on issues relevant to themselves and the organization (Michael, 1993).

According to Iwhiwhu, (2005). Records play a vital role in the development of mankind. Records are necessary because they contain information vital to the daily operation of a business, organization, government and associations, and as well as to the role of institutions, and private persons. Without records, for example, a business could not function. Many businesses have ceased to exist as a result of losing their records through fire, natural disaster or negligence. In the case of government agencies, loss of records, especially through fire, which is a common feature in some African countries, results in hardship to individuals and bodies dealing with those government agencies (http:/www.extension.iastate.edu/Publications/PM1452.pdf). In universities an individual may wish to prove date of birth, year of entry into the university, faculty/department it belongs, date of graduation or tax assessment for purposes of reference or identification. Failure to find a record for reference or other purpose may lead to frustration. In the business sector, failure to obtain a record often costs money and loss of goodwill. Individuals, organizations and institutions therefore need to keep complete and accurate records (Michael, 1993).

He further state that in many African countries, among the high producers of records are commercial companies, educational institutions, associations, governments and their agencies, industries, health institutions, the armed forces, etc. Naturally, the highest producer of records in African countries, as elsewhere, is government. Records are generated daily by the various levels of government, namely, federal, state and local governments, education industries and district councils. In many sectors of records generation, it is discouraging to note, records-keeping has not been given the requisite attention by organizations and individuals. In some offices filing is not done regularly; hence the problem of inability to retrieve needed records. In other offices, records are not properly taken care of and deteriorate fast or even disappear as a result of exposure to the element or through theft. Samuel and Dee (2005) revealed that the prevailing condition in school record management in Nigeria is disheartening and discouraging. The country seems to be living in prehistoric times in the educational management while even developing countries in Africa such as South Africa, Kenya, Uganda and Tanzania are far ahead of Nigeria in ICT applications. Despite its huge material resources and population endowment, Nigeria cannot be counted among progressive nations using ICT in record management, as technology has become a critical tool for achieving success in education.

Before the advent of computers and information technology, universities in Nigeria are using the traditional-paper based documentation system. Information are received, store and recorded on paper by filling it as a record. Even up till now, most universities are still managing records in physical format of paper based documentation system, which looks tasking to the students and the administrator of the universities.

University is an organization that maintains details and adequate record of students and the personnel. The academic affairs units of the registry of university are largely responsible for this task. Record management is a vital task that universities hold in sacrosanct. This information concerning students' entry qualification, biographies results mention a few. This information is equally regarded as private and confidential. Record management in universities serves various purposes.

- To make information available for taking decision on academic matters.
- To determine the historical background on an individual in the university communities.
- To make information concerning students to academic matters available for the usage of relevant organization and agencies.
- To keep information and record for future usage and reference. (Granath, Alariksson, and Axelsson, 2004).

All these can be only be achieved through appropriate registration. Therefore, there is a need for registration. Registration according to advanced learners' dictionary revised edition 1999. Is to make a rating and formal record of something in a list in other words, registration is collections of data about someone which could make him relevant to a particular organizations or enlisted as a member of an institution. These registrations are made into records which will be kept for future needs. Record keeping is a simple, easily implemented, and cost effective management tool. Complete and well organized records can help ensure proper maintenance of facilities and equipment and can aid in determining the population of the students and staffs in a university community Wright (1990). In other words, records in the university environment, comprises of registration, which involves collection of demographic data of every individual within the university setting, computation of students result, that is, collation of all the results of the students according to the department of registration to easy the issue of statement of results and transcripts to student after leaving school. Also, time-tabling which connot the resumption date, time of lectures and date of examination which also called university calendar. While record-keeping can be ascribe to filling/ storage of the records members of the university community in a separate entity for easy identification, retrieval and easy access. All these can be referred to as record management.

Changes in technology and multimedia have brought new types of records into existence. They are more difficult to identify and therefore challenge the ability of the record keepers and those who are involved in managing these records, to capture them in a static or permanent form that will enable them to provide evidence of business or administrative transactions. In traditional paper-based document systems, the media and format used for a record has been the same for the entire history of the record from creation, transmission, use, and reference, through to storage. There is no difference between preserving the form and preserving the content because of the permanent relationship between the physical format of the paper and the information it contains. For electronic documents, the media and format of information can be changed during the lifecycle of document, and the actual encoded format during authoring or creation, transmission and storage is almost certainly different in order to support the processing required at each stage (Hofman, 1999).

Abimbade (1997) described computer managed instruction as an approach involving the use of the computer in scheduling courses/ subjects, space, utilization, inventory and personnel control, recording and reporting attendance, school accounting, storage and retrieval of student information marks management (computation and reporting of marks) and word processing. He further explained that, computer managed instruction can be used to improve educational efficiency in the following areas:

- *Organization of Information:* Microcomputers can be used, for example, to categorize data on students by sex, class, state of origin, performance in school etc. The data are organized into an easily accessible format and can be easily stored in and retrieved from the microcomputer. The data on staff, facilities and finances can be similarly treated, thus, the microcomputer enable us to have electronically maintained database.

- *Computation and Processing of Paper Work:* Computation is of course the traditional function of computers. Microcomputer software and hardware enable even untrained personnel to do complex computation very rapidly and accurately. Similarly, the microcomputer, through word processing enable us to draft, revise and produce reports of high quality at least in terms of presentation without much hard labour, frustration and waste of time.
- *Improvement of Communication:* With the installation of microcomputers, there is usually a tendency for their users to interconnect them in order to promote communication linkages between microcomputers. The linkage might involve the use of telephone or fax, communication facilities.
- *Enhancement of Planning:* The database is established through the organization of data on various elements of the school pupils, staff and resources. It can be used to plan and make decisions on the basis of accurate and readily available facts.
- *Progress Monitoring:* We can use the microcomputer to monitor progress in many areas of education. That is, continuous monitoring and assessment of students learning and achievement.
- *Enhancement of Instruction:* It can also use as instruction delivery. Specifically, it is used for drill and practice, lesson, reinforcement etc. in particular, it has been found that the microcomputer is very effective in the teaching of visual recognition and linear problem solving. In other words, computer managed instruction is capable of generating, the demographic data of students and university personnel, production of results online, retrieving on lecture timetable online and enlisting of courses and registration through online.

While conventional programme can be referred to as a way of collecting of data or information on students and staffs through the filling or supplying to already programmed paper and collate together to form a record of an individual in university or in an organization. That is, is a programmed paper that designed for collection of data in order to have record of individual in an organization. Every member of the organization coming inn newly or reporting needs to fill this document in order to produce record for them.

Statement of the Problem

Most universities in Nigeria are still using the traditional paper based documentation system which slows down the method of processing of documents, filling system in keeping records, and delay processing of documents in and out of the university. Therefore, this study investigated how university students' perception of computer managed package on records management in Nigerian universities.

Research Question

Specifically the paper addressed the question.

1. What is the students' perception of computer managed packaged on record management in two universities?

Hypotheses

Two hypotheses were formulated and tested in the study. These are:

1. There is no significant difference between male and female students' perception of computer managed packages for records management.
2. There is no significant difference between the perception of OOU and Unilag students of computer managed package on record management.

The study investigated the students' perception on effectiveness of computer managed package and conventional programme on records management in Nigerian universities. The scope of this study covers two universities in two states of South-west Nigeria, (Lagos and Ogun state). Two hundred (200) students were randomly selected in each university. The study could have covered more state but due to time and financial constraints it was restricted to two states.

Research Methodology

This section focuses on the methodology that was employed in the study, which includes the research design, variables of the study, selection of participants in the study and research instrument. It also outlines the procedure as well as the statistical tools used in the study.

This study adopted the descriptive research which employed survey design to investigate the perception of students on the use of computer package for records management. It described the status quo of the variables and made rational explanation for them. The population comprised of undergraduate students in Nigerian universities.

The sample technique for this study was the stratified random sampling to select six universities in South-western Nigeria. Nigeria is divided into six geo-political zones, namely South-west, South-east, South-south, North-west, North-east and North-central zones out of which South-west zone purposively selected was for this study. The zone comprises of six states which include Ekiti, Lagos, Ogun, Ondo, Osun, and Oyo states. Also the purposive sampling technique was used to select two states: Lagos and Ogun states. Two hundred (200) students' from each university were randomly selected among the final year students' and those that have spent up to four years in the university while the remaining one hundred students' were drawn from students' in part one to three in each university.

The rationale for the choice of the participating students' is based on the facts that. In most universities in the last four years there are still using conventional mode of registration, therefore, they are exposed to this mode. While those that gained admission in the last two years were exposed to computer package of registration.

Instruments

The following instruments were be used for the study:

I. Students' Perception of Computer Managed Packages Questionnaire (SPCMPQ).
II. Conventional Record Keeping Questionnaire (CRKQ).

SPCMPQ is a self developed structured questionnaire with two sections viz., A and B.

Section A comprises of Biodata of the respondent while section B consists of 20 likert scale responded items. CRKQ was prepared by the researcher and it consists of two sections viz., A and B.

Section A: This section seeks information on demographic data of the respondents that is, gender, university name and level of studentship. Section B: This section consisted of 20 items on conventional programme of record management on a 4-point likert scale ranging from Strongly Agree (SA), Agree (A), and Disagree (D) to Strongly Disagree (SD).

The CRKQ was prepared and show to experts to access its face and content validity. It was tried out among the undergraduate students of Tai Solarin University of Education. Cronbanch was used to measure the internal consistency and a reliability value of 0.74 was obtained.

The SPCMPQ was also validated through a pilot study was conducted in the same university. Cronbach Alpha was used to measure its reliability and the value obtained is 0.76.

Procedure

The researcher took time to visit the 100 level and 200 level students during general studies (GNS) to distribute the questionnaire while the course advisers for final year students were employed to help in administer the questionnaire and collection were made at end of the day.

The data collected were analyzed using descriptive statistics such as frequency counts' means standard deviation and chi-square test.

Results

The results of the study were presented below:

Research Question 1

What is the students' perception of computer managed packaged on record management in two universities?

Table-1
Students' Perception of Computer Managed Package on Record Management

S.No.	*Statement*	*SA*	*A*	*D*	*SD*	*Mean*	*Std.*
1.	Computer package make registration easier.	117 (58.5%)	39 (19.5%)	31 (15.5%)	13 (6.5%)	3.3	.9563
2.	Registration on computer is easier and more accessible.	117 (58.5%)	39 (19.5%)	31 (15.5%)	13 (6.5%)	3.3	.9563
3.	Registration on computer saves time.	117 (58.5%)	39 (19.5%)	31 (15.5%)	13 (6.5%)	3.3	.9563

Contd...

S.No.	Statement	SA	A	D	SD	Mean	Std.
4.	Online registration is less stressful.	117 (58.5%)	39 (19.5%)	31 (15.5%)	13 (6.5%)	3.3	.9563
5.	Computer registration minimize error during registration.	117 (58.5%)	39 (19.5%)	31 (15.5%)	13 (6.5%)	3.3	.9563
6.	Registration with computer is very fast and quick.	117 (58.5%)	39 (19.5%)	31 (15.5%)	13 (6.5%)	3.3	.9563
7.	Manual registration is very reliable.	13 (5%)	31 (5.5%)	139 (19.%)	117 (58.5%)	3.3	.9563
8.	Manual registration is very boring.	117 (58.5%)	39 (19.5%)	31 (15.5%)	13 (6.5%)	3.29	.9605
9.	Manual registration is very effective than registration on computer.	117 (58.5%)	39 (19.5%)	31 (15.5%)	13 (6.5%)	3.3	.956
10.	I prefer manual to online registration.	117 (58.5%)	39 (19.5%)	31 (15.5%)	13 (6.5%)	3.3	.9563
11.	No student needs to be computer literate before he can register online.	117 (58.5%)	39 (19.5%)	31 (15.5%)	13 (6.5%)	3.3	.956
12.	Registration on line depends on availability of electricity therefore make registration unpredictable.	117 (58.5%)	39 (19.5%)	31 (15.5%)	13 (6.5%)	3.3	.956
13.	Registration online is very costly compared with manual.	13 (5%)	31 (5.5%)	139 (19%)	117 (58.5%)	3.3	.956
14.	Registration on computer requires typing skills and therefore it makes registration difficult.	13 (5%)	31 (5.5%)	139 (19%)	117 (58.5%)	3.3	.956
15.	Registration online promotes easy access to academic information.	117 (58.5%)	39 (19.5%)	31 (15.5%)	13 (6.5%)	3.3	.956
16.	Registration online is cumbersome due to information required.	117 (58.5%)	39 (19.5%)	31 (15.5%)	13 (6.5%)	3.3	.960

Contd...

S.No.	Statement	SA	A	D	SD	Mean	Std.
17.	Online registration can be done anywhere.	117 (58.5%)	39 (19.5%)	31 (15.5%)	13 (6.5%)	3.3	.956
18.	Manual registration gives authentication of the student than online registration.	13 (5%)	31 (5.5%)	139 (19%)	117 (58.5%)	3.3	.956
19.	Online registrations give room for certificate forging.	13 (5%)	31 (5.5%)	139 (19%)	117 (58.5%)	3.3	.956
20.	Computer registration is reliable.	13 (5%)	31 (5.5%)	139 (19%)	117 (58.5%)	3.3	.956
	Weighted average	3.3					

From Table 1, the study revealed that majority of the students responses tends towards agreement (SA and A) for most of the items. Specifically the means are 3.3 which are above the 2.5 middle point score. The weighted also confirmed this. Therefore, the study found that the students' have positive perception towards the computer managed package for record management, which also indicated that the students' have high perception towards computer managed package. This suggests that the students' prefer to use computer for their record processing, although some students' see the computer managed packaged as means of fraudulent act in certificate forgery.

Hypothesis 1

There is no significant difference between male and female students' perception of computer managed packaged on record management.

Table-2

Chi-square Analysis of Male and Female Perception of Computer Managed Package on Record Management

Variables	x^2	*df*	*Sig.*
Gender * Item 1	1.709[a]	3	.635
Gender * Item 2	1.709[a]	3	.635
Gender * Item 3	1.709[a]	3	.635
Gender * Item 4	1.709[a]	3	.635
Gender * Item 5	1.709[a]	3	.635
Gender * Item 6	1.709[a]	3	.635

Contd...

Variables	x^2	*df*	*Sig.*
Gender * Item 7	1.709[a]	3	.635
Gender * Item 8	2.004[a]	3	.572
Gender * Item 9	1.709[a]	3	.635
Gender * Item 10	1.709[a]	3	.635
Gender * Item 11	1.709[a]	3	.635
Gender * Item 12	1.709[a]	3	.635
Gender * Item 13	1.616[a]	3	.656
Gender * Item 14	1.616[a]	3	.656
Gender * Item 15	1.709[a]	3	.635
Gender * Item 16	2.004[a]	3	.572
Gender * Item 17	1.709[a]	3	.635
Gender * Item 18	1.616[a]	3	.656
Gender * Item 19	1.616[a]	3	.656
Gender * Item 20	1.616[a]	3	.656

NS = Not Significant at 0.05 alpha level of df = 3.

Table 2 above show that both male and female students have the same perception of computer managed packaged of record management that is, the mean scores of both male and female students in all the items indicate that they have good perception of computer managed package on record management. The implication of this is that no difference in the perception of male and female students' on computer managed package on management record. Hence the hypothesis that state there is no significant difference between male and female students' perception of computer managed packages for records management is hereby not rejected.

***Hypothesis* 2**

There is no significant difference between OOU and Unilag students' perception of computer managed package on record management.

Table 3, revealed that both students' from the two universities have positive or high perception of computer managed packaged on record management, this is because the mean score of both students' from OOU and Unilag in all the items shows that they have equal perception of computer managed on record management. This implied that there is no significance difference between the students'

Table–3

Chi-square Analysis of the Universities Students' Perception of Computer Managed Package on Record Management

Universities vs Items			
Variables	x^2	*df*	*Sig.*
Universities vs Items 1	2.207[a]	3	.531
Universities vs Items 2	2.207[a]	3	.531
Universities vs Items 3	2.207[a]	3	.531
Universities vs Items 4	2.207[a]	3	.531
Universities vs Items 5	2.207[a]	3	.531
Universities vs Items 6	2.207[a]	3	.531
Universities vs Items 7	2.207[a]	3	.531
Universities vs Items 8	2.207[a]	3	.531
Universities vs Items 9	2.207[a]	3	.531
Universities vs Items 10	2.207[a]	3	.531
Universities vs Items 11	2.207[a]	3	.531
Universities vs Items 12	2.207[a]	3	.531
Universities vs Items 13	2.582[a]	3	.461
Universities vs Items 14	2.207[a]	3	.531
Universities vs Items 15	2.800[a]	3	.424
Universities vs Items 16	2.207[a]	3	.531
Universities vs Items 17	2.582[a]	3	.461
Universities vs Items 18	2.582[a]	3	.461
Universities vs Items 19	2.582[a]	3	.461
Universities vs Items 20	2.582[a]	3	.461

NS = Not Significant at 0.05 alpha level of df = 3.

from the two universities in perception of computer managed packaged on record management.

Discussion

From the study, it can be deduced that majority of the students' have positive and high perception of computer managed package on record management. This suggests that many of these students have basic knowledge of computer; also it revealed that the students' are familiar with the use of computer packages on record management. It also shows that the students preferred to do their documentation on computer than doing it manually.

REFERENCES

Abimbade, A. (1997): *Principles and Practices of Educational Technology.* Ibadan: International Publishers Limited pg. 167.

Advanced learners dictionary (1999) Revised edition.

Barata, K. and Cain, P. (1999). Managing electronic records and managing public sector records: a study programme. London: International Records Management Trust.

Barry, R.A. (1997). Electronic records management ... the way we were ... the way we are: one man's opinion: Records Management Journal, 7(3), 157 -189.

Base: Paper presented at the Seminar on Accountability in Government in an Electronic Age, held on 25-26 June, Kuala Lumpur.

Brubach, N. (2001). Electronic records – preparing future archival professionals for.

Cain, P. (1998). Effects of the failure to manage records and the erosion of the evidence.

Canalejo, E.C. (1999). The contribution of archives to the information society: Paper presented at the DLM-Forum on Electronic Record of the European Communities, held on 18-19 October, Brussels.

COMMA: Curators and Records Managers in Africa. International Journal on Archives, 1/2, 37, 43.

Dearstyne, B. (1999). Records management of the future: anticipate, adapt and succeed.

Department of Information Services Malaysia (2003): Malaysian Official Year Book. Kuala Lumpur: Government of Malaysia.

Dherent, C. (1999). The archives of France: policy on storing electronic documents.

Directory of Archival Education and Training Institution. (2002): International Council on Archives. Retrieved March 23, 2004 from ICA web site:http://www.ica-sae.org.

Dollar, C.M. (1990) Electronic records management and archives in international organizations: In Peter Walne, Selected guidelines for the management of records and archives: a RAMP reader. Paris: UNESCO.

Duff, W. (1995): Defining transactions: to identify records and assess risk. Retrieved June 6, 2001, from University of Pittsburg web site: http://www.lis.pitt.edu/nhpr 5.html.

Duranti, L. (1996): The preservation of the integrity of electronic records. Paper presented at the DLM-Forum on Electronic Records of the European Communities, held on 18-20 December, Brussels.

Duranti, L., & MacNeil, H. (1996). The protection of the integrity of electronic records: an overview of the UBCMAS research project. Archivaria, 42, 46-67.

Duranti, L., & Thibodeau, K. (2001): The INTERPARES international research project, Information Management Journal, 35(1), 44-50.

Durrance, C. (Ed.). (1989). Management of recorded information: converging discipline. New York: K.G. Saur Verlag.

Eastwood, T. (1992): Building standards of competence for archivists: Proceedings of the Maastricht Centennial Symposium Archives and Europe without Boundaries. Janus, 1992. 2, 207-215.

Eisenbeis, K. (1995): Privatising government information: the effects of policy on access to land sat satellite data. Metuchen, New Jersey: The Scarecrow Press, Inc.Emmerson, p. (1989). What is record management? In Peter Emmerson (Ed.), How to manage your records: a guide to effective practice. Cambridge: ICSA

Enamiroro, Patrick. O. (2006): Retrieved from http://www.krepublishers.com/02-journals/JSS/JSS-13-0- 000-000-2006-Web/JSS-13-3-000-000-2006-Abst-Text/JSS-13-3-205-213-2006-391-Oghuvbu-E-P/JSS-13-3-205-213-2006-391-Oghuvbu-E-P-Text.p.

Enemute Basil, (2005): Being A Paper Presented At An International Conference On Preservation And Access For Digital College And University Resources Held At Arizona State University, Tempe. USA. February 28 – March 1, 2005.

Engel, A., & Wettengel, M. (1999). Disposition and archiving of authentic electronic records in the information network Berlin-Bonn. Paper presented at the DLM- Forum on Electronic Records of the European Communities, held on 18-19 October, Brussels.

Erlandsson, A. (1997). Electronic records management: a literature review. Paris: International Council on Archives.

European Communities, (1996): Proceedings of the DLM-Forum on Electronic Records, held on 18-20 December, Brussels.

European Communities, (1999): Proceedings of the DLM-Forum on Electronic Records, held on 18-19 October, Brussels.

Evans, F.V. (1980). The establishment of an archival regional training centre in Asia.

Fredriksson, B. (2002): The changing role of archivists in the contemporary society.

Fresko, M. (1996): Long term preservation of electronic materials. London: The British Library (Research and Development Report No. 6328). Google automatically generates html versions of documents as we crawl the web.

Government of Malaysia, (1997): Electronic government flagship application: electronic government information technology policy and standards. Retrieved June, 13, from the United Nation website:http://www. unpan1. un.org/intradoc/groups/public/document/APCITY/U NPAN015130.pdf.:Information Management Journal, 33(4), 4-19.

Granath, P., Alariksson, S., & Axelsson, S. (2004), creating a system for public information: the Swedish aid agency's transformation to electronic administration. Records Management Journal, 14(1), 25-32.

Granstrom, C. (1996): Relationship between creators, users and custodians of information. Paper presented at the DLM-Forum on Electronic Records of the European Communities, held on 18-20 December, Brussels.

Michael Afolabi, (1993): Education and Training of Archivists, Manuscript New and dynamic tasks: Paper presented at the European Conference for Archival Educators and Trainers, held on 24-25 September, Marburg, Germany.

2

Effects of Computer Assisted Instruction on the Achievement among Students

Dr. K. Anandan, India

The present day students are being influenced by a number of new media such as TV, Video, Computer etc. Among all other media, computer has been accepted as an important tool to amplify the learning capacity. The large amount of information stored in computer is made available to the learner more rapidly. The dynamic interaction between the student and instructional programme is possible through computer than any other media. The excessive verbalism in the conventional method of teaching has lost its efficacy and students' interest in subject.

According to Batra (1989), Computer Assisted Instruction (CAI) refers to a learning situation in which student interacts with (and is guided by) a computer through a course of study aimed at achieving certain instructional goals. Kulkarni (1986) stated that aids like chalkboard, charts etc. Radio and television went further and broke the walls of a classroom and took over many functions which no human teacher can ever perform and that too at a place and time convenient to the learner.

Review of Related Studies

Since the usage of computer for classroom instruction is less popular in the schools in India and its development is in initial stage, only few studies at Ph.D. and M. Phil. level have been conducted. Studies conducted in Science (Natchimuthu, 1986; Shilaja and Lalitha, 1986; Chandra, 1987; Mohan, 1987; Singha, 1988) and studies done in Mathematics (Sharma, 1979; Sivaraj, 1988; Palaniappan, 1989; Stella, 1989) showed that CAI made more effective achievement of the students' in Indian context.

Notable studies and projects have been reported in many of the countries like United Kingdom, USSR, Germany, Japan, Denmark, Ireland etc. CAI students' score higher than the control group students in more studies (Tailor, 1980; Pamela, 1983; Abraham and Sandma, 1984; Ester, 1984; Opera and Mika, 1984; Porincheck, 1984; Saesar and John, 1984; Delton, 1985 and Maxhensy, 1985).

Need for the Study

Many Aided and Matriculation Schools in India are already having computers and have started to use CAI. The State and Central Government are giving much concentration in integrating computers for classroom instructions in government institutions, particularly rural institutions. The measures taken by the government reveal that it tries to make use of the advantages of CAI found in different studies conducted abroad and in India.

The present investigator felt that there was a need to conduct a study to measure the effectiveness of CAI in the existing conditions over the conventional methods of instruction in our country. Economics, being the investigator's major subject in post graduation, the study was conducted in measuring effectiveness of CAI in Economics.

Objectives of the Study

The major objective of the study was to find out the effectiveness of CAI in Indian Economics of 11th Standard English Medium students'. The specific objectives were:

- *(i)* To construct and validate a criterion test and CAI package in Indian Economics.
- *(ii)* To find out the effect of CAI package on the achievement in the components, namely, knowledge, comprehension and application in Indian Economics.
- *(iii)* To find out the effect of CAI package on achievement after keeping intelligence and socio-economic status of 11th Standard students as covariates.

Methodology

The nature of the experiment was Pre-post Equivalent Group Design. Teaching of Indian Economics through CAI for 11th Standard was independent variable and achievement in Indian Economics was the dependent variable. The co-variates in the study were intelligence and socio-economic status of the students. Group test of Ahuja and socio-economic status of Kuppusamy were used. Two experimental groups, namely, Experimental-I and Experimental-II had the student strength of 19 and 14. The strength of the Control Group was 34. Achievement Test in Indian Economy (ATIE) was constructed and validated by the investigator for measuring the dependent variable. Duration of the experiment was 12 weeks.

Development of Criterion Referenced Test

In order to measure the dependent variable, Achievement Test in Indian Economy (ATIE) was developed. Investigator decided to have multiple choice items. The framed items were on three levels, namely, Knowledge, Comprehension and Application according to Blooms (1954). Mainly correct answer type and the best answer type items were developed for the present study. After the investigator was himself satisfied with the items prepared, it was shown to two economics teachers of 11th Standard and two teacher educators for verifying the suitability of the items for the target students. After carrying out the additions and deletions of items, there were 95 items in all the 10 units in Indian Economics. All the items were cyclostyled and administered to the sample for item analysis. According to the norms pointed out by Ebles (1966) and Marshall and Hales (1971), 75 items were selected as 24, 25 and 26 for the components of Knowledge, Comprehension and Application respectively. Split-half method was followed to find the reliability of the tool. It was found to be 0.86 which showed a high reliability of the tool.

Development of CAI Software

The development of CAI package consisted of two phases: *(i)* development of Programmed Learning Material (PLM) in Indian Economics for 11th Standard students, and *(ii)* converting the developed PLM in CAI.

First the list of ideas to be taught under the topics selected was prepared. The ideas thus collected were arranged in sequence. Based on the sequence, each idea was considered for the development of the frame. The number of teaching frames were-94, testing frames-20, bar diagrams-2, pie diagrams-2. While constructing frames different types of frames were prepared. After completing the first draft of all the frames, a thorough review was made followed by editing. It was edited in three phases, viz., Technical Accuracy edit, Programming Technical edit and Composition edit. Then it was cyclostyled for individual try-out. After carrying out the classifications it was again cyclostyled and administered for group try-out. With the revisions made as the result of the group try-out, field try-out was conducted.

The developed PLM was converted into CAI package. The BASIC Language was selected for developing the CAI. One can select his own topic from the menu presented in a frame by pressing the appropriate serial number of the units to be learnt. After taking his own time to read the content in the frame, he has to press any key in the key-board. Now the student has to respond to the question by taking either in capital or small letter. The answer will be checked by the computer. If the answer is correct, it will say, 'Good' you can proceed. If the responded answer is wrong, computer will say, 'answer is wrong'. Then the same frame will be presented again to read the content carefully. The CAI package was tested among 10 students of Kendra Vidyalaya, Madurai. Eight students scored around 85 per cent while the other two scored around 75 per cent. From this, it was surmised that the developed software was valid for external use.

Data Analysis

The investigator wanted to find out whether there was any significant difference in the mean achievement in Indian Economics between the pairs of groups. For that, t-test was applied. The results of the same pre presented in Table 1.

Table–1
Significance of Difference of Means of Achievement in Indian Economics between Control and Two Experimental Groups (ATIE-t-TEST)

S.No.	*Groups*	*N*	*Mean*	*SD*	*'t' value*	*df*
1.	Control	34	30.1471	3.3767	10.3614**	51
	Experimental-I	19	40.4737	3.4216		
2.	Control	34	30.1471	3.3767	5.2021**	46
	Experimental-II	14	38.6426	4.8613		

** Significant at 0.01 level.

The t-values of 10.3614 with df 51 and 5.2821 with df 46 in Table 1 are considered to be significant at 0.01 level. From the observation of the means achievement, the achievement of two Experimental groups is superior than the Control group.

Table-2
Significance of Difference in Achievement in the Components of Indian Economics Among Control and Two Experimental Groups (ATIE-'t'-TEST)

S.No.	Groups	N	Mean	SD	't' value	df
1.	**Knowledge**					
	(a) Control	34	10.3824	2.4743	10.1802**	51
	Experimental-I	19	16.8421	1.9794		
	(b) Control	34	10.3824	2.4743	6.4029**	46
	Experimental-II	14	15.7143	2.8670		
2.	**Comprehension**					
	(a) Control	34	8.3235	1.7705	8.0480**	51
	Experimental-I	19	12.2105	1.5839		
	(b) Control	34	8.3235	1.7705	4.4087**	46
	Experimental-II	14	11.2857	2.1636		
3.	**Application**					
	(a) Control	34	11.4706	1.8461	0.8909 NS	51
	Experimental-I	19	11.4211	1.9527		
	(b) Control	34	11.4706	1.8761	0.2795 NS	46
	Experimental-II	14	11.6429	1.8650		

** Significant at 0.01 level; NS-Not Significant.

It is inferred from Table 2 that the Control group students stay behind significantly from Experimental group-I and Experimental group-II students' in their achievement in Indian Economics for the two components, namely, Knowledge and Comprehension. But for the component of application under achievement in Indian Economics, there is no significant difference between the pairs of the sample groups of students. The t-values of 0.8909 with *df* 51 and 0.2795 with *df* 46 are not significant.

In order to find out the level of significance of mean differences on the achievement in the components of Indian Economics after adjusting the initial differences on Intelligence among the pairs of the sample groups of 11th Standard students, t-test was used. Table 3 presents the result of the analyses.

The observed t-values of 8.3916, 6.6708, 6.1259 and 3.8172 in Table 3 between Control group and Experimental group-I and Control group and Experimental group-II for the components of Knowledge and Comprehension are found to be significant at 0.01

level. There is no significant difference on the adjusted means for the component of application under means achievement in Indian Economics.

Table-3

Significance of Difference in Achievement in the Components of Indian Economics after Adjusting Intelligence Between Control and Two Experimental Groups

S.No.	*Groups*	*N*	*Myx adjusted*	*'t' value*	*df*
1.	**Knowledge**				
	(*a*) Control	34	10.38	8.3916**	51
	Experimental-I	19	16.38		
	(*b*) Control	34	10.38	6.6708**	46
	Experimental-II	14	15.71		
2.	**Comprehension**				
	(*a*) Control	34	8.33	6.1259**	51
	Experimental-I	19	12.21		
	(*b*) Control	34	8.23	3.8172**	46
	Experimental-II	14	11.28		
3.	**Application**				
	(*a*) Control	34	11.44	0.0280 NS	51
	Experimental-I	19	11.42		
	(*b*) Control	34	11.44	0.2503 NS	46
	Experimental-II	14	11.64		

** Significant at 0.01 level; NS: Not Significant.

The observed t-values of 9.0667, 6.7344, 5.4512, 3.8817 with df of 51 and 46 (Table 4) respectively for the components, such as, Knowledge and Comprehension between Control group and Experimental group-I and Control group and Experimental group-II are found to be significant at 0.01 level. But the t-values of 0.0362 with df of 51 and 0.3241 with df of 46 for the component of Application after adjusting the initial differences of socio-economics status are not found to be significant.

Findings

(*i*) From the perusal of the data analysis, it was found that CAI had produced significant positive effect on the achievement on Indian Economics when compared with traditional method.

Table-4
Significance of Difference of Means in Achievement in the Components of Indian Economics after Adjusting Socio-Economic Status Between Control and Two Experimental Groups

S.No.	*Groups*	*N*	*Myx adjusted*	*'t' value*	*df*
1.	**Knowledge**				
	(*a*) Control	34	10.36	9.0661 **	51
	Experimental-I	19	16.83		
	(*b*) Control	34	10.36	6.7344**	46
	Experimental-II	14	15.73		
2.	**Comprehension**				
	(*a*) Control	34	8.31	5.4512**	51
	Experimental-I	19	12.20		
	(*b*) Control	34	8.31	3.8817**	46
	Experimental-II	14	11.29		
3.	**Application**				
	(*a*) Control	34	11.44	0.0362 NS	51
	Experimental-I	19	11.46		
	(*b*) Control	34	11.44	0.3241 NS	46
	Experimental-II	14	11.64		

** Significant at 0.01 level; NS: Not Significant.

(*ii*) It was found that significant favourable achievement was made in the components of Knowledge and Comprehension but not in Application.

(*iii*) It was also observed that there were significant differences favouring CAI even after controlling the intelligence and socio-economic status of the students.

Educational Implications

As the study has demonstrated that CAI produced significant positive difference in the achievement upon the Knowledge and Comprehension aspects, CAI can be confidently used as an effective technique of teaching for Knowledge and Comprehension aspects of Indian Economics to the Higher Secondary students. As the availability of computers in schools is increasing, the CAI technique could be good alternative to the lecture method. The government can prepare and distribute the validated software to the schools to enjoy the maximum return on the investment made on education.

REFERENCES

Abraham, Sandma (1984) The effect of CAI on first grade Phonics & Mathematic Achievement Computations. *Dissertation Abstract International*, Michigan : University Microfilms International, Vol. 45, No. 04, October.

Chandra, S., (1987) Comparative study of effectiveness using computer and CCTV for instruction in Science for IX standard pupils, *M. Phil. Thesis*, Coimbatore: Bharathiar University.

Dalton, L.B., (1986) The Effects of Different Amounts of Computer Assisted instruction on the Biology achievement and attitudes of High School students. *Dissertation Abstracts International*, Michigan: University Microfilms International, Vol. 47, No. 1, July, p. 141-A.

Ebels Robert L., (1966) *Measuring Educational Achievement*, New Delhi : Prentice Hall of India Pvt. Ltd. p. 319 and 364.

Mohan, R., (1987) Mobile computer assisted instruction for inservice teacher education, *Journal of Technology Systems*, p. 2(4), 305-313.

Mukhopadyay, P.M., (1989) Low Cost PC: Boon to Computer Education, *Educational Technology*, November, Vol. 2, No. 6.

Nachimuthu, K., (1989) Development of Computer Assisted Instruction Program *M. Phil. Thesis*, Madurai Kamaraj University.

Palaniappan, V.P., (1988) Computer and Education, *Educational Technology*, December.

Stella, M., (1989) Development of CAI on Number sets for VII standard students, *M. Phil. Thesis*, Coimbatore : Bharathiar University.

Tailor, R.P., (1980) *The Computer in the School, Tutor, Tool, Turee:* Teachers College Press, New York.

3

TYPO3–e Government-O.S.I.R.I.S. Open Source Based Integrated Regional Information System for Virtual Town Halls

Andreas Beckar, Thailand
Dr. Austin Njiribeako Nosike, Spain

eGovernment is IN. Many Communities try to get there wide range of services online. Most of them invest huge sums in expensive unextended (by free) systems instead of using an approved open source enterprise CMS. TYPO3 offers its users not only a complete eGovernment system but also an excellent training and support community. As TYPO3 and its eGovernment Extension "civserv" are Open Source no costs will be caused by the software itself.

Since the 90's civserv has been developed by Muenster University. Since 2004 it is developed by citeq. Missing software support for eGovernment services often causes problems installing virtual town. With O.S.I.R.I.S. you can also integrate services of Counties and Provinces into local virtual town halls.

Also the coordination of information in a recent visual context causes problems. Using O.S.I.R.I.S. Communities will be enabled to manage their information and design by themselves.

O.S.I.R.I.S. will be delivered with a complete CSS-design and can run in a single or multi-client setting. This means more then only one community can run on the same O.S.I.R.I.S. System and still each community can have their own layout.

As TYPO3 and MySQL support UTF8 it is full suitable for Asian languages.

TYPO3 – A Short Introduction

TYPO3 is an Enterprise Content Management System which predestines itself for the use in public institutions and smaller and large Enterprises. It is Open Source with a GNU licence and developed by thousands of developers which have been mainly located in European Countries. Meanwhile big TYPO3 Enterprises have been established in India, China, Brazil, and the US. LisAndi Co. Ltd. located in Phuket promotes TYPO3 in Thailand and offers various services and packages. More and more companies and NGO Organisations as well as private people use TYPO3 to present themselves online.

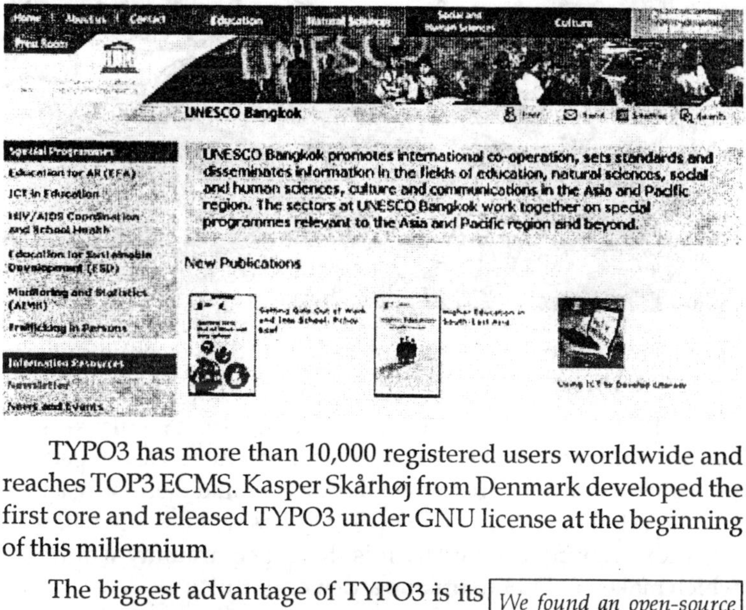

TYPO3 has more than 10,000 registered users worldwide and reaches TOP3 ECMS. Kasper Skårhøj from Denmark developed the first core and released TYPO3 under GNU license at the beginning of this millennium.

The biggest advantage of TYPO3 is its graphical and multilingual abilities and the strict separation from structure, design and content. Its huge worldwide community helps to support beginners and advanced users. A TYPO3 User Group for South-east Asia named ThaiPo3 has been established by UNESCO Bangkok and Andreas Becker in 2005. ThaiPo3 is having several workshops and seminars throughout the year, mostly held in Bangkok or Phuket.

We found an open-source content management system called Typo3, which is an enterprise CMS that rivals commercial products costing $60,000. A local firm in Colorado with experience on the LAMP platform customized it for Typo3. (Kent Morrison – Steamboat Springs)

eGovernment with TYPO3

TYPO3 is used in many Communities around the world (TYPO3 eGovernment 2007).

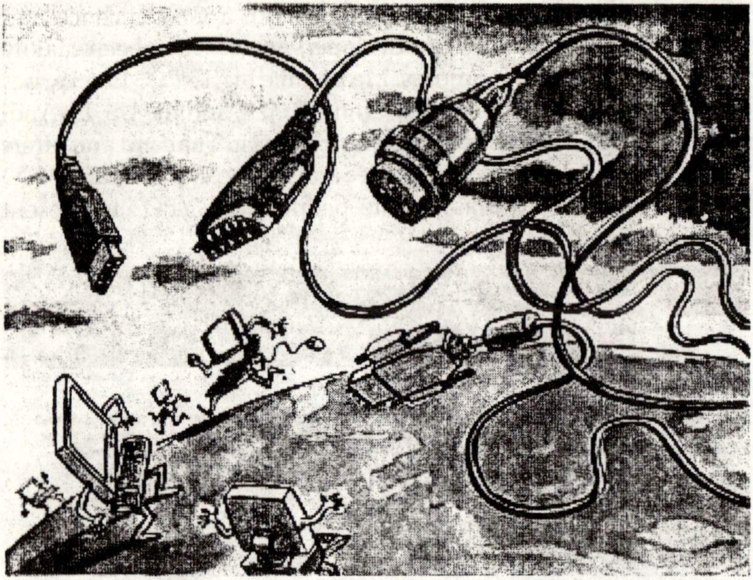

Steamboat Springs in US-Colorado based their community site on TYPO3 (Marson 2006).

TYPO3 gives communities independence from regular and cost intensive updates circles of commercial products. Developed and published extensions are under GNU licence and therefore easily to be integrated into all other TYPO3 websites without any follow up costs for i.e., updates. Finally it is the big community worldwide which makes TYPO3 so unique and wonderful.

Meanwhile complete TYPO3 package solutions like those from Web Empowered Church (Web Empowered Church 2007) (developed in USA) or T3Pack.com (Becker 2008) (developed by LisAndi Co.Ltd./Thailand) help beginners and advanced users to deploy TYPO3 websites instantly.

Both are using the futuristic TYPO3 TemplaVoila Templating Machine accompanied with already installed and configured common extensions like News, Blog, Forum, iCalendar, Staff Directory, Guest book, Gallery, GoogleMaps and more.

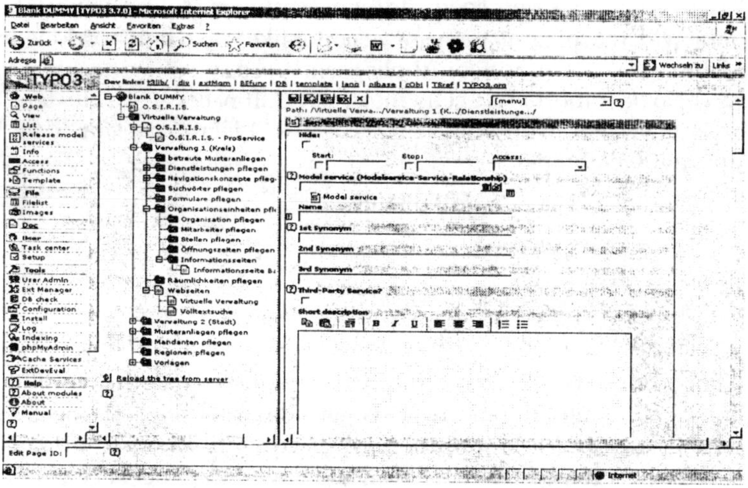

Those packages are a great start for any TYPO3 website. "Civserv" a TYPO3 eGovernment extension can be integrated easily. Communities could have their complete website and their eGovernment systems running within the same base system. No extra training will be necessary for the editors and administrators.

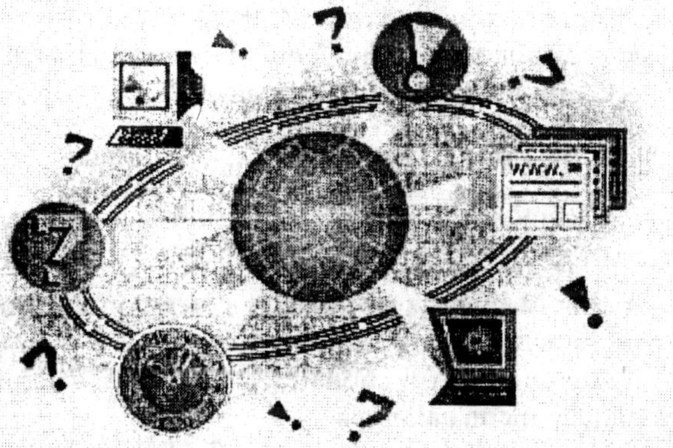

TYPO3 offers a decided User Management System and Versioning, Work flow and Workspaces. The access to each site and content element can be restricted to its specific needs by persons and by tasks. Intranet and worldwide web applications can be managed in the same site. TYPO3 is capable to integrate other existing databases (i.e., Oracle, Postgres, ...) using the dbal or adodb interface.

Institutions won't need additional software. All editing can be done with the integrated wysiwyg editor like you where working in a common Word-processor Application. Word and office documents can also be imported directly into TYPO3. If necessary a clustered TYPO3 System using different servers will increase security and uptime availabilities.

The basic system requirements:

- Apache Server
- PHP5.2
- MySQL4/5
- ImageMagick or GraphicsMagick

In times where huge financial resources aren't available anymore, Open Source products get more and more in focus of enterprises and communities. Most communities are already standing with the back to the wall and have empty pockets. On the other hand there is a need for them to present their communities and offer services online. An informativ Touristik site can attracts people from all around the world and local people will enjoy the easiness and availability of eGovernment 24/7 services. TYPO3 can offer you both.

Websites need to be maintained as nobody will visit websites which provides no updated data. Without any additional software TYPO3 can be edited from anywhere as long as an internet access is available. Communities with a slow internet connection could also use a local TYPO3 System which regularly synchronizes its data with an online TYPO3 System i.e., during nighttime automatically.

The system itself needs to qualify with the following characteristics:

- It should be able to manage a large amount of text and multimedia content.
- It needs other functionalities like news, calendar, event-management, gallery, ...
- Citizens need to be able to find the right partner to communicate with i.e. A staff register could help.
- Formular should be available online for reading and editing.
- In western countries like US and Germany websites also need to fulfill certain criteria for Accessibility. Since 2006 all Community websites in Germany need to be accessible also for people with disabilities.

- The design of a website "opens the eyes" of the clients and interests them. Therefor the system should offer easy templating and CSS designing. I should present all content in a CI – Look and Feel.
- Community workers are no IT Professionals, so the system should offer them an easy access to maintain and process their information data and content.
- The system should be expendable with multilingual content and offer full UTF8 support.
- It should be possible to integrate or communicate with other web applications.
- Its hould be a secure system which offers a modern and secure user management and work flow system.
- It should be capable to integrate also community features like a forum or online support live chat.

TYPO3 has got a backend where the content gets created, edited-maintained and the frontend where it has presented. We have backend and frontend users who can be registered. The backend user don't need any programming knowledge to maintain his information data. A context sensitiv help systems eases the usability.

O.S.I.R.I.S.

Open Source based Integrated Regional Information System forms O.S.I.R.I.S.

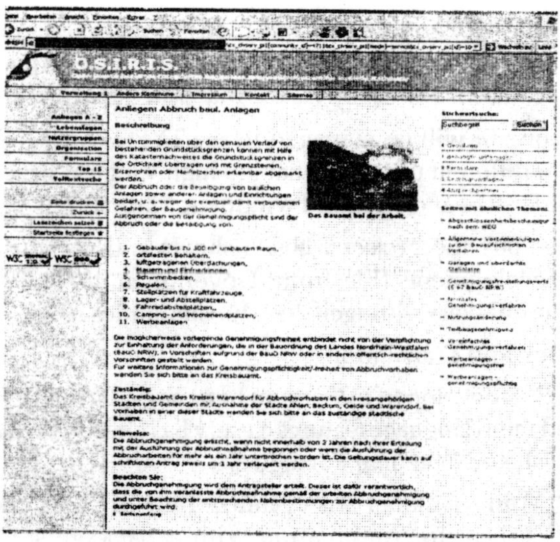

It is developed on TYPO3 base in Germany by University Muenster and Citeq – the communal service provider of the town Muenster. The TYPO3 Extension inheriting O.S.I.R.I.S. is called "civserv". A virtual town hall which offers its services for citizens online in the internet.

O.S.I.R.I.S. fulfils all SAGA (Standards and Architectures for Governmental Applications) standards. It is also conform to BITV (Federal Ordinance on Barrier-Free Information Technology 2008) standards, accessible also for visitors with disabilities.

It integrates connectors to OSCI-Format, a XML format to exchange data and is able to integrate a virtual post office and portal server.

Through the image of the entire service offering, detailed contact data or online forms, O.S.I.R.I.S. fulfilled a number of demands on the user side.

The process time is shortened by electronic forms which simplify the process data. The complete presentation is uniform with a usable and accessible navigation.

It is possible to manage several clients in one O.S.I.R.I.S. system. This reduces doubled workload, and increases accessibility for visitors and will increase also the content quality. Sub Districts can be integrated with same CI or their own one.

It enables governmental institutions to share content virtually even over province and district borders. Customisations of new formular can be made easily via the integrated real text editor.

All content will be managed in the TYPO3 backend. Storage folders for different purposes enable a highly logical structure like a page/folder tree and standard windows, Mac or linux systems.

Since 2004 the project website shows and demonstrates the newest developments (Electronic Government in Organisationen der Kommunalverwaltungen des Münsterlandes 2007).

Adaptation and Translation

O.S.I.R.I.S. is developed in German Language, but as TYPO3 offers very good multi language features civserv has already been translated into Danish and Brazilian Portuguese.

TYPO3 in Version 4.2 is optimized for PHP 5.2 and up and supports UTF8. In combination with a package solution like described above (i.e., T3Pack) "civserv" will be able to show its full power and glance. The T3Pack Package contains all necessary extensions and can be enhanced with even more features. It will be supported here in Asia (LisAndi Co. Ltd., Phuket), the ultimate TYPO3 user group in South-east Asia "ThaiPo3" and also by Workshops (i.e., given at UNESCO, Bangkok).

As the Packages from Web Empowered Church and T3Pack are well coordinated templates and extensions can be shared and modified easily. Some Hope Churches in Thailand started to use TYPO3 as a base and also the schools website "Rajaprajanugroh. com" is based on T3Pack. The TYPO3 Core parts are already available in Thai and many other Asian Languages. Extensions can be translated with an integrated translation tool (T3Pack). As T3Pack is developed also for purposes of UNESCO, Bangkok its extensions and templates get optimized for Asian needs which integrates the use of RTL (Arabic, Hebrew, ...) and LTR support. It is fully UTF-8 and can display any Asian language.

Communities in Tourist Regions will be able to maintain multilingual sites. Together with LisAndi Co. Ltd. a translation service will be formed to help communities, churches and commercial business owners to build and organise multilingual TYPO3 sites.

Vision

Combined with its good SEO features and a well organised multi domain site structure TYPO3 can help communities to receive better search engine ranking and therefore more people looking at their sites resulting in more customers hopefully.

Communities will be able to build complex Community websites using only one System for all. This will reduce time for training officers and employers immense as well as costs for updates (0), administration and future developments.

Using TYPO3 for websites will enable communities to bundle all their efforts to one. Community Services, Governmental Services as well as touristic serves, a job board, several online market places, shops and communicational tools like a Forum can be managed in one system.

Extensions which have been developed for one TYPO3 site could be integrated and customized in other TYPO3 sites. The global community of developers and users is fast growing. It makes community and TYPO3 users more independent. Upgrades and bugs will be resolved much faster – normally there is no need for awaiting a new release like in most high cost software products. Support is available all around the globe. TYPO3 is gaining more and more attention in Asia.

REFERENCES

Becker, Andreas. *TYPO3 for All.* 2008. http:/t3pack.com (accessed 09 01, 2008).

Electronic Government in Organisationen der Kommunalverwaltungen des Münsterlandes. 2007. http://www.regiokomm.de (accessed 09 01, 2008).

Federal Ordinance on Barrier-Free Information Technology. 2008. http://www.einfach-fuer-alle.de/artikel/bitv_english/ (accessed 09 01, 2008).

Marson, Ingrid. *Rocky Mountain high for open source.* 2006. http://news.zdnet.com/2100-9593_22-6043049.html (accessed 09 01, 2009).

TYPO3 eGovernment. 2007. http://www.t3gov.de/1191.0.html (accessed 09 01, 2008).

Web Empowered Church. 2007. http://www.webempoweredchurch.org (accessed 09 01, 2009).

4

In Support of Technological Developments on Educational Communication and the Feel Bad Factors for the Marginalized Class: A Study

Arjun Das, India

Due to rapid advancement of science and technology it has brought tremendous opportunities for the development of education and education related communication in the era of globalization. No doubt present day higher education is handicapped without having modern communication aids that too in a big country like India. Education plays an important role and it is the backbone for a nation. In a democratic country like India education can play the key role towards advancing knowledge so as to maintain healthy democratic spirit and values among cross-section of people. Our education policy and prospect should be framed in such a way so that it touches upon the heart and mind of the mass people enabling them to join for the nation building activities. At no point people should feel isolated from attaining higher education. In this regard it is observed that the benefit of higher education now goes to a section of people who can afford the financial liabilities and thereby grasp the opportunities that has been brought by the economic liberalization. On the other hand a large section of meritorious people cannot afford higher education because of financial disadvantages and they feel deprived. In this context this paper is an attempt to analyze various factors leading to the disparity that has been created in the field of higher education for the urban elite and the rural mass. And at the same time the paper is also an attempt to study the technological advancement and opportunities so far educational communication is concerned as we need to take a fresh look for the entire educational system in the context of ongoing globalization. We need inputs from all to make concrete progress in the field of education because in the context of globalization education assumes a greater meaning. It is more so because greatness of a nation should not be measured by its ranking in global economic power, but by its ability to provide quality education which can ultimately safeguard the national interest. Here in lies the importance of this present chapter.

I

With the process of globalization, knowledge economy gains momentum in the decade of 1980s. Since then large-scale changes are taking place in the higher education sector both at national and international arena. Considering the positive agenda for higher education more than 5000 participants and representatives of more than 180 countries at the World Conference on Higher Education, adopted a declaration and action plan. Those are perceived in many countries as the guidelines for concrete action and reforms in the field of higher education, including its internationalization keeping in mind that higher education must serve sustainable development and must help to build a better society or, as it would be said today, to build a fair globalization, which all societies in the world deserve. Higher education exists to serve the public interest and is not a commodity, a fact that WTO Member States have recognized through UNESCO and other international or multilateral bodies, convention, and declarations which states:

"The mission of higher education is to contribute to the sustainable development and improvement of society as a whole by: Education highly qualified graduates able to meet the needs of all sectors of human activity; advancing, creating and disseminating knowledge through research; interpreting, preserving , and promoting cultures in the context of cultural pluralism and diversity; providing opportunities for higher learning throughout life; contributing to the development and improvement of education at all levels; and protecting and enhancing civil society by training young people in the values which form the basis of democratic citizenship and by providing critical and detached perspectives in the discussion of strategic choices facing societies. Given this public mandate, authority to regulate higher education must remain in the hands of competent bodies as designated by any given country. Nothing in international trade agreements should restrict or limit this authority in any way."

In the light of the above if we consider the Indian scenario in higher education we find that though India claims to have the second largest education system in the world, in view of its vast population it is regarded as one of the backward countries in respect of education, especially higher education. India, with a population of more than a billion (the second largest in the world) has a tremendous potentiality of human resources and a large potential market provided higher education is imparted and extended minimizing the rural urban gap so far using Information and Communication Technology (ICT) is concerned. India started implementation of ICT during the decade of the 1980s and could witness the rapid development of its software industry contributing significantly to the world ICT market. But the rapid development of its software market has not been matched by other ICT sectors such as hardware or telecommunications. Also all regions have not been a part of this massive software boom. All this implies that there exists a Digital Divide in India. Geographical diversity and divergent economic policies among the states have perhaps fuelled this digital divide. However, there has been no serious attempt to measure the extent of digital divide among different states of India. In the present global context there remains hardly a more topical issue than the impact of technology on society. But the key challenge facing decision-makers is how to harness the potential of these revolutionary technologies to the complex goals of human development and education. Not surprising, therefore, that investment in education emerges as a major priority for political leadership anywhere, raising in its wake questions about reform and innovations needed in education, underlined with how to spread the benefits of improved relevance efficiency and value for investment of education to all citizens. It is also concerned in this context that previous investments in technologies such as language laboratories, radio and educational television of new ICTs and their promise of more cost effective and feasible solutions to the problems of education for the deprived and marginalized can raise justifiable skepticism.

Nevertheless, there is unanimous agreement that in the face of the inexorable advance of the knowledge and information age stimulated by the rapid developments in ICT, changes in education are inevitable with quantum leaps in investments in integrated solutions using technology for education.

II

Due to rapid convergence of educational technologies such as computer, CD-Rom, audio-video and web conferencing, high speed internet, broadband and television for instance all these has made possible to develop learning into a reality in the age of science and technology. The digital world today enables children to learn anything from mathematics to music from teachers across the country and the globe. Students' in higher education can attend lectures and tutorials from their homes and community centres; youngsters with profound disabilities have found unprecedented inclusion as universities and colleges have built learning networks opening new opportunities for home-makers just as educational software and digital collections have reinvented museums and libraries. However, the challenges today are not about technology itself but relate to the role of technology in promoting systemic change in education and how it can enhance the way we deal with key issues of access and equity, management and efficiency, pedagogy and quality as we prepare citizens for an era of globalization dominated by technologies related to knowledge, information and communication with its innovating ways of producing, storing, transmitting, accessing and using knowledge and information. Technology only acquired value to the extent that it proves useful for and is beneficial to human purposes. In the context of education, nothing is more important than the need for sound policies and pragmatic strategies relating to investment in technology for education.

In the changing scenario in the global context the knowledge and information is now widely accepted as a new form of wealth, a driving force for the development of individuals, communities and nations. The challenge, therefore, is to enable the population in general to have access to the skills for coping with and the ability to function effectively in this age of information and knowledge, empowering them thereby with improved life chances and quality of life. The adoption of the knowledge-based society by the Indian society has increased the gap between the 'haves' and the 'have-nots' in India. The financial and consultancy assistance by the World Bank and various international organizations that were embraced by the Indian Government in 1991 were taken hostage by the middle class to benefit itself while further displacing people of lower classes, lower castes and women. According to the World Bank, as of 2001, approximately 433 million people are living on less than US$1 per day in India, which includes 36 per cent of the total poor in the world (World Bank 2001). The gap between the haves and the haves-not continued to increase at such a rate that since 1991 it has become more difficult for the less fortunate to break the hold the upper and middle class have on the economic and social dominancy of the Indian society. One area in particular that the middle class has utilized to control the inequalities based on class, caste, and gender has been the higher education sector.

III

The divide between the urban and rural has at times been synonymous with the divide between the middle class and the people of lower classes, lower castes and women. Based on numbers alone, according the 2001 census of India, the population of India is 1,027,015,247; where 741,660,293 live in the rural areas and 285,354,954 live in the urban areas. Since the liberalization of the economy took place in 1991, in addition to the reforms of the higher education sector, the income gap between rural-urban and the have and have-nots have increased many fold. The emphasis from the Indian Government to provide all necessary resources to the middle classes and the IT sector has allowed them to move forward, but it has also forced the people living in the rural areas to wait for these benefits and resources to trickle down to them. And because of this process, people in these areas, majority of which are people of lower classes, lower castes and women, have been left behind the middle class and India's stride towards becoming a knowledge-based society and modernization. It is a fact that IT sector has contributed to students' from an elite-urban background in their pursuit to gain employment outside of India, instead of focusing on assisting the less fortunate or the marginalized class with their economic and social hardships. Perhaps because of the above phenomenon from 1991 onwards the Indian Government continued to be influenced by the middle class more vigorously and therefore, the rural-urban gap has not only been sustained but has increased since India's adoption of a liberalized economy and the knowledge-based society in 1991. And with this transition, two factors have come into play that has assisted in the gap between the middle class and people of lower classes, lower castes and women, in addition to the rural-urban divide to increase, these are the continual lack of higher education institutions within rural areas and the digital divide.

Among other third world developing countries the digital divide is far more than a gap in access to ICT in India so far its population strength is concerned. It is a major impediment to the social and economic development of poor nations. In the twenty-first century, knowledge and information and a highly skilled labor force are increasingly important determinants of growth in the global economy. Since ICT has already revolutionized economic life and business in the industrialized countries and is transforming these societies in equally profound ways. It has become an identified fact that ICT is a key weapon in the war against world poverty. When used properly, it offers huge potential to empower people in developing countries to overcome development obstacles, to address the most important social problems they face, and to strengthen communities, democratic institutions, a free press, and local economies.

It is a matter of concerned that in India the development of information and communications technology is increasing the gap between the rich and the poor, the knowledgeable and the knowledge deprived, the information rich and the information poor. Instead of closing the divide, the introduction of more ICT exacerbates social and economic divides- not only between rich and poor countries, but also among various socioeconomic groups within countries. It is a fact that there are stark differences in access across the world according to gender, geography, income, education, age, occupation, and even ethnicity and race. So the groups with the greatest access to new information and communications technology are generally well-educated, high income urban males. For example, in India the poor illiterate females in rural areas are least likely to have access to ICT and herein fails our policy makers to adopt comprehensive decision in the higher education sector for ICT so as to minimize the differences between urban elite and rural mass. No doubt the global dimensions of the digital divide are most prominent in education. At the beginning of the twenty-first century many industrialized countries had begun to gear up their education systems for the knowledge economy by making major investments in computers for classrooms, in networking their schools, and in training teachers to use technology in their teaching. But in contrast most of the developing countries including India with few exceptions, were more concerned with very difficult educational issues such as low primary and secondary school enrollments, inadequately trained teachers, little or no access to textbooks, and ineffective school management rather that with improving ICT. The exceptions were a small number of countries in Asia, Latin America, and other parts of the developing world that began introducing computers in classrooms, networking schools, and developing digital content to address the educational requirements of the global knowledge economy. Among Asian countries, Singapore, Malaysia, Korea, China, and Thailand were making important investments in ICT in higher education.

IV

The developing countries face massive challenges in bridging the digital divide in education. If we take the case of India we find that according to statistics listed on the CIA website, the total number of households with Internet users in India is around 20,481,000. Looking at the total number of people in India, in addition to the number of literates one would think that the majority of Internet users are located within the rural areas. But, this is not the reality. The total numbers of Internet users are located in the urban hubs. Due to the lack of willingness by the Indian Government to break the inequalities created a new digital divide has accrued within the rural areas of India, while at the same time allowing the middle class and the urban areas to move towards becoming a knowledge-based society. The digital divide established in the rural area is due to two factors. One is the high cost of Internet use outside of the urban areas and two, the lack of infrastructure being developed to lay connections to the rural areas. Yet, both of these factors are directly related to the lack of higher education institutions located in the rural areas. Because of lack of higher education institutions, there has been an increase in the alienation of knowledge of social ethos.

In order to bridge the digital divide in education, developing countries like India will first need to overcome the key constraints to the development of ICT in higher education. Too often programs fail to address the problems in a comprehensive and sustainable way. To reduce the technology gap developing countries including India need to discover ways to expand information infrastructure, increase access by improving markets, and reduce the cost of service, especially for Internet access. A reduction in Internet costs both telecommunications company charges and Internet service provider charges in developing countries is necessary for a broadening of the information society there, and for more widespread and cost-effective use of new technologies to improve education. Even with the best of intentions, however, achieving these goals will not be easy for developing countries. They lack both the funding and the technical expertise to overcome infrastructure and human resource constraints due to geographical variations and other administrative factors. Many international financial organizations, aid agencies, and private players are committed to help developing countries to bridge the digital divide and are being mobilized into action by the United Nations, the World Economic Forum and such other bodies. While access to computers and telecommunications networks is necessary to bridge the digital divide, access alone is not sufficient to ensure that education systems in developing countries benefit from the Internet revolution. The respective governments in the third world countries also need to train teachers and trainers to exploit the potential of learning technologies; offer free or inexpensive Internet access to educational institutions; foster capacity to develop content and instructional resources in their own language; build networks and well maintained facilities for both accessing knowledge and providing affordable lifelong learning and skill upgrading and preserve the freedom of teachers and students to explore the myriad educational resources on the web without filtering and censorship .

Further, both industrialized and developing countries must also seek to address the digital divide between rich and poor. In the developing countries like India, public policies to promote competition and to make new technologies more accessible will ultimately influence availability and adoption of technology and access. However, special community-based programmes by governments and nongovernmental organizations involving marginalized or rural communities, women, and minorities are also essential for bridging the digital divide. In this direction policy makers for higher education should play pivotal role.

Conclusion

Having discussed in the aforesaid paragraphs all about higher education, globalization and its implication on higher education and the use of information and communication technology for the higher education sector and the problem.and prospect for rural and urban mass we may safely conclude that the Indian Government continues to provide the rural area with little or no attention at the higher education level to tap into the necessary knowledge that is relevant to the people located in these regions. The Indian government continuous their procedures to make plans and recommendations, but do very little to implement them and follow through. According to the Indian Government's thinking and planning, people within the rural area are poor, lack services and opportunities and have fallen behind people located in the urban area because of their inability to find employment within the rural area. Instead of that the government should consider the fact that there remains a vast gap between rural and urban people in regard to what knowledge is necessary for the development of rural mass. Herein lies the importance why we should try to minimize the problem of digital divide so far we talk about higher education and the benefit of information technology.

It is a known fact that the system of higher education in India faces serious challenges. And it needs a systematic overhaul, so that we can educate much larger numbers without diluting academic standards. This is imperative because the transformation of economy and society in the twenty-first century would depend, in significant part, on the spread and quality of education among our people, particularly in the sphere of higher education.

REFERENCES

1. Bhatnagar, Subhash 2000, Information Technology and Development: Foundation and Key Issues, New Delhi.
2. Agarwal, Ranjana 2003, Equal Opportunity in the Information Technology Sector, Reality or Myth: A Case Study. In NIEPA, International Conference on Globalisation and Challenges for Education. Focus on Equity and Equality, New Delhi.
3. Castles, Manuel 1998, End of Millennium. Malden, MA: Blackwell.
4. Castells, Manuel 2001, The Internet Galaxy. New York.
5. United Nations Development Programme. 2001. Human Development Report 2001: Making New Technologies Work for Human Development. New York.
6. World Bank 1998, World Development Report: Knowledge for Development, Washington DC and OUP.
7. World Bank 2005, World Bank Report: India and The Knowledge Economy Leveraging Strength and Opportunities, Washington, D.C.
8. Knight, Jane 2002, Trade in Higher Education Services: The Implication of GATS-Report.
9. Sadgopal, Anil 2003, Political Economy of Education in the Age of Globalisation, New Delhi.

5
Applications of Communication Technologies

Ayesha Mariam, India

Introduction

The process of transferring information with the use of a medium in which the communicated information is understood easily by both sender and receiver is called communication. It requires that all parties understand a common language that is exchanged. This process requires a vast repertoire of skills in intrapersonal and interpersonal processing, listening, observing, speaking, questioning, analyzing and evaluating. Use of these processes is developmental and transfers to all areas of life: home, school, community, work, and beyond. Communication is usually described along a few major dimensions: Content (what type of things communicated), source, emisor, sender or encoder (by whom), form, channel (through which mediums) destination, receiver, target or decoder (to whom) and the purpose of pragmatic aspect. Therefore communication is a social interaction where at least two interacting agents share a common set of signs.

Types of Communication

1. A language is a syntactically organized system of signals, such as voice sounds, intonations or pitch, gestures or written symbols which communicate thoughts or feelings. There are thousands of human languages and these seem to share certain properties.
2. A dialogue is a reciprocal conversation between two or more entities.
3. Nonverbal communication is the process of communicating

information's through sending and receiving wordless messages. Written texts also have nonverbal elements.

4. In the 21st century, however, it includes other media used to disseminate news, such as, radio, television, mobile phones, websites, MP3 players and documentaries.

Radio and Television to Assist Teaching and Learning

Pioneers of wireless telegraphy (radio), working 100 years ago, believed the new technology would soon be put to useful purposes. After 1922, the British Broadcasting Corporation (BBC) began to use "wireless" to assist learning. John Reith of Britain, a public service broadcaster aimed to "educate, inform and entertain", set up the National Advisory Committee on Education. Separate committees were set up for school and Adult Education and the systems flourished with most subjects and the systems flourished with most subjects on the curriculum treated.

The British System of educational broadcasting was widely studied and used as a model in many countries. It was realised in at radio had great potential in both formal and informal education by adding to what teachers could provide and acting as an agent of in-service training.

By the mid-1960s, a comprehensive system of school broadcasts was being provided both by the BBC and independent television, which had started school broadcasts. The visual medium added a new dimension to learning.[1] In under developed countries, educational broadcasts became a tool in social and political development. By the 1960s there was considerable evidence that educational broadcasting was a powerful branch of distance learning. When in 1969, a major step was taken in United Kingdom with the setting up of the Open University. This combined the practice of correspondence learning, a well-known distance learning technique, with educational broadcasts. The Open University model is now being used worldwide and uses a very broad range of new educational technology.

Technology in Educational Broadcasting

The Internet is the latest new technology to propel a development in educational broadcasting. Prominent examples in the past have been the transistor, which allowed many more people to use radio conveniently, especially in developing countries where teachers were scarce; stereo sound; black and white television, followed by colour television, which was an important addition to programmes dealing with subjects such as natural history and geography; improvements in recording techniques, casetting and disc recording (CD-ROMs); and the growth of transmission systems, such as cable and satellite, resulting in much-increased coverage. Efficient postal systems, the telephone (fixed and mobile), and various recording and playback systems based on computer technology all have a part to play in educational broadcasting in the new millennium. The Internet and its websites are now familiar to many children in developed countries and among educational elites elsewhere, but it remains of little significance to very many more.

Information Communications Technology

Information Communication Technology is an umbrella hem that includes all technologies for the communication of information. It encompasses: any medium to record information (whether paper, pen, magnetic disk/tape, optical disks–CD/DVD, flash memory etc...) and also technology for broadcasting information–radio, television; any technology for communicating through voice and sound or images–microphone, camera, loudspeaker, telephone to cellular phones. At present, it is apparently culminating to information communication with the help of personal computers networked through the Internet that can transfer information using satellite systems or intercontinental cables. A PC connected to the Internet has become a vital tool for communication during the past few decades since its proliferation among the masses.

Information Technology in Education

The pace of change brought about by new technologies has had a significant effect on the way people live, work and play worldwide. New and emerging technologies challenge the traditional process of teaching and learning and the way education is managed. Information Technology is having a major impact across all curriculum areas. Easy worldwide communications provide instant access to a vast array of data, challenging assimilation and assessment skills.[2] Rapid communication plus increased access to IT in the home, at work and in educational establishments, could mean that learning becomes a truly lifelong activity–an activity in which the pace of technological change forces constant evaluation of the learning process itself.

Initial strategy focussed on encouraging teacher training in new technologies and the provision of hardware in educational establishments, with the general aim of stimulating schools and local authorities to support curriculum and management use of IT. The curriculum identities a core set of IT capabilities and stresses that these should be developed by applying them across subject areas.

The provision of hardware and software resources varies substantially in colleges. Learning resources centres now often contain learning materials published on CD-ROM and most colleges are connected to the Internet. These technologies have the potential to develop "Virtual Campuses" and thus increase student access and participation. Although there is a trend towards individualized programmes of study for students, little-use is made as yet of computer managed learning.

IT and the Curriculum

As part of the IT curriculum, learners are encouraged to regard computers as tools to be used in all aspects of their studies. In particular, they need to make use of the new multimedia technologies to communicate ideas, describe projects and order information in their work. This requires them to select the medium best suited for conveying their message, to structure information in a hierarchical manner and to link together information to produce a multidimensional document. It has an impact on most other curriculum areas. Science uses computers with sensors for logging and handling data; mathematics uses IT in modeling, geometry and algebra; in design and technology, computers contribute to the pre-manufacture stages; for modern languages, electronic communications give access to foreign broadcasts and other materials and in music, computers enable pupils to compose and perform without having to learn play traditional instruments. For those with special educational needs, IT provides access to mainstream materials and enables students to express their thoughts in words, designs and activities despite their disabilities. Learners can absorb more information and take less time to do so using IT. Learners may be more productive, challenge themselves more, be bolder and have more confidence.

Integrated Learning Systems (ILS)

Another use of IT in learning is currently undergoing trials in the UK; the integrated learning systems. These involve learning through rather than about IT, by providing structural, individualized tuition in numeracy and literacy. Using the system for short, regular sessions, learners progress through the programme at a steady but challenging rate. The system keeps a progress record; assess the learners' rate of performance and produces reports for teachers, learners and parents.[3] This approach provides highly structured, targeted and assessed learning for short periods of time. Pupils and Teachers alike find the individual ILS reports helpful and motivating and teachers have never before had such detailed and accurate analysis of students' abilities. The multimedia attributes of the system make it possible to demonstrate complex concepts and students can proceed at their own pace free from the pressure of their peers.

Communication Technologies in Education and Training

The use of communication tools such as e-mail, fax, computer and video-conferencing overcomes barriers of space and time and opens new possibilities for learning. The use of such technology is increasing and it is now possible to deliver training to a widely dispersed audience by means of on-demand two-way video over terrestrial broadband networks. Schools and Colleges are making increasing use of the Internet. They use the Internet both the access materials, people and resources and to display their own Webpages created by students and teachers. The use of video-conferencing is growing slowly and has helped some students learn foreign languages by talking directly to other students abroad.

Achievements

The Internet has opened up many opportunities, from finding out information, conducting communications globally, e.g., through e-mail, voice-mail, skype, e-commerce. One often wonders: How did people manage before the time of the Internet? How much hard was it to communicate and find out information quickly and easily? A PC connected to the Internet whether through a dialup connection, broadband or Wi-Fi has indeed made it a facile act for many peoples. Apart from Internet a PC allows communication of information through Compact Discs, Pen Drives, Printers, whether laser or inkjet, flash memory cards and exchange or information within a local network. PC based ICT has also emerged as a source of employment in many emerging economies through Business Process Outsourcing (BPO) or Knowledge Process Outsourcing (KPO) from companies in the developed world. People now have the chance to conduct remote logon, in which they can access their work computers (in office) from home. This has opened up many more opportunities for those struggle to find time to leave their house to go to work, so they can now just work from home.

Future Trends in Teachnology and Learning

Radical Technological developments in miniaturization, electronic communications and multimedia hold the promise of affordable, truly personal, mobile computing. The move to digital data is blurring the boundary between broadcasting; publishing and telephony by making all these media available through developments are not only giving learners' access to vast libraries and multimedia resources, but also live access to tutors and natural phenomena throughout the world.[4] Easier access for students to information, tutorials and assessments together with the use of IT tools such as word processors and spreadsheets, will help them learn more productively. In areas of curriculum that are structured and transferable to electronic format, students will work at different levels and on different content.

Developments in communications technology and the increase in personal ownership of technology will allow learning in schools and colleges to integrate with learning elsewhere. The boundaries between one institution and another and between institutions and the outside world will become less important.

The technological revolution creates rapid and disruptive changes in the way in which people live, work and play. As the technological advance shows no sign of slowing, the challenge is in learning to adapt to changes with the minimum of physical and mental stress. To make this possible, the learning systems and those who manage them must prepare people to work with new technologies competently and confidently. The nature of technology is that it not only poses problems but also offers solutions constantly creating opportunities and providing new and creative solutions to the process of living and learning.

REFERENCES

1. Cahoon, B., "*Teaching and Learning Internet Skills*", In Adult Learning and the Internet, edited by B. Cahoon, pp. 5-13, New Directions for Adult and Continuing Education, No. 78, San Francisco: Jossey- Bass, 1998.
2. Forsyth, I., "*Teaching and Learning Materials and the Internet*" (2nd ed.), London: Kogan, 1998.

3. Rapaport, M., *Computer Mediated Communications*: Bulletin Boards, Computer Conferencing, Electronic Mail, and Information Retrieval, New York: John Wiley & Sons, 1991.
4. Roberts, L., "*A Transformation of Learning*: Use of the NII for Education and Lifelong Learning", In D.P. Ely and B.B. Minor (eds.), Educational Media and Technology Yearbook 1995/1996, pp. 50-66, Englewood, CO: Libraries Unlimited, 1996.

6

Group Formation in Collaborative Learning–Need for Effective Approach

S.R. Balasundaram, India
B. Ramadoss, India

e-Learning

There has been a steady increase in the use of the Internet and in particular the World Wide Web for both academic and training activities. Due to the convenience and the flexibility of operations, this new type of teaching and learning process through technologies, otherwise called e-Learning is being adopted in most of the universities, institutions and organizations worldwide. Some of the major potential advantages experienced through e-Learning are the freedom of choosing anytime-anywhere learning models, the possibility of learning the content in different forms using multimedia technologies and the ability to cover more information in short span of time.

Instead of defining e-Learning systems as another mean for teaching and learning process, they can also be thought of for exploiting the principles of educational technology in their models to offer more benefits to the administrators, instructors and especially to the learners. Research shows that e-Learning can be defined employing theories of social and active learning through collaborative activities (Vygotsky, 1978; Sudweeks and Simoff, 2000; Tiffin and Rajasingham, 1995). The social nature of cognition as theorized by Vygotsky (1978) provides a basis for learning requiring social interaction, because Vygotsky viewed learning as a particularly social process giving importance to interaction between the peers of a group or the persons associated with the environment. Though e-Learning can provide enhancements to the teaching and learning process, the biggest impact occurs when it can enable social and collaborative interaction where all participants in the system can actively participate and contribute.

Collaborative Learning

The idea behind collaborative learning is to group learners or form teams for solving some problems or performing discussions to arrive at a solution. The growth of technologies has made it possible to define different forms of collaboration–through mails, chats, conferencing, blogs etc. In a collaborative e-Learning context, learners are responsible for each other's learning. The success of collaborative learning lies in the maximization of information exchange, utilizing the skill levels of one by the other, and motivating the peers.

Johnson and Johnson (1986) stress that there is high evidence that teams of collaborative learning can achieve higher levels of knowledge and retain more information when compared to those who learn individually. Also, as highlighted by Totten *et al.*, (1991), collaboration enables learners to engage in discussion and define utmost responsibility of their activities. This in turn makes the learners to become critical thinkers.

Group Formation

In the context of collaborative learning, the learning normally takes place when the learners are active and collaborate with each other during problem solving. But, the collaboration process need not always give positive results. That is, much has to be thought of in the formation of groups associated with the collaborative activity. Most of the time, the skill levels of the individuals or members present in the group, play a significant role in determining the outcome of the group. That is, if the group members have good understanding level in terms of communication and subject, the group can perform well. Otherwise, even though a group has some highly competent members, due to the improper mixture of members or poor formation of the group, the contribution from the groups may not be appreciable. Though technologies can enhance the collaborative process in an e-Learning environment, there is no measure to take care of the knowledge or communication skill related attributes of the group members. In this regard, the 'group formation' needs to be given attention in any collaborative learning process.

Earlier Research on Collaborative Learning

Literature shows that there has been lot of research activities done in the area collaborative learning. Ogata, Matsuura and Yano (1996) focused on Computer Mediated Communication associated with collaborative learning: Comparison of face-to-face and online learning was focused by some researchers (Johnson, Aragon, Shaik, and Palma-Rivas, 2000; Tiene, 2000; Sumner and Hostetler, 2002).

How to form Groups?

To define an effective collaborative learning situation, it becomes mandatory to consider the benefits of proper group formation. Some of the important parameters that can be thought of while forming groups are:

(a) Communication skills
(b) Understanding level
(c) Team size
(d) Knowledge or skill levels of the members

There are different types of assigning the members to groups. Some of the familiar approaches are:

(i) Random Method
(ii) Self-Selection
(iii) Task Based
(iv) Selective Method

1. *Random Method* – Assigning students or members to each group in random fashion. In an e-Learning environment, this can be done using random numbers generators applied to the list of enrolled or registered members. Though it is a good practice, there may be chances where a group may be formed with 'poor' skilled members.
2. *Self-Selection* – Members choosing their own co-participants. In a traditional class room environment, this may be feasible. But, in an e-Learning situation, especially, where members are not known to each other, it is not a suitable method.
3. *Task Based* -- In this method, list of topics or tasks are given for the learners. Groups are formed based on the individual's interest or expertise or preference on a particular topic or task. Though groups may be formed having well identified members in each group, managing the contributions from the individual groups and evaluating the performance of groups may be difficult, especially in an e-Learning scenario.
4. *Selective Method* – This focuses on forming groups based on some criteria. In a traditional class room situation, this may be based on several parameters.

(a) Individuals may prefer to form their groups–known persons, friends etc. Sometimes, groups may be based on scoring high marks.

This chapter focuses on the last method where groups have to be formed with the expectation that the talent or skill levels of each group are almost the same. For this, we have considered the marks of a 'Pre-test' conducted before the actual collaborative task to be done.

Methodology

The course 'Object Oriented Analysis and Design' is one of the essential subjects for any Computer Science or Information Technology related disciplines. For an assignment on applying object oriented analysis to a situation, the learners are expected to analyse the given problem statement and finally specify the list of classes, objects, associations needed for the design and implementation of the same. In this context, in an e-Learning environment, the learners are given problem statement. As the initial step, a preliminary test on 'Basics of objects and classes' was conducted. Based on the individual's performance, the test scores were utilised to form the groups. The groups could have members of distributed skill levels or knowledge levels. The total skill levels of all groups were almost equal. This enabled the system to have a smooth collaborative learning process. The algorithm used for forming groups is given below.

Algorithm for Group Formation

Aim

Groups have to be formed and the members have to be allocated to the group according to the rule that all groups must have almost equal weightage (here, the scores of a preliminary test).

Inputs

1. Number of members and their weightage.
2. Total number of groups to be formed.

Algorithm

Step 1: Let n be the number of members.

Step 2: Consider the individual's test scores.
Let them be w_i where $1 <= i <= n$.

Step 3: Define the number of groups (ng).

Step 4: Find $Avg = \sum_{i=1}^{n} wi / ng$

Step 5: Find the smallest and the largest value of w_i.
Min = small(w_i)
Max = large(w_i), $1 <= i <= n$

Step 6: Divide the range from Min to Max with ng equal divisions.

Step 7: Arrange the range values in ascending order and choose the values one from each range.
If the Sum of values ≠ Average value, then choose the next value from the range currently present, until the value is approximated to the average value.

Step 8: Thus the persons are allocated to various groups.

Member ID	*Weightage*
1	15
2	20
3	18
4	25
5	28
6	78
7	47
8	92
9	76
10	84
11	66
12	52
13	48
14	39
15	62

GROUP 1

Member ID	*Weightage*
1	15
14	39
11	66
3	18
7	47
9	76

GROUP 2

Member ID	*Weightage*
2	20
13	48
6	78
4	25
12	52

GROUP 3

Member ID	Weightage
10	84
5	28
15	62
8	92

Conclusion

When the knowledge levels of individuals are distributed or heterogeneous, care must be taken to form groups so that the entire learning process is made a meaningful one. In this chapter, the selective based technique related to group formation is considered. As a next move, the data clustering techniques will be tried out for forming the groups.

REFERENCES

Bowen, D.D., and Jackson, C. N. (1985-86). "Curing those 'ol 'Omigod-Not-Another-Group-Class' blues". Organizational Behaviour Teaching Review, 10(4), 21-23. Discusses a list of features needed for defining better groups for collaboration.

Vygotsky, L.S. (1978). Mind in Society: The development of the higher psychological processes. Harvard University Press,Cambridge, MA.

Sudweeks, F. & Simoff, S. (2000). Participation and reflection in virtual workshops. Proceedings Western Australian Workshop on Information Systems Research, Edith Cown University.

Tiffin, J. & Rajasingham, L. (1995). In search of the virtual class: Education in an information society. Routledge, London.

Johnson, R.T., & Johnson, D.W. (1986), Action Research : Cooperative learning in the science classroom. Science and Children, 24, 31-32.

Totten, S., Sills, T., Digby, A. & Russ, P. (1991), Cooperative learning, A guide to research. New York: Garland.

Ogata, H. Matsuura, K. and Yano, Y. (2000), Active Knowledge Awareness Map: Visualizing learners activities in a Web based CSCL environment. International Workshop on New Technologies in Collaborative Learning, Tokushima, Japan.

7

Implementation of Knowledge Management in School Organization for Enhancing Student Learning

Dr. Cheng Chi Keung, Hong Kong

Introduction

Rapid advances in technology and communications have greatly accelerated the emergence of new knowledge. Student should be well equipped with learning skills to explore knowledge in a self-regulation manner (Zimmerman, Bonner and Kovach, 1996). In order to supporting student learning, school should consider to establish a KM system for supporting and complementing their traditional teaching. KM system enables school education to be delivered to the student's home, breaking the boundaries of a traditional classroom. The tools for developing a learning community such as real-time discussion chat rooms and bulletin boards are usually provided in the KM system to allow information exchange and idea sharing round-the-clock. KM system also provides versatile information and functions so the teachers can interact more effectively with the students as well as provide study advice to students online. For enhancing the effectiveness and efficiency of students' learning, KM system should be incorporated in schools to help students construct their knowledge through knowledge sharing and discussion and facilitates deep learning of students.

What is Knowledge?

Sallis and Jones (2002, p. 8) defined Knowledge as "information in use," and "interaction of information with the human mind that gives it meaning and purpose." in their book "Knowledge Management in Education: Enhancing Learning and Education." Knowledge is constructed through an "*accumulation of facts, procedural rules or heuristics through our daily experience and study.*" It also involves the intelligence to acquire and apply what one has understood through learning and experience. There are two types of knowledge, namely, explicit knowledge and tacit knowledge. The former can be codified and digitized in organizational documentation and can be transmitted or expressed easily. Capturing explicit knowledge is not difficult. The latter is originated from experience, action, ideals, values and emotions of an individual (Sallis and Jones, 2002). As remarked by Awad and Ghaziri (2004), "*[it is] embedded in the human mind through experience and jobs.*" It is however difficult to codify and store in database. It can only be expressed or transmitted through metaphor and by analogy. Thus, it is a laborious task to manage and capture tacit knowledge.

Knowledge is important to civilization of mankind, and of course plays an important role in school education process. With the accumulation of knowledge among people, the lifespan of civilization can be maintained. Given a person's limited lifespan and resources, it is impossible to construct knowledge all on his or her own. The sharing of knowledge among individuals is therefore necessary. Students do not need to construct their knowledge from the very beginning every time but they can base on what have been constructed by others.

What is Knowledge Management?

Knowledge management refers to things which enable the gathering, organizing, sharing and analyzing individuals or collective knowledge, and application of knowledge and other intellectual capital assets to maximize the organizational knowledge-related effectiveness and prosperity (Wiig, 2004). The concept of KM is originated in the business field. A well-organized knowledge plays an important role in the success of an organization. With the sharing of knowledge among staff, problems can be tackled in an effective manner. Without harnessing the knowledge, knowledge asset will be lost once the staff with this knowledge leave the organization. This will hinder productivity and learning opportunities of other staff. Effective management of knowledge is therefore important for the benefits of a business organization (Sallis and Jones, 2002).

The application of new technologies is usually required to establish an effective KM system. These technologies include a large space of repositories of database, software, use of Internet and Intranet. KM involves the embedding and storing of tacit or explicit knowledge from various outside sources. The resulting knowledge is organized and represented in the form of databases and documents. Furthermore, knowledge can be enriched through the culture and incentives of an organization when it is transferred and shared (Awad and Ghaziri, 2004). Applying KM in school education is a way that could assist students to share and construct their knowledge in the learning process.

Can Knowledge Management Applied in School Education?

There have been debated in the field of management studies on deriving education practices for potential benefits from knowledge management. Sallis and Jones (2002) describe KM in education as the process of constructively using the information and knowledge that is inherent to any organization to enhance performance, management and operation. They assume that we are entering a period when economic success will depend increasingly on the knowledge component within enterprise, and that techniques exist to foster, develop and benefit from the human resources in any organisation. They suggested that the benefits of such approaches which have proved effective in commercial circles can deliver equivalent benefits to educational agencies.

In recent year, school education is moving from the old culture to a new culture that is ready to embrace Knowledge Management. There are significant opportunities for schools to apply KM to support their missions (Kidwell, Vander and Johnson, 2000). A knowledge repository is built for curriculum revision and interdisciplinary curriculum development. It cannot only improve the speed of curriculum updating and development but can also enhance the quality of the curriculum and the programs by identifying and leveraging best practices and monitoring the outcome. Administrative services related to teaching and learning can be improved by the implementation of a knowledge portal which include best practices, lessons learned, teaching material sharing, etc.

Knowledge Management in school organization can be thought of as a framework or an approach that enables teachers and students within the school organization to develop a set of practices to collect information and share what they know, leading to action that improves teaching and learning outcomes. In seeking to balance school information culture and its technology culture, KM brings together three core organization resources—people, process and technologies (Australian Standard AS5037, 2003). The people element drives goals such as building a learning environment, knowledge sharing and innovation through collaboration. The process element encompasses a range of qualitative and quantitative approaches to facilitate knowledge creation, and to capture, validate, transfer, and disseminate knowledge throughout the organization. Technologies that enable KM include groupware, databases, enterprise knowledge portals, taxonomies, search engines, data mining systems, knowledge-based systems, collaborative tools, etc. Integrating KM requires understanding how to align, with a specific organization context, these three core resources.

Those schools that invest in new technology without understanding their existing organizational and human patterns of information sharing are not reaching the potential of their investment. Likewise, those invest heavily in information-sharing processes but do not have effective means for tracking student outcomes are tying the hands of their teachers. Improved decision making, enhance creativity and innovation, and stronger lines of lateral, and vertical, communication are important outgrowths of knowledge management. For school, however, the full promise of KM lies in its opportunity for improving student outcomes. The ultimate benefit of the KM system, of course, is to students and the education community as a whole.

How can Knowledge Management System Enable Student Learning?

The knowledge management system provides a means for teachers to discuss different ideas of teaching and posting resources for students learning. The KM system involves systematization of database, web forum, e-mail account, chat rooms, video conference and personnel webpage etc. Before constructing the KM system, it is necessary to construct a knowledge database. Teachers are encouraged to provide resources, for instance, articles and past paper of different subjects and video clips for illustrating tacit knowledge, like demonstration of experiments and sports.

Students are enabled to exchange their ideas with teachers and peers by video conferencing via the KM system. Specific lessons can be arranged to meet such purposes. By installing Integrated Services Digital Network (ISDN) phone lines and web-cams in school, users can communicate with people in another location with similar devices and share ideas and products with each other face-to-face. Thus, tacit knowledge can be exchanged. By providing training courses or user manual, students are encouraged to use the system. Teachers are encouraged to post teaching resources and carrying discussion in the discussion forum. Teamwork is important for the running of the KM system. Group projects of different subjects should therefore be assigned to the students. When they submit their products, they are required to put their products in the KM system. This can encourage students to use the system and enable others to browse and read their products. Furthermore, they can also exchange opinions or share information about these projects on-line.

Students are enabled to form into groups for sharing knowledge based on their duties and their respective subjects via the KM system. Students' information can be obtained from the system database and they will be assigned to different groups by the system automatically. Under the system, different groups would have their own repositories of documentations and discussion forums. Each student is assigned with a login ID and password. Before entering the system, the user has to input the login ID and password for security reason. The system is able to recognize their identity by matching the login ID with their users' information. Then, the user login their own personal account and can access to their respective groups. Through the KM system, a forum is provided for students to carry out discussion and exchange knowledge. This facilitates student learning when they share their experience and knowledge.

Students are enabled to search resources and knowledge by using a search engine provided in the KM system. Students are only required to input keywords or subjects for searching information and can post documentation to the system. The system will assign the documentation to different groups according to their subject automatically. Users will be notified with e-mail when there is any new entry added to their groups. Useful materials to all members in the school can be put in a common repository which can be accessed by all groups in the KM system.

What will be the Student Learning Outcomes?

The Knowledge Management System creates a virtual learning community which provides a suitable learning context for students to undertake knowledge conversion. The process of knowledge conversion involves socialization, externalization, internalization and combination (Nonaka and Takeuchi, 1995). The knowledge management system provides a context for "socialization", in which students may exchange information and ideas with experts, teachers, peers, parents and web-citizens by using broadcast, personal or interactive communications. It also provides a context for "combination", in which students may develop knowledge by accessing information from the Internet, Intranet and Extranet. Students may also share their knowledge with people from all over the world; develop knowledge through the KM system, or record knowledge in their Personal Portfolio. The collaborative learning environment of the KM system provides a context for students to "Internalize" and "externalize" knowledge, in which students externalize their learning outcomes by collaborating with experts, teachers, peers, parents and web-citizens and internalize knowledge by discussing with those parties. Through the process of knowledge conversion, the virtual learning environment, enable students to develop their personal learning paths, communication and sharing with others, disseminate knowledge, and enhance their own personal knowledge based. With this acquisition of knowledge, students can build and create knowledge infinitely, unrestricted and unlimited in the virtual learning community constructed under the KM system. Virtual learning community could support constructive learning (Von Glasersfeld, 2001).

The virtual learning community could promote student self directed learning. The roles of the teacher and student are no longer as clearly defined in the virtual learning community as they have always been in physical classroom setting; a relatively blurred teacher-student relationship naturally follows. Students' can be teachers when they give advice in the virtual community and publish learning projects on virtual forum. Teachers can be students' when they join any learning activities in the virtual forum. Nevertheless, teachers remain important in students' learning process; they act as facilitators, providing guidance in students' learning process. Students can communicate and interact with others to construct meaning through self-directed inquiries, guided activities, and community-based collaborative learning. They are encouraged to construct their own knowledge and become a self regulated learner (Zimmerman, Bonner and Kovach, 1996). Since knowledge of different subjects is shared in the KM system, the developments of competence among students can be facilitated and this further helps them to cope with future challenges.

The virtual learning community could sustain collaborative learning and knowledge construction among students. The success of collaborative learning relies on all participants to act as knowledge-contributors (Kreijns, Kirschner and Jochems, 2003). Knowledge and ideas from teachers, parents and community members provide multiple perspectives in the virtual learning community. They contribute and present their ideas and question others views to obtain a shared understanding or to solve problems. As Riel and Fulton (1998) predict that communicative technologies make it possible for people anywhere in the world to be a part of a classroom lesson, and thus, the classroom is no more dominant by one expert, the teacher, but supported by a world of experts. The virtual learning community becomes a place for knowledge dissemination, which provides a means to enhance and broaden participants' perspectives as well as allow participants to consider an issue in a more complex way. With access to various resources, ideas, and perspectives from people around the world, learners can work with and learn from others who are distant in time and location. The virtual learning community breaks the walls of classroom and allows students to learn from and learn collaboratively with other students.' It is expected that students' fully utilize the privilege to actively engage in communicative and collaborative learning and in higher-order thinking, as well as to adopt a constructivist learning approach and to enhance their own personal growth with the establishment of knowledge sharing culture.

School education should see a paradigm shift from teacher-centre to student-centre, in which communication, collaboration and self directed learning are encouraged under the virtual learning community. In such a context, learning is surely a lifelong process. The KM system enable students' to develop their personal learning paths, communicate and share with others, disseminate knowledge, and enhance their own personal knowledge base. Although the system plays an important role in supporting collaborative knowledge construction by connecting classrooms to the world and by providing a medium for storing, organizing, and reformulating the ideas that are contributed by people all over the world, it is obvious that building physical communicative network is not the same as building a collaborative virtual learning community. The network, in and of itself, does not define community. It is the interaction and partnerships among the people who gather in the forum that make the learning community possible. What important is a collaborative school culture, in which students' teachers and staff are willing to share and disseminate knowledge.

How to Implement KM in School Successfully?

The implementation of KM in school organization is not without problems, several barriers make it difficult to use and share data and information effectively. For example, many technological tasks of the KM system could be done automatically by installation of appropriate equipments and software, but convincing student to share their knowledge with others could be a challenge for implementing KM. As Awad and Ghaziri (2004) remark that, "secure and mature people are less reluctant to share what they know with others." The problems can be tackled when a culture of sharing knowledge is established among teachers and students' in the schools. It may be solved by assigning group-works to students' and by that they are encouraged to put their works in the KM system.

Teacher facilitation skill for motivating students' to participate in the discussion is also essential for knowledge sharing culture. The role of a teacher is to bring the best out in students' as they work to achieve results in interactive events, which involve fostering collective effort, building cohesion and teamwork, and managing interpersonal conflicts (Schuman, 2005). For encourage student knowledge sharing in the KM system, it is important for teachers to have working knowledge of KM system and the facilitation skills in the virtual community. School should seek and prepare valuable guides and techniques in enabling teachers to reflect on their work and knowledge that would be of value to student learning within any human development context. For teachers there is much in the development of the "knowledge worker" that echoes the "reflective practitioner" in the work of Schon (1983), and the techniques described could add to the stock of those used in the school.

School administrators should exercise collegial management practices (Bush, 2005) to reduce the bureaucratic control and enhance teacher professional autonomy for knowledge sharing within the virtual learning community. In view of the fact that, there is a need to let student know and share the tacit knowledge they have for mutual benefit in order to release the capacities of those in school organizations, it is necessary to increase the degree of independence of the teachers, to foster the willingness and the skills to work collectively for the collective good, and to acknowledge both risk and the possibility of failure. Sallis and Jones (2002) acknowledge that this approach stands in contrast to much management theory which stresses tight control and accountability. For teachers it also raises the degree of freedom to go down this road in states which are increasingly imposing on schools outcome measures which tend to remove choice and intensify knowledge sharing. A similar issue arises around the freedom of teachers to innovate within systems that are increasingly narrow around both curriculum and modes of delivery. If so, it might appear that the "benchmarks" of good practice emerging from industry may not be in harmony with the possibilities in much of the educational field. But the problem of whether it is possible to transfer certain aspects of work developed in the commercial world to a field as highly contested as education remain unsolved.

The success or failure in the implementation of KM depends not on simply how much money has been invested in equipping hardware and other IT facilities in schools or in the installing of software. It is, however, highly relied on the school culture. If students' are reluctant to share their knowledge, it will be difficult to promote the use of KM. To implement KM effectively, Petrides *et al.*, (2003) recommend school to build on vocabulary and practices of the organization context to develop a knowledge sharing culture, and to focus on students' and their needs for improving learning rather than settle for procedural tinkering focus.

Conclusion

The concept of Knowledge Management can be integrated in the school organization for enhance student learning. By discussion with different individuals or groups in the virtual learning community, student shares their learning experience and knowledge with each other. It provides opportunities to students to learn actively and facilitate their construction of knowledge, and thus learning will not be limited in schools only. It also allows student to work cooperatively with others for achieving effective learning. Successful implementation of KM in school organization brings together three core organizational resource—people processes, and technologies, to enable the organization to use and share information more effectively. With such system, students could continue their learning after their graduation from schools to cope with the continuous changes of the world in a long run. KM is one of the effective concepts in enhancing students' learning.

REFERENCES

Standards Australia, 2003. AS5037. *Interim Australian Standard on Knowledge Management*. Australia: Standard Australia.

Awad, Elias. M. & Ghaziri, Hassan. M., 2004. *Knowledge Management*. Upper Saddle River: Pearson Prentice Hall.

Bush, T., 1995. *Theories of Educational Management*. Second Edition, London: Paul Chapman.

Kidwell, J.J., Vander Linde, K.M. and Johnson, S.L., 2000. Applying corporate knowledge management practices in higher education, *Educause*, 4, pp. 28-33.

Kreijns, K., Kirschner, P.A. & Jochems, W., 2003. Identify the pitfalls for social interaction in computer –supported collaborative learning environment: A review of research. *Computers in Human Behaviour*, 19, pp. 335-353.

Nonaka, I. & Takeuchi, H., 1995. *The knowledge-creating company*. New York: Oxford University Press.

Petrides, Lisa A. & Nodine, Thad R., 2003. *Knowledge Management in Education: Defining the Landscape*. USA: Institute for the Study of Knowledge Management in Education.

Riel, F., 1998. *Technology in Classroom Tools for doing things different things*. Paper presented at the Annual Meeting of the American Educational Research Association, San Diego, April 1998.

Sallis, E. & Jones, G., 2002. *Knowledge Management in Education: Enhancing Learning and Education*. London: Kogen Page Ltd.

Schon, D. A., 1983. *The reflective practitioner: How professional think in action*. London: Temple Smith.

Schuman, S., 2005. *The IAF Handbook of Group Facilitation: Best Practices from the Leading Organization in Facilitation*. San Francisco: Jossey Bass.

Von Glasersfeld, E., 2001. Radical constructivism and teaching, *Prospects* 31, pp. 161-173.

Wiig, Karl M., 2004. *People-Focused Knowledge Management: how effective decision making leads to corporate success*. USA: Elsevier.

Zimmerman Barry J., Bonner S., & Kovach R., 1996. *Developing self-regulated learners: Beyond achievement to self-efficacy*. USA: American Psychology Association.

8

Business Education for IT Professionals

Chrisantha Silva, Sri Lanka
Neeran Gautham, India

Introduction

What contributes most for the success of Information Technology in an organization? The technology itself cannot provide the facilities and the infrastructure required for a successful IT environment. It is the knowledge, skills and the efforts of the IT professionals that contribute significantly for the success use of information technology. How much of their technical knowledge contributes to the success use of information technology? There are gaps between technical know-how and the business knowledge of workers in the IT industry. The lack of business knowledge of IT professionals has an impact the performances of IT professionals. It is not only the technical knowledge that contributes to the success of an IT system. The awareness of the organization's vision, the business knowledge and the relationship with other staff play a vital role when achieving the results. We have observed that most of the IT professionals lack this knowledge and capabilities. Their main concerns are the technical knowledge and the technical work that they are good at and involved in. In today's environment this is not sufficient for the successful operation of an organization. There are vast amount of material documented and discussions have been held on the importance of aligning the IT plan with the business plan. Much have been discussed how to bridge the gap between IT and the business. In this context the business knowledge of IT professionals becomes an important contributing factor but unfortunately most of the time this has been overlooked.

In this paper we discuss why IT professionals or technologists need business knowledge and how it can contribute for the success of both IT and business. There are various IT professionals from technical to IT management. The categories such as Managers, Business Analysts, Project Controllers are not considered as pure technical jobs. This paper is about IT professionals who are involved purely in technical work. Further the strategy required to educate IT people is reviewed and possible action plans are discussed. This paper is based on experience gained in various business organizations.

Characteristics of IT Professionals

Being knowledge workers IT professionals identify themselves with their profession rather than organizations. They drive primarily by the pride of accomplishments. Keep their knowledge up to date with latest technology developments is passion for them.

IT professionals work in a challenging environment. They are a set of knowledge workers with high degree of education and specialized in technical areas. Their work is based on knowledge, problem solving, analysis and design. Primarily their passion is for their profession that involves many technical tasks. They are first loyal to their profession that is the technical area that they have specialized in other areas such as the business knowledge and soft skills are secondary to them.

The complexity of today's systems needs the interaction of various components of hardware, software and middleware. Back end data bases, business logic layers, application layers, application interfaces, user interfaces, web services are some of the examples. In IT there is no one person expertise in all these areas. It is the contribution of team of experts in various areas that produces effective systems. Team work plays a vital role in IT projects. IT professionals always have to work as teams and it is important that they maintain a healthy relationship with other IT experts.

The Importance of Business Knowledge

With more and more automations organizations are highly dependent on IT and therefore are compelled to invest on IT. In the last few decades IT has been promoted aggressively as the potential route to increase productivity. The role of IT is to support the business. Information Technology does not have a role to play without the business. How does IT increase productivity? It is not merely the processor speed, hard drive size and bandwidth. What matters is how IT supports business to achieve its goals. One primary objective of IT investment is to gain the business advantage through Information Technology. That means IT has to participate in a role that goes beyond technology. IT should enable the business units to identify the problems and then assist them in defining solutions that address the most important business functions first. This shows us a valid reason why business competence of information technology professionals is important.

Business competence focuses on the areas of knowledge that are not specifically information technology related. At a broad level, it comprises the organization-specific knowledge and the interpersonal and management knowledge possessed by IT professionals.

As mentioned above the technical knowledge alone will not increase the productivity of IT professionals. The IT systems are developed and implemented to fulfil user requirements. The success of the system depends on to what extent the system has met the user requirements. In other words the success depends on to what extent the requirements were understood by the IT professional. This can only be achieved by having a better understanding of the business and by having a good relationship with users. One may argue that a complete user requirement specification enables the software developer to build a system that meets user requirements. This is again a case of what the book says verses the practical situation. All specifications should be aligned with the practical situations.

The need to communicate with people from different functional areas in the business requires IT professionals to develop some commonality of vocabulary and business knowledge, and of working experience with business people.

To build a successful system one has to consider the following factors:

- How the automated system impacts the business users?
- What contribution will this make the organization to reach its goals and vision?
- How can IT provide more than what is requested and add value to the business?

This leads to a situation where the IT professional has to act proactively. The technical knowledge alone will not allow them to do this. We need a business education that enables IT professionals to apply their technical knowledge in ways that are beneficial to the organization and to act cooperatively with their business partners.

Another important area that has impact on the successful system is project management and planning. A feasible project plan can only be prepared by considering the practical issues in the business areas.

Our Experience

The importance of providing business education and soft skills to technologists was a major topic during the last few years. Our observation is that most organizations have not achieved success in this area. In the following section some possible reasons and cases are highlighted:

- IT professionals do not consider that business knowledge and soft skills as part of their job description. Further they do not believe that those skills will enhance their productivity and contributes more to the business.
- Some are on the view that the business knowledge accumulated on the job is sufficient to perform their tasks and therefore methodical and structural training is not required.

Quest for Technical Knowledge

With today's organizations more and more dependency on IT, the staff at IT have to work under pressure to meet target dates. IT professionals prefer to learn and experiment with new techniques and methods. This they do even at the cost of the target dates. Further they have to keep their knowledge up to date to cope up with the rapid technological changes in IT. This has lead to a situation where IT professionals are stuck in an island of technologies separated from the business. We have observed that they have a passion to acquire technical knowledge. Most of the time the business knowledge and soft skills are not been considered as a part of their job.

During the annual appraisal process the training requirements are discussed and the training plan for the next period is prepared. Most IT professionals request for training only on technical areas.

Most organizations today want their staff to attend on soft skills training and in some instances this is compulsory. There are cases where IT staffs apply for the training, make arrangements to attend the course or workshop but never turned up. There are always no shows by the IT staff. The reason given was that their technical tasks are more important than the soft skills. Even if they attend those courses they easily forget what was discussed and do not apply those concepts in their daily activities. However there is always high demand for technical training. Their enthusiasm to try out what they have learned is high.

Another observation is that most of these staffs are not aware of company vision, mission and values. What the organization wants to achieve during the next few years and the business plan is not a part of their technical job. These were highlighted during some of their interviews for promotions. Their responses for questions related to business knowledge were poor.

Impact on Systems Development

We have observed that there were many incomplete specifications prepared during the systems development especially in the area of user requirements. In cases where technologists are involved in the user requirements studies they are unable to look at the requirements from the business perspective. In cases where the requirements are properly documented by the business analyst the Software Developers were unable to translate these to program code due to lack of understanding of the business processes. The result is that the business process is not properly reflected in the automated system. During system testing when functional errors were reported, the technologist was not in a position to fully understand the issue due to lack of business knowledge. The result is long discussions between the developer and the user without reaching any solutions.

Providing Business Education

Providing business education to IT professionals requires a structured approach. The objective is to provide them the business knowledge and soft skills that are required to perform their technical work. The conventional approach will not be effective in the case of IT staff.

Strategy

The approach for education starts with a strategy. The purpose of the strategy is not only to provide business education but also make this more appeal to the technologist. When formulating such a strategy one has to consider the followings:

- IT professionals are knowledge workers and they have a passion for their profession rather than the organization they work for.
- They are specialized in technical areas and want to keep their technical knowledge up to date.
- Their motivational factors are different from those of other workers.
- They are highly mobile set of people.

The technical work of IT professionals is based on knowledge, problem solving, analysis and design. They need strong analytical and critical thinking skills to perform their jobs. Their skills in these areas are limited to the technical aspects that they are specialized in. In other words IT professionals are very good analytical and critical thinkers from technical point of view. They need to expand this in terms of business perspective.

The strategy may vary from organization to organization and the by specific type of tasks handled by the IT staff. For example, senior IT professionals must be business people first and need more commercial and management skills to manage teams of people. Software and system engineers may need the same skills at a different level. Another requirement is the requirement of work as a team. The complexity of today's automated systems requires the contribution of different expertise and no IT professional can work in isolation. Some of these technologists may work on technical tasks at the back end and no interaction with the functional users. Even these staffs have to interact with the members of the IT team. This implies that soft skills such as interpersonal relationships are a must for IT professionals. This is another important area one has to focus on when formulating the strategy.

Therefore, the training should takes place at two levels:

(a) Organization specific knowledge that covers the areas organizational overview, organizational unit, organizational responsibility, vision, mission, values of the organization and IT – business integration.

(b) Interpersonal and soft skills development that includes interpersonal communication, leadership, team work and knowledge networking.

Once the levels are identified, then a training matrix by type of training and type of work involved is prepared for each level.

Types of Courses

Selection of courses and training programmes for IT professionals is a challenging task. What are the areas of knowledge that represent business competence of IT professionals? One should understand that some of the courses on Management and Business Studies are not popular among the IT staff. Topics such as leadership, company vision, motivation are not in their vocabulary. The contents of the courses should convey a message that makes them understand the relevance of these courses to their job. It is important to make them understand the relevance of these courses to their work. Therefore we suggest the following types of training programmes and courses. If provided in the proper sequence this will be highly effective.

Team building—this may include out bound training, work shops that involve lots of role play.

Soft skills training—this may include presentation skills, negotiation skills, conducting effective meetings, stress management, time management.

Leadership training—discuss the topics in leadership such as inspiring the others, appreciate the others, have a vision, be a model, credibility.

Organizational culture—company vision, mission and values, work as a team to achieve departmental and organizational goals, how to create a culture that everyone can work in harmony.

Management concepts—this may include general management topics.

On the job training—to complement the above the organization can arrange on the job programme to train IT staff. This may be a real project related to leadership or organizational culture that needs team work. The project may require the team to perform a study on organizational behaviour and come up with suggestions to improve the relationships within the department. This is a good opportunity for them to apply what they have learned in the classroom environment.

Problems and Issues

Motivate for Training

The main problem in educating IT professionals is making them believe in business education. It is the responsibility of the relevant manager to convince them to understand the business. One should understand that in most cases it is not possible or advisable to force IT professionals to participate in business education. This has to be handled by considering what motivates the IT professional. To inspire and motivate them for training their manager needs leadership qualities that are accepted by the IT professionals. As mentioned in the previous section one has to carefully select the training courses relevant to each professional. The training matrix plays a vital role to select the courses.

The order or the sequence of training is also important. A technologist involved only in technical work will not be prepared to attend training in management concepts. To make this more appeal initially send them for an outbound training or team building workshop and then consider the other training in business.

Time Management

Organizations high dependency on Information Technology has made the staff at IT to work under pressure to meet the target dates. In most projects they are compelled to work extended hours and work during weekends. This has made them fully occupied only on their technical work. During the little time available they prefer to gain knowledge on technology. Our experience is that in some instances their supervisors are reluctant to release their technical staff attend for non-technical training due to tight target project completion dates.

The solution is to have proper time management on the tasks of the IT professionals. Acquiring business skills should be a part of the work of IT professionals. As mentioned in the above section if IT professionals are motivated on acquiring business knowledge then they will find time for business education. They should understand that time management is a part of their profession.

Follow Up

Unless you apply what you have learned in a practical situation then the training becomes futile. The business knowledge gained at the classroom or at the work shop should be followed by applying these concepts in day to day work. Therefore a follow up is required to evaluate the effectiveness of the training. We suggest the following indicators to measure the business knowledge and soft skills of IT professionals.

- Improvements in soft skills such as presentation skills, negotiation skills.
- Reducing the conflicts among the team members and with the user departments indicating an improvements in interpersonal relationships.
- Ability to identify and document the user requirements during the requirements study stage. This will be reflected in the complete and accurate requirements specification.
- Promptly identify the reasons for system errors and be able to explain those in functional terms instead of technical terms.
- Ability to handle conflicts between IT and functional departments.
- Awareness of the company vision, mission and values and understanding of how IT systems can contribute the organizations to achieve its goals.

Conclusion

IT professionals are knowledge workers and are a set of highly technologically literate people. They attempt to keep their technical knowledge updated and ignore the importance of business skills. In today's business environment in addition to their technical skills they need an awareness of the business and soft skills to perform better. Although the importance has been discussed, our experience is that this has not seriously addressed by most organizations. This chapter discussed why business awareness is important to IT professionals and highlighted a feasible approach to provide business education.

REFERENCES

Kouzes James M and Posner Barry Z, "The Leadership Challenge", Jossey-Bass Publication. USA, 2003.

Goleman Daniel, Boyatzis Richard and McKee Annie, "The New Leader: Transform the art of leadership into the science of results", Time Warner Paperback, UK, 2002.

Hargrove Robert, "E-Leader: Reinventing Leadership in a Connected Economy", Perseus Publishing, Cambridge Massachusetts, 2001.

Dr. Ivancevich John M, Dr. Duening Thomas N, "Managing Einsteins; Leading High-Tech Workers in the Digital Age" McGraw-Hill, USA, 2002.

9

E-Learning and Barriers to Realization of its Potential in Mauritius

Dr. H. Chittoo, Mauritius
Rakesh Ramchurn, Mauritius
Bhissum Nowbutsing, Mauritius
Mohun Prasadsing Odit, Mauritius
Sareetah Devi Motee, Mauritius

Introduction

E-learning represents one of the most dramatic changes to impact education and training in the history of education. The internet and multimedia technologies are reshaping the way knowledge is delivered allowing e-learning to emerge as a solution to the problem of lifelong learning and workforce training (Zhang *et al.*, 2004). What makes e-learning content different from other educational materials is that it can be disassembled as individual learning objects, tagged, and stored for reuse in a variety of different learning contexts (Harris, 2005). These learning objects can be assembled into different configurations depending on the requirements of an individual educational situation. This reuse of educational content is one of the core values of e-learning systems (Harris, 2005). The possibility of turning education into e-education has created enormous opportunities to cut the costs of education, allow for life-long learning at anytime convenient to a learner that it is naïve to even think it will take time for it to gain grounds.

There are lots of debates on the meaning of e-learning and even some of the drawbacks associated with it. Whatever be the debates on the meaning of e-learning and its drawbacks, the potentials it offers are so numerous and far-reaching to democratize access to education at a much lower costs that it is futile to even think that e-learning will meet with a bleak future and that we can adopt a wait and see approach. It can only become popular to the extent of gradually replacing traditional forms of delivering education/ training.

Why is it, therefore, that in Mauritius, a country which has the highest level of web-readiness index in the whole of Africa and among the highest among Asian countries, e-learning is practically inexistent. This paper will assess only from the demand-side perspective, the barriers that may be preventing the supply of e-learning to take-off bearing in mind that the supply-side as well may be a hindrance to the development of e-learning. The data has been collected mainly from secondary sources.

In order to achieve the objective of this chapter, section 2 will review some literature on e-learning. Section 3 assesses the e-learning potential and constraints in Mauritius before the conclusions and some policy implications are reached in section 4.

E-Learning-Literature Review

The Debate on E-Learning Definitions

Jay Cross, a CEO of e-learning Forum, a 1,200-member think tank and advocacy group, and founder of internet time group and a veteran of the software industry as well the training business coined the term "e-learning" in 1998. There is a very wide and ongoing debate as to what is e-learning and different authorities have their own viewpoints. E-learning is a vast and a multifaceted topic and it is hard to find a generally established definition (Dublin, 2004) says that the truth is that the term e-learning means different things to different people. E-learning is the delivery of course, content via electronic media, such as internet, intranets, extranets, satellite broadcast, audio/video tape, interactive TV, and CD-ROM (Urdan and Weggen, 2000). Urdan and Weggen (2000) seem to infer that: "Terms like e-learning, technology-based learning, and web-based learning are defined and used differently by different organizations and user groups." As per Zemsky and Massy e-learning is "a concept in search of consistent definition." It became popular in the USA in 2001 and was often referred to as computer-based training (CBT) delivered over intranets and the internet. Several questions regarding the definition of e-learning emerge. As per some authorities it means online coursework/assignments for learners at a distance while others use this term to imply virtual learning environments to facilitate the deliverance of education in universities. Many others say it is just an online tool to augment, develop, apply and broaden collaboration. So it is yet to be established that it is blended learning or just online learning (OL).

The definition of e-learning as per OECD is dynamic moving from none or trivial on-line presence to mixed-mode and finally completely on-line teaching/learning adopted as a substitute to professional learning. As per Khan (2001) e-learning technologies such as web-based learning (WBL), internet-based training (IBT), advanced distributed learning (ADL), web-based instruction (WBI), OL and open/flexible learning (OFL) are the same.

Hall and Snider (2000) define e-learning as the process of learning via computers over the Internet and intranets. Hall and Snider extended that e-learning is also referred to as web-based training, online training, distributed learning or technology for learning. Distance learning, however, was not included in the e-learning definition and was defined as its own entity as a learning process meeting three criteria: A geographical distance separates communication between the trainer and participant; the communication is two way and interactive; and some form technology is used to facilitate the learning process.

Hall (2000) contends that e-learning will take the form of complete courses, access to content for "just-in-time" learning, access to components, and the separation of "courses" to acquire and test knowledge vs content as an immediate, applicable resource to resolve an immediate, perhaps, one time only problem. Learning is and will continue to be a lifelong process, that could be accessed anywhere at anytime to meet a specific need or want. Hall added that more links to real-time data and research would become readily available. Given the progression of the definitions, then, web-based training, on-line learning, e-learning, distributed learning, internet-based learning and net-based learning all speak of each other (Hall and Snider, 2000; Urdan and Weggen, 2000).

Similar also to e-learning and its related terms is technology-based learning (Urdan and Weggen, 2000). Urdan and Weggen shared that e-learning covers a wide set of applications and processes, including computer-based learning, web-based learning, virtual classrooms, and digital collaborations. For the purpose of their report, they further customized their definition to the delivery of content via all electronic media, including the internet, intranets, extranets, satellite broadcast, audio/video tape, interactive TV, and CD-ROM. They warned, however, that e-learning is defined more narrowly than distance learning, which would include text-based learning and courses conducted via written correspondence. Like Hall and Snider, 2000), Urdan and Weggen (2000) have set apart distance learning and e-learning in their glossaries, making, however, e-learning inclusive and synonymous to all computer-related applications, tools and processes that have been strategically aligned to value-added learning and teaching processes.

Reverting to Halls (2000) contention of e-learning in all-inclusive form, distance learning as planned interactive courses, as the acquisition of knowledge and skills at a distance through various technological mediums would seem to be one of e-learning possible disguises. Interestingly, Urdan and Weggen (2000) saw e-learning as a subset of distance learning, on-line learning a subset of e-learning and computer-based learning as a subset of on-line learning. Given the review of definitions on all these terms 'subset' does not appear to be the most likely word to describe the relationship among these words and their forms. The definitions show a great depth of interdependence among themselves. While one person may narrowly define a term, another person could give it the all encompassing power. This communicates that e-learning, if given the all encompassing form, can be the larger circle of which all other terms would be overlapping at different times and extents given their user's intention. Another rationale for this choice is that "just-in-time" learning is a major advantage of e-learning but not of distance learning. Distance learning purports planned courses, or planned experiences. E-learning does not only value planned learning but also recognizes the value of the unplanned and the selfdirectedness of the learner to maximize incidental learning to improve performance.

Training Effectiveness in E-Learning

The use of technology in education and training is transforming the way that people learn in today's academic and corporate settings. According to a 1999 Training Industry Report, technology training budgets in the corporate setting increased 13 per cent from 1998 to 1999. While stand-up classroom instruction is still the most common delivery method for training, web-based training is quickly gaining ground (Bernstein and Auerbach, 1999). The shift from traditional face-to-face classroom instruction to technology-based instruction is expected to continue at an accelerated pace into the new millennium.

The rapid growth and integration of e-learning programs has prompted experts, authors, and researchers to question how best to evaluate the effectiveness of such programs. The change in training delivery methods comes at a time when corporate training departments are increasingly charged with demonstrating how their efforts add value to the organization (Hackett, 1997; Phillips, 1997; Holton, 1995; and Parsons, 1995). Regardless of the delivery method, organizations are looking to training professionals to identify how training helps the organization. Instruction delivered via electronic mediums, like any other instructional process or procedure, requires the use of evaluation to measure its effectiveness. Hence e-learning initiatives are subject to the same effectiveness measures as traditional training programs. Many questions regarding the effectiveness of e-learning have surfaced. One of the most common questions raised is simply "How effective is it?" (Thompson, 1998; Edwards and Fritz, 1997; Chute, Thompson, and Hancock, 1999). Measuring the overall effectiveness of e-learning requires a multilevel evaluation approach that requires systematic analysis of different sources and types of information. According to Chute, Thompson, Hancock (1999) both scholarly research and practical experience have shown that distance learning is educationally effective, offers business value, and is in many cases more cost-effective than other approaches. They suggest ten key points to a successful distance learning programme:

- Determine needs up front.
- Look to distance learning as a way to revitalize and innovate existing training programmes.
- Use multilevel evaluation approaches.
- Keep the focus on what is learned, not on the technology that is helping you learn.
- Market distance learning programmes internally and externally.
- Use on-site coordination.
- Obtain local field manager commitment.
- Make sure the instructors are well trained.
- Design programmes specifically for distance learning.
- Use reliable equipment.

The popularity of e-learning interventions is growing exponentially. To remain competitive in today's tight labor market, organizations are exploiting advances in technology to train employees more rapidly, more effectively, and at less expense than the past (Urdan and Weggen, 2000). The debate over the effectiveness of e-learning has got a lot of attention lately. Trainers, educators, researchers, and authors have discussed the significance of moving instruction to the web (Goodwin, 2000). However, the recent popularity of e-learning has not come without scrutiny. E-learning delivery methodologies can require a paradigm shift in the way that training is viewed and delivered.

This paradigm shift required trainers and educators to rethink how to best train and educate employees and students. A change of this magnitude is not easily accomplished without a compelling argument to do so. According to Chute, Thompson, and Hancock (1999), the first step in starting an e-learning programme is usually to understand and convince others of the advantages of the delivery method. Since supporters of e-learning often promote its cost effectiveness and increased access as primary advantages, many question if it compromises educational effectiveness to get these benefits (Chute, Thompson, and Hancock, 1999).

One of the most common ways to measure the effectiveness of e-learning is to compare it to traditional instructor-lead education and training. For many years educators and other experts have studied different forms of distance learning and teaching in order to identify if there are any significant differences when compared to traditional education and training. Chute, Thompson, and Hancock, 1999 related, "After looking first at correspondence, audio conferencing, videoconferencing, and computer conferencing, 35 these researchers have overwhelmingly reported that there is no significant difference in the achievement of students in well designed distance learning programmes, based on standard performance measures."

Competitive Advantage of E-Learning

Because of its potentials, e-learning was identified as a tool for the support of the knowledge creation process. Urdan and Weggen (2000) identified a paradigm shift in the way education is looked at and delivered and the emergence of a knowledge-based economy, and huge knowledge gaps as significant trends that have given rise to e-learning. A new industry, which is coming up, has revolutionized higher education. Whether it is called distance education, asynchronous studies, on-line instruction or e-learning, IBT has gained a significant foothold in the realm of professional education. In addition to the time and geographic flexibility, its modalities can be changed to fit the need of the user (Beck and Gary, 2004). The very question that traditional face-to-face teaching is the best has been challenged and questioned (Harasim *et al.*, 1998). As per Hiltz *et al.*, (1999) on-line education can be instrumental in achieving high rates of learner participation and group interaction which cannot be offered by traditional teaching. Traditional institutions offering higher education that we know of are structures of concrete consisting of buildings, which house the various disciplines, libraries, classrooms and laboratories. There is an auditorium, which is used occasionally for ceremonial occasions. The university is linked to the world beyond through its front doors, by snail mail, telephone or the world wide web. ICT has its own implications for universities and has become inevitable. ICT infrastructure has become an essential criterion upon which students and researchers chose their school and therefore is an indispensable duty for a university willing to remain competitive (McCredie, 2003). First of all, a global ICT infrastructure is coming up; a virtual world or so as to say in other words, the universities' educational setting is acquiring another shape in the form of a virtual educational environment. Secondly, subject material is no longer contained in people and books, but can be accessed through the infrastructure of computers internet-worked with each other. The third upshot is organizational in nature. The functional framework of universities will have to be re-structured. The academicians will retain their autonomy for those tasks where autonomy is essential and a natural outcome of their work. This implies, for instance, that the bureaucratic management to arrange financial support for fundamental research will have to be dismantled to a certain degree. Last but not the least, ICT makes things more transparent and the significance of educational functions clearer. Concealing things in terms of teaching such as quality of instruction, guidance and evaluation of educational processes and student performance becomes difficult.

E-learning is coming up as a challenge to the "bucket theory" or the "banking concept of education" which works on the assumption that the instructor owns the knowledge and deposits it into the passive students' attending the class (Freire, 1993). Traditional teaching suffers from "narration sickness" and interactive web-based education if used carefully is the perfect solution to the problem because the emphasis is on "learning by doing". Moreover, teaching in a traditional set-up has its own limitations and a traditional teacher can never provide 24 × 7 services to his/her students, which can be delivered through e-learning. The benefits of any-time access to e-reserves also ensure that students can obtain academic materials at any time, eliminating frustrations such as "The library was closed."

New delivery systems that increase the effectiveness of learning at a distance, new organizations such as virtual universities, and other models of teaching and learning are forcing higher education to change the way they do business (Berge, 2000). Fry (2001) is of the viewpoint that that if universities are to compete in a global higher education market they must embrace the technological advancements such as e-learning and use them as a strategic tool so that they are capable of transforming educational and business practices. E-learning has its own benefits such as it provides many ways to increase communication between class members and faculty, including discussion boards, chats, and e-mails which results in increase in motivation among the students.' E-mails can be used by instructors to remind learners about forthcoming events and how they have performed academically and (Stephenson, 2001). On-line education instills in the students' a sense of equality whereby each student can express himself or "speak up" by posting his views on discussion forms which is boon for shy and anxious students.' This promotes more confrontational and direct communication between students.' Traditional teaching relies primarily on physical attendance and if students' wish to work on joint projects they must coordinate schedules but with the use of web-based collaborative tools and IJEM asynchronous discussions this is no longer an issue and reliance on physical attendance can be done away with. Using e-learning and web-based advanced techniques there is a growing emphasis on leveraging advanced technology. In the area of case teaching, for example, the field is witnessing a steady increase in the use of CD-ROM cases and web-based materials. Web-based integrated software packages for e-learning have recently been developed that provide two sets of capabilities:

1. Assembling multimedia content created by a variety of authoring/publishing software programmes into a course; and
2. Managing course registration, administering and recording tests on-line, and tracking course and programme completion.

The benefits of e-education in the present day education scenario today are many and, with advancements in technology; they promise to deliver even greater returns in the future, which is all the more reason as to why it should be pursued.

Some Trends in E-Learning

Some of the main evolution features in the e-learning markets are presented in the following Table:

Table–1
Trends in E-Learning

Sector	*Trends*
Schools	■ Although many schools have introduced platforms for sharing information and supporting the pupils in their learning, it is likely to take years before the teaching staff and culture is ready to adopt comprehensively pedagogical approaches that take full advantage of e-learning. In the medium term, learning material publishers will continue to introduce text-based curricula resources supplemented by e-learning elements, but these will typically require access to different external platforms and will be linked directly to specific textbooks.
	■ On the platform side, if in-house developments and the open source tools succeed in overcoming problems of reliability, interoperability, documentation, continuous development and standards integration, commercial offerings will have a very tough time trying to achieve market shares in the school market.
	■ As teachers become more ICT literate, they will be developing more of their own learning materials and sharing these with each other and pupils, making these suitable to individual learners.
Higher Education	■ Open source e-learning platforms are likely to gain a foothold in this sector.
	■ The universities will increase in the number of courses offered in e-learning format (as stated in the study "Virtual Models of European Universities", European Commission 2004).
Vocational Education and Training (VET)	■ Open source e-learning platforms will offer a serious competitive alternative for users in the VET market and this is based on the fact that there is already a solid base of in house developed learning platforms at VET institutions.
Workplace Learning	■ Strong e-learning sectors in the workplace market will continue to be the ICT, business services, financial and pharmaceutical

Contd...

Sector	*Trends*
	sectors. In the public sector, it will continue to be the national health services, the defence departments and public including local government authori ties. ■ In this sector, apart from internal education and training for employees, there is likely to be more focus on training through e-learning to external partners and customers.
Consumer Market	■ The consumer e-learning segment will consist of Internet and CD-ROM based edutainment products primarily for children and young people and in the long term, also mobile, location independent edutainment to handheld devices. It will also include standard and individualized language learning products for the same media, and educational products that allow parents to supplement their children's education with online or CD-ROM based learning opportunities. ■ In future, more and more guidelines and manuals associated with complex domestic appliances and small machines will be multimedia based with simulations of the assembly process, maintenance, cleaning and/or usage. It will be possible to access the simulations from various devices (PDA, Mobile phone, TV connected to Internet or a PC).
Lifelong Learning	■ Although it is an obvious market for e-learning products and services, it is unlikely to show much growth in the future because the motivation of learners to choose lifelong learning via e-learning is limited unless it is part of a formal postgraduate education financed by employers or required education in order to change or advance in careers while still in employment.

Future Development in the Sector of E-Learning Suppliers

The evolution of e-learning supplies can be characterized as follows:

(a) Many small e-learning operators in all product areas (technology, service and content) will have disappeared, merged with others (both international and national) or evolved into a different sub sector. Those that survive will have identified a valuable niche or built strong ties to a loyal customer base.

(b) New operators could emerge either in niche areas (game based learning, simulations, open source integration) or by complementing their current offerings with e-learning services. In the future telecommunications operators and

professional associations are expected to enter the market as suppliers of e-learning services for their customers.

(c) The international (predominantly US and Canada-based) e-learning operators can be expected to continue their strong market presence and in some areas they will increase their dominance. Firms offering L(C)MS and enterprise suites include companies like IBM, Oracle, SAP, SumTotal and SABA, all mainly addressing the needs of large organizations. Within education segments, they will include companies like WebCT, Blackboard and Microsoft. Within live e-learning platforms, they will include Centra, Interwise and Webex.

(d) Strong international entrants can also be expected within emerging segments such as game based learning. US-based operators like Horn Interactive, Digital Mill, Socratic Arts, Breakaway Games, ACLS Interactive could be tempted to enter the European markets.

Given all the benefits of e-government, why is it, then, that it is practically inexistent in Mauritius. The section that follows tries to give explanations by analyzing the demand-side of e-learning in Mauritius.

Analysis of Demand-Side Factors of E-Learning in Mauritius

What constitutes the market for e-learning initiatives? They are the users of e-learning, comprising mainly of citizens, businesses, government officers.

Demands for E-Learning in Mauritius

Demand for e-learning can only come from people who can have access to computers and the Internet to get engaged in electronic learning, on the one hand, and more importantly these people should be able to use computers. I think on both counts, the demand side of the e-learning market is not yet ready in Mauritius. This could partly explain why the government or private providers of education are in no hurry or are under no pressure to move education provision on-line.

A recent survey conducted by the National Computer Board (of Mauritius) (NCB, 2003) to measure 'ICT Penetration within Mauritian Households' revealed the following:

- Computer ownership in Mauritian households having telephone connectivity stood at 29.4 per cent in June 2002.
- In the rural areas computer ownership has increased from

18 per cent in 2000 to 27 per cent in 2002. Furthermore, the proportion of rural and urban household to own a computer was as follows:

Table-2

Distribution of Computer Ownership by Household in Urban and Rural Areas in Mauritius as at June 2002

Urban	31%
Rural	27%

Source: NCB (2003).

- There has been a marked increase in Internet penetration with 23.8 per cent of households having telephone connectivity reporting having access to Internet in June 2002 compared to 12 per cent in September 2000.
- Internet penetration among households having telephone connectivity and owning computers has registered an increase from 58 per cent in year 2000 to 81.1 per cent in 2002.
- It has been observed that although males have a tendency to surf more on the net than females yet this gap has considerably declined since 2000.

Table-3

Use of Internet by Males and Females in Mauritius as at 2002

Year	*Male*	*Female*
2000	72%	28%
2002	57%	43%

Source: NCB (2003).

- More households having telephone connectivity have one e-mail account in 2002 (13%) compared to year 2000 (11%).
- Internet access and usage have increased in lower income group.

Table-4

Internet Access by Income Group in Mauritius as at June 2002

Income Group (Rs.)	*2000*	*2002*
20,001–30,000	28%	39%
More than 30,000	55%	55%

Source: NCB (2003).

Note: Re. 1 = 0.25 RMB or US $ 0.033(approximately).

- Main reasons for Internet usage are:

Table–5

Main Reasons for Internet Usage in Mauritius as at June 2002

E-mail/Chat	66%
Entertainment	29%
On-line Banking	7%
Discussions Group	5%
Job Search	1%

Source: NCB (2003).

- On-line purchases have increased from 1 per cent in year 2000 to 2.2 per cent in 2002.
- Businesses: ICT Penetration.

(i) 83.3 per cent of business have at least one PC.
(ii) Most widely used software are office tools: 96 per cent.
(iii) 90 per cent of computerized establishment have access to Internet.
(iv) 21.3 per cent of establishments have websites.
(v) 8 per cent purchase goods and services from the Internet.
(vi) 3.6 per cent sell goods over the Internet.

Source: NCB IT Usage Survey 2005.

- ICT Penetration: Education Sector:

(i) Primary Schools: 280 schools have at least 1 PC and one printer.
(ii) Secondary Schools: The 34 state secondary have a computer laboratory with and average of 15 PCs.
(iii) 70 out of 91 private schools have computers.
(iv) Vocational and Continuing Education and Training: 65 institutions registered with the IVTB offer IT Courses, 5, 598 students' are enrolled in award courses and 10,164 are enrolled in non-award courses.
(v) Tertiary Level: 1,291 students' are following a programme in IT in Mauritius, 202 are studying degree programmes in IT abroad.

Source: Interim Report of the Task Force on Education and e-Training 2005.

The statistics should, however, be interpreted with care as they are government statistics which may be positively inflated to reflect an increase in computer ownership, access to internet, increase in computer penetration among lower income groups, among others. The true picture is totally different and is better represented by the UNDESA (2003) statistics. The latter reveals that, in fact, only 1.3 persons per 1000 in Mauritius are on-line or have access to the Internet.

The other reality often hidden by crude statistics is one of education. The Internet language and the official language of government in Mauritius is English. Whatever the statistics say, some 80 per cent people in Mauritius use a local dialect for daily communication and what more is that this dialect is not a language which can be written. As it is, some 40 per cent of 11 year old fail from primary school and cannot read or write English or count properly. This situation has been so for the past 30 years. No amount of effort can effectively bring these people to start using computers at any time in the near future. Besides many of the people receiving training in ICT are mainly for personal use of office tools, and probably are not making people 'technologically ready' for confident use of ICT for e-learning purposes.

That is a condition non-conducive for the provision or consumption of e-learning. The market is simply not ready. It can be forecast that even if government were to put education on-line in the near future, Mauritius will be among the first countries in the world to suffer from an 'e-learning bubble' i.e., the supply will by far exceed demand resulting in underutilized investment. To support the argument—a finding from a 2001 survey about e-commerce in Mauritius which revealed that: Private sector businesses faced a number of constraints in adopting e-commerce as a strategy; the main reasons reported were limited size of the market, inadequate IT infrastructure, shortage of IT skills and that goods and services produced were not sellable over the Internet. On the other hand, not doing so, keeps the capable people of the Mauritian society from achieving the full potential of living in the information age, and become internationally competitive citizens.

Conclusions and some Policy Implications

The tools of e-education and e-learning have created a new technological environment for both citizens and education providers. Different institutions and societal groups with different organizational cultures will have different cultural responses to the possibilities that these new technologies provide. As Hood (1998: 199) put it, 'a cultural theory analysis suggests that any given technological change can lend itself to very divergent visions of social modernization'. This paper supports that claim and makes clear the inadequacy of techno-determinist approaches that forecast that, in and of themselves, the advance of computers and automation would produce pre-determined and common organizational responses.

The point made in this paper is that investment in Telecommunication infrastructure and Human Resources as well as the acquisition of ICT by educational providing organizations are pre-requisites for the development of e-education/learning. They are, however inadequate, in that they will not by themselves lead to an increase in e-learning. What may be required are strategies to overcome the institutional, organizational, cultural, social and psychological barriers to e-learning. The greatest resistance or barrier remains people leading some researchers to claim that the potential of e-learning can only be tapped when the present technology-savvy generation takes over from the old and present generations of educators and citizens. I disagree with this overly pessimistic view.

What may be required is to increase the 'Technology Readiness' of education officers and citizens alike. By 'Technology Readiness' I mean people's propensity to embrace and use new technologies for accomplishing goals in home life and at work. People as consumers simultaneously harbor favourable and unfavourable views of technology, and the relative dominance of favourable will vary across individuals. People's/Consumers' propensity to embrace technology may vary widely, resulting from an interplay between drivers (optimism, innovativeness) and inhibitors (discomfort, insecurity) of technology readiness. Indications are that massive investments will be required not only in physical ICT infrastructure, but also in terms of education and training of both officers within education providing organizations and of citizens outside government. IT literacy may not be adequate. What may be required are ICT 'proficient' educationists and citizens. Increased access to ICT by the largest possible number of people is another very important strategy—increasing the number of access points, decreasing cost of access, increasing the number of people having access and also the ease with which access may be obtained, may be important ingredients. We may very well be in a process of social re-engineering of educational organizations and society/citizens in trying to increase the uptake of e-education/learning by increasing the Technological Readiness of the population of a country and its access to ICT.

No doubt there are certain areas, which need to be worked upon for the successful implementation of e-learning but traditional institutions offering higher education in any country should give it a thought. They need to become more customer centered and take a lesson from businesses which regard customer to be the king. Focusing on blended learning, rather than insisting on teaching students' at my place at my pace using an industrial model that is now becoming obsolete is what they need to look at.

Universities need to leverage their competitive advantage in terms of the ICT revolution and the new model of e-education has to be relied upon in the future. Successful management of these initiatives requires strategic planning and positioning that can demonstrate a clear picture of returns in terms of resources, time and money.

Peter Drucker made a sensational statement a decade back that: "Thirty years from now the big university campuses will be relics. Universities won't survive.... It's as large a change as when we first got the printed book" (Lenzner and Johnson, 1997) so that higher educational institutes shake off their inertia and utilize ICT to its best. This evoked a response from higher educational institutions in the western world, which realized the potential of ICT and started offering online education. Institutes of higher education should also critically appraise what he meant to say and think of making the best use of ICT for their respective institutions.

Government intervention in such a initiative would go a long way in paving sharing of quality knowledge resources across the platform amongst user community. Emerging educational technologies, particularly those in the area of ICTs are providing new ways of educating, training and learning to supplement and complement education resources to meet the challenges of the twenty-first century. Introducing a well-coordinated ICT programme in teaching institutions should go beyond providing computers and content. Education models that are innovative, cost-effective, scalable and sustainable are required to inspire students' and persuade parents and communities, and engage governments for the long-term. Meeting citizen's basic needs such as quality education complemented by more initiatives in the field of e-learning and its adoption by the traditional institutions of higher education will be a move which will prove to be like a real catalyst in Mauritius's or for that matter any country's knowledge economy. The time to start is only now if education/training institutions are not to become good only for the museum of industrial history.

REFERENCES

Beck, E.C. and Gary, S.R. (2004), "Theory and practice for distance education: A heuristic model for the virtual classroom", in Caroline, H., Karen, S. and Discenza, R. (Eds.), Distance.

Learning and University Effectiveness: Changing Educational Paradigms for Online Learning, Information Science Publishing, Hershey, PA, p. 121.

Berge, Z.L. (2000), "Why not reengineer traditional higher education?", in Lisa, P.A. (Ed.), Case Studies on Information Technology in Higher Education: Implications for Policy and Practice, Information Science Publishing, Hershey, PA, pp. 209-11.

Bernstein, D. S., & Auerbach, S. (1999). 1999 state of the industry report. Inside Technology Training, 12-16.

Corporate e-learning: Exploring a new frontier. WR Hambrecht + Co.

Hall, B., & Snider, A. (2000) Glossary: The hottest buzz words in the industry.

E- Schreiber, D. A., & Berge, Z. L. (1998).

Chute, A,G., Thompson, M. M., & Hancock, B W. (1999). The McGraw-Hill handbook of distance learning. New York: McGraw-Hill.

Dublin, L. (2004), "The nine myths of e-learning implementation: ensuring your real return on rour e-learning investment", available at: www.astd.org/NR/rdonlyres/6267344B-F4A0-449E-8B43-6DEECF80C71D/2990/DublinREV.pdf (accessed 21 November 2006).

Edwards, C., & Fritz, J. H. (1997). Evaluation of three educational online delivery approaches. ED430516.

Freire, P. (1993), Pedagogy of the Oppressed, Continuum Books, New York, NY.

Fry, K. (2001), "Elearning markets and providers: some issues and prospects", Training and Education, Vol. 43 No. 4, pp. 233-9.

Hackett, B. (1997). The value of training in the era of intellectual capital. The Conference Board, report 1199-97-RR.

Hall, B. (2000). New study seeks to benchmark enterprises with world-class elearning in place. E-learning, 1 (1) 18 -29.Urdan, T. A., & Weggen C. C. (2000).

Hall, B. (2000). How to embark on your e-learning adventure: Making sense of the environment. E-learning, January-March.

Harasim, L., Hiltz, S.R., Teles, L. and Turoff, M. (1998), Learning Networks: A

Field Guide to Teaching and Learning Online, MIT Press, Cambridge, MA.

Harris, J. (2005), "E-learning strategy: repurposing content", Chief Learning Officer, October, pp. 24-8.

Hiltz, S.R., Copolla, N., Rotter, N. and Turoff, M. (1999), "Measuring the importance of collaborative learning for the effectiveness of ALN: a multi-measure, multi-method approach," available at: www.sloan-c.org/conference/proceedings/1999summer/papers/ 99summer_hiltz.pdf (accessed 21 March 2006).

Holton, E.F. (1995). In search of an integrative model for HRD evaluation. Proceedings of the 1995 Academy of Human Resource Development Annual Conference (pp. 4-2). Baton Rouge, LA: Academy of HRD.

Hood, C. (1983) *The Tools of Government* (London: Macmillan).

Hood, C. (1991) 'A Public Management for all Seasons' *Public Administration,* 69/1: 3-19.

Hood, C. (1998) *The Art of the State: Culture, Rhetoric and Public Management* (Oxford: Clarendon Press).

Khan, B.H. (2001), A Framework for Web-based Learning, Educational Technology Publications, Engelwood Cliffs, NJ.

Lenzner, R. and Johnson, S. (1997), "Seeing things as they really are", Forbes, 10 March, available at: www.forbes.com//forbes/1997/0310/5905122a_7.html (accessed 12 March 2006).

McCredie, J. (2003), "Does IT matter to higher education", Educause Review, Vol. 38 No. 6, available at: www.educause.edu/ir/library/pdf/erm0360.pdf (accessed 17 March 2006).

Phillips, J. J. (1997). Handbook of training evaluation and measurement methods (3rd ed.). Houston, TX: Gulf Publishing.

Parsons, J.G. (1995). The impact of values on the financial analysis of HRD. Proceedings of the 1995 Academy of Human Resource Development Annual Conference (pp.4-2). Baton Rouge, LA: Academy of HRD.

Stephenson, J. (Ed.) (2001), Teaching & Learning Online. Pedagogies for New Technologies, Kogan Page, London.

Urdan, T.A. and Weggen, C.C. (2000), Corporate E-learning: Exploring a New Frontier, W R Hambrecht & Co, San Francisco, CA.

Zhang, D., Zhao, J.L., Zhou, L. and Nunamaker, J.F. (2004), "Can e-learning replace classroom learning?", Communications of the ACM, Vol. 47 No. 5, pp. 75-9.

10

Effectiveness of E-Content Material on rDNA Technology in Tertiary Level

A. Felix, India

Introduction

'Knowledge is power' and this power is explicitly seen in every field, based on the input of information and communication technology. There is a drastic paradigm shift in pedagogical system in this modern era because of the advancement of digital technology for dissemination of knowledge.

Teacher are one of the sources of knowledge as there are different sources are available in this modern scientific world. But teacher can never be replaced by any advancement in technology and the required emphasis is on the equipment of different operational aspect of technology. They disseminate the knowledge to the learners in the best possible and productive way by the concept of educational technology. Therefore, the conventional classroom instructional techniques can be modified based on the technological advancement in the field of education.

E-Content: The Possible Meaning

An application of computer in the teaching and learning process is e-content. This may be intranet based which include text, video, audio, animation and visual environments.

E-content is the advancement of technology design, deliver, select, administer and extent learning. E-content today is mostly viewed as a way to preserve and carry forward cultural historical heritage, to disseminate, life style, scientific, educational and business information in some digitalized format or to provide some interactive service to assess.

"E-content is digital information delivered over network based electronic devices, i.e., symbols that can be utilized and interpreted by human actions during communication processes, which allow them to share visions and influence each others knowledge, attitudes and behaviour."(From the book e-content: A European outlook–Springer).

So "e-content" is a package of data in an electronic digital form." In short the term "e-content learning material" means the concept of packaging the knowledge (lessons) in the forms of presentations like PowerPoint, E-books, PDF format using Aerobat Reader and HTML file for educational instruction.

Technology Development at CEC

CEC has attempted to develop the technology for generation of e-content.

- The technology for e-content development, keeping in view the instructional design and built in supporting evaluation for learning.
- It is attempting to develop technology for learning object repository.
- It is proposing to develop internet based video streaming with variable bandwidth.

Development of E-Content

There are different types of e-content according to CEC namely:

- Assembled e-content.
- Short course/unit/module.
- Full courseware.
- Short reusable learning objects or SLOs.

Technology Applications

The content development can follow simple conversion of knowledge/information into digital form. This is often seen in various websites, which does not qualify to be called as learning resources with specific objective and outcome of learning. It is an open ended system of information sharing.

Instructional Design

The other could be based on scientific method of instructional designs, which guides the students to achieve specified objectives and aims at outcome based learning. It is an integrated system with facility of navigation.

Learning Object Repositories Form

The third could be short re-useable learning objects and put in learning object repository in archival server and it is in searchable made.

CEC Road Map

The CEC's aim is to provide quality knowledge resources pertaining to higher education for face to face and self paced learning. CEC, bestowed with this responsibility, has chalked out the following road map for achieving above goals for packaging the knowledge resources and distributing the same.

Having gained considerable experience in packaging knowledge through video programmes, CEC is now aiming at packaging the knowledge in web based educational programmes having video, hyper text, animation by adhering to instructional design of international standard.

Most of e-content resources are predominantly hyper text based with some animation. The video and hyper text/XML based educational programmes are a few and far. This is partly because of bandwidth problem. But now the problem of bandwidth is over as technology is advancing very fast. As CEC is planning for future, it is basing its approach towards future system of e-learning. Therefore mix of video and hyper text and animation is being attempted.

In this investigation the e-content material is in the form of short learning objects (SLOs) which is developed using the following production software:

1. ULEAD.8 for video editing software.
2. Microsoft FrontPage , for web publishing.
3. Flash to Audio Video converter used for flash presentation into video.
4. Powerpoint for slide presentation.
5. Microsoft word for preparing text contents.
6. Hyperlink of media player to play video clips.

DEMO OF THE E-CONTENT DEVELOPED
(It will run for 4 – 5 minutes)

Validation of E-Content for Effectiveness

Validation is different from evaluation, the distinction is drawn between validation when experts give their opinions on contents, accuracy, relevant, pedagogical treatment and so on and evaluation, which is especially concerned with measuring the results achieved by the materials when used by the learners.

There are 3 general types of validity, namely 1. Face validity, 2. Content validity, 3. Construct validity. In this work objective is to go for content validity based on the achievement test conducted to the M.Sc., Biotechnology students. The expected result for validation is 90 per cent of students should get 90 per cent marks in the achievement test.

Achievement Test

S.No.	*Content*	*Yes*	*No*
1.	Insulin is a human hormone.		
2.	DNA is Deoxyribonucleic acid.		
3.	rDNA is recombinant ribonucleic acid.		
4.	Insulin is also produced by rDNA technology.		
5.	Genetically modified DNA fragments are termed as rDNA.		
6.	There is a single step involved in rDNA technology for production of Insulin.		
7.	Vector is known as Plasmid.		
8.	Donor organism is not needed for the rDNA technology.		
9.	Host cell alone is needed for the rDNA technology.		
10.	Cloning does not take place in rDNA technology.		
11.	Insulin is the final product of rDNA technology.		
12.	Human growth hormone promotes growth in children.		
13.	Interferon helps the cells to resist viruses.		
14.	Interleukin stimulates the proliferation of RBCs in immunity.		
15.	Renin inhibitors do not decrease blood pressure.		

Achievement Test Analysis

No. of students	=	27
No. of questions	=	15
Maximum marks allotted	=	15

Achieved Marks

No. of Students	*Obtained Marks*
2	13
15	14
10	15

90 per cent of the students = 25
The ranges of marks obtained by 27 students = 13–15
90 per cent of the students got 90 per cent and above marks in the achievement test.

Since 90 per cent of the students got 90 per cent of marks and above the e-content is validated based on the achievement test conducted to the students.

Pie Diagram

This pie diagram clearly shows the percentage of students with respect to the percentage of marks obtained in the achievement test.

1. 7.40 per cent of students who have scored 86.67 per cent of marks in the achievement test conducted for validating the developed e-content.
2. 55.56 per cent of students who have scored 93.33 per cent of marks in the achievement test conducted for validating the developed e-content.
3. 37.04 per cent of students who have scored 100 per cent of marks in the achievement test conducted for validating the developed e-content.

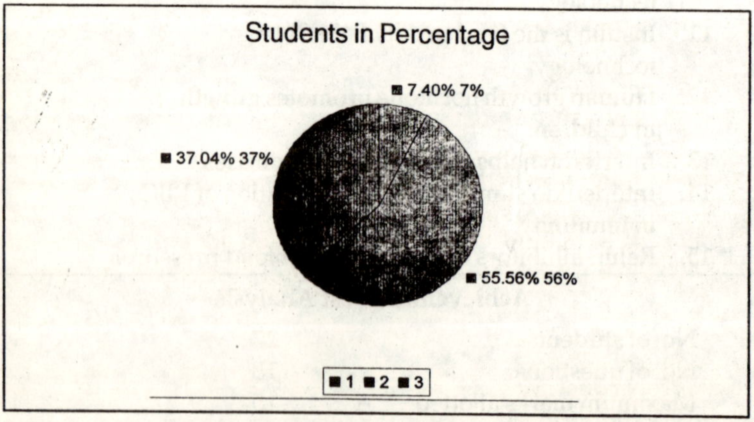

Conclusion

The teacher today has at his command a wide range of aids to choose from using the right type of aids at the right time in the right way can help the teacher in

- Motivating the students.
- Focusing attention.
- Reducing verbalism.
- Inducing greater attention.
- Classifying concepts.
- Bringing the world into the class room.
- Making abstract concepts into concrete.
- Adding interest and involvement.

And thus make learning more enjoyable, dynamic and permanent. This e-content development is an effort from the part of investigator to take the concept of rDNA technology to the student's community in an effective manner.

REFERENCES

1. Davidson, K. (1998) Education in the Internet linking theory to reality (on–line). Available: http://www.oise.on.ca/-kdavidson/cons.html
2. Fillip Neven and Erick Dual., "Reusable learning objects: a survey of LOM-based Repositories, Belgium: Available: http://www. CAI.com/
3. Sharma, G.D. Prof. "Knowledge packaging for face to face and self paced learning". Consortium for educational communication, NSC Campus. Aruna Azaf Ali Marg, New Delhi.
4. http://www.rDNA.com/
5. http:/www.insulin.com/

11

Code Switching and Collusion: Classroom Interaction Between Chinese Bilinguals

Jackie Yeoh Lay Kean, Malaysia

Introduction

Malaysia, being a multi-ethnic and multi-lingual country consists of three main ethnic groups, namely Malay, Chinese and Indian. The people speak a multitude of languages, ranges from Malay, English, Mandarin, Tamil, other Chinese dialects such as Cantonese, Hakka, Hainanese, Teochew, Hokkien, and other languages of indigeneous groups in Sabah and Sarawak.

Malaysians are generally bilinguals, if not multi-lingual. Basically, we can categorise Malaysians into two types of bilinguals. The first type of bilingual is that the indigeneous groups need to know more than one language for socializing purposes. The second type of bilingual is one which is acquired, i.e., through the compulsory learning of school subjects such as Malay and English from primary level onwards.

Let's look at a brief overview of the language education in Malaysia. Although Malay is the national language of the country, English is taught as an important second language. Generally, there are two types of schools in the country, namely the national schools and the national type schools.

The national type schools comprise of Chinese-medium schools and Tamil-medium schools where Chinese and Tamil is the medium of instruction respectively, Malay is taught as the second language and English as the third language. In the national schools, the medium of instruction is Malay and English is taught as a second language.

With the type of language situation in Malaysia, it is an accepted phenomenon that Malaysians alternate the use of two or more languages. Asmah (1982) did a study on verbal communication among the Malaysians shared her observation:

> "... bilinguals are on the increase. The role of Malay ... as the national and official language, contributes to the presence of bilingualism among individual in Malaysia. Coupled with this, the English Language which ... at the moment remains as the second most important language in Malaysia, has also brought about the rise of bilinguals of Malay-English, Cantonese-English, Tamil-English and so on."
>
> *(Asmah, 1982: 119)*

In a multi-ethnic and multi-lingual country like Malaysia, it is a common phenomenon among students to alternate the use of two or more languages. It is common to hear students switching from Malay to English, Mandarin, Hokkien, Cantonese, Hakka or Tamil. Switching of this kind is an inevitable process in a multi-lingual and multi-ethnic setting in Malaysia. (Asmah, 1982).

The more common form of switching among school children especially among Chinese students who studied in the Mandarin medium schools from Year 1 to Year 6 is the switching from Mandarin to Bahasa Malaysia or English or vice versa. This is so due to the fact that these Chinese students only communicate in Mandarin or other dialects even when they are at home. This is seen in terms of Appel and Muysken's (1987) classification, where the Chinese ethnic in Malaysia would fall in the category of a Type II bilingual society. The Type II category consists of people who have the command of two and often more language and the entire society can be considered as bilingual. Thus, most Malaysian Chinese are able to converse in at least two, if not more languages, one being Mandarin and the other Malay or English.

Due to the factor stated above and some socio-cultural factors, switching from Mandarin to English and vice versa at the word, phrase, clause, sentence or discourse level is a natural and prominent phenomenon. This is also true even if the students are fairly competent in English. This phenomenon of switching from one language to the other is technically known as code switching.

The earlier studies of code-switching in multi-lingual societies focused on the sociological aspects, where code-switching was felt to be triggered by a number of socio-cultural factors. Since code-switching was found to be neither random nor meaningless, it can be assumed that code-switching can be said to be rule-governed.

In an observation by Abdullah (1979) on code-switching among Malay-English bilinguals, discussions concerning studies will lead to exchanges in English. Bilingual Malay students often use English to refer to concepts that are specifically Western. Another factor that contributes to code-switching is the setting. Azlina (1975) in her study on code-switching stated that Malay bilinguals code-switch in informal situations more frequently than in formal situations.

An analogy can be made based on Abdullah's and Azlina's studies when the results of the current observation carried out on Mandarin speaking students arrived at the same results. The above findings provide views relevant to this study, on the general use of Mandarin and English in the daily conversations of Chinese bilinguals.

Gumperz (1972) has argued that if the goals of bilingualism are to be achieved, there must be some understanding of the nature of code-alternation and its meaning in everyday interaction. With that in mind, this present study seeks to look at the purposes of code-switching which are identified as conversational functions. These conversational functions are intended to arrive at the social meanings of code-switching.

Language choice and language variation have always been the main concern for people who are interested in studying the language behaviour of both children and adults. Sociolinguists in Malaysia attempt to find out what motivates a speaker to choose Language A rather than Language B or what causes a speaker to switch from Language A to Language B. A study which aims to answer the above question, namely the when, why, where and whom, is indeed significant so that sociolinguists in general and educators in particular would be able to understand better the patterns used among Malaysians, within the culturally and linguistically diverse setting.

This present study hopes to offer insights into the characteristics of code-switching behaviour among Chinese bilingual students who habitually alternate Mandarin and English as they communicate with their peers and teachers. This study also hopes to contribute towards a better understanding of the phenomenon of code-switching which has, in the past been referred to in derogatory terms such as bastardized, corrupt to name a few. (Kamwangamalu, 1989)

According to Gumperz (1972) the incidence of code-switching in human groups, its persistence overtime, its linguistic characteristics and its functions in human interaction when treated as a communicative phenomenon in which speakers build on each other's knowledge of alternatives, can generate important conversational inferences. This study which focuses on a detailed analysis of natural conversations may provide important clues to the phenomenon of language choice and language variations among bilingual speakers.

Code-switching is a very useful social skill which reflects linguistic competence or lack of it. Bilinguals employ it as a communicative strategy to fulfill a broad range of communicative functions. It is with this view in mind that the present study hopes to investigate code-switching in order to throw some light on the relationships between interactional strategies and social meanings in the Malaysian context. This present study also hopes to provide more information and understanding of this code-switching behaviour so that this speech phenomenon would be able to gain more acceptance as a communicative strategy in a multi lingual and multi cultural setting.

This research aims at:

(i) Interpreting the social meanings of code-switching used by bilingual Chinese students by attempting to study the different types of conversational functions of code-switching in the natural conversations of the bilingual Chinese students/Mandarin speaking students.

(ii) Determining whether code-switching is related to the proficiency of bilingual speakers in their languages

Definitions of Code-Switching

The author has looked at various definitions proposed by various linguists. For the purpose of this study the author has confined the discussion to four definitions of code-switching.

The term code-switching was defined as follow:

"code-switching has become a common term for alternative

use of two or more languages, varieties of a language or even speech style."

(Hymes, 1978)

"... the use of two or more linguistic varieties in the same conversation or interaction. The varieties may be anything from genetically unrelated languages to two styles of the same language."

(Scotton and Ury, 1975)

"... the use of more than one language by the communicants in the execution of a speech act."

(Di Pietro, 1978)

"... the alternating use of two languages on the word, phrase, clause or sentence level. Such alternation differs from linguistic interference and integration in that in code-switching, there is ordinarily a clean break between phonemic systems. In essence, code-switching involves introducing into the context of one language stretches of speech that exhibit the other language's phonological and morphological features."

(Guadalupe Valdes-Fallis, 1978)

The definition of Guadalupe Vales-Fallis has been selected for the purpose of this research to further clarify the interpretation of code-switching. Code-switching in this study refers to the alternate use of two genetically unrelated languages of Mandarin and English at the word, phrase, clause or sentence level in the conversations of bilingual Mandarin speaking students.

Some possible reasons for the switching from one language to the other as suggested by Crystal (1987) were explored. Firstly, we need to consider whether a speaker may not be able to express himself/herself in one language so chooses to switch to the other language to compensate the language deficiency. Secondly, switching may occur when the speaker wishes to express solidarity with a particular social group. Here, the speaker may choose to exclude others from the conversation.

Studies of Code-Switching in Other Settings

The studies done on code-switching in other settings are divided into two categories, namely sociolinguistic and linguistic.

Sociolinguistic studies are concerned with how language choice relates to socio-cultural and individual factors and language functions whereas linguistic studies look at the structure of language.

Language alternation between various pairs of languages has been found to be characteristic of communities bilingual in Swedish and English, Greek and English, French and English, Yiddish and English, Italian and English, German and English, two dialects of Norwegian and English, two dialects of Hindi and English, Hindi and Punjabi and English and Spanish (Valdes-Fallis, 1978:7). Findings from these studies have found code-switching to be neither random nor meaningless. Rather, code-switching is used a device to convey important social information ranging from role relationships between speakers to feelings of solidarity, intimacy and so forth.

The above findings have helped the author to look for the social and linguistic aspects of code-switching among bilingual Chinese students.

Blom and Gumperz (1972) have made a study by looking into the factors which account for speakers switching between one variety of a language and the other. In teir study, they investigated the language use in the village of Hemnesberget where all the residents spoke both the standard language, Bokmal and the local dialect, Ranamal. Blom and Gumperz discovered two types of code-switching, "metaphorical code-switching" and "conversational code-switching." The first type of code-switching was used to convey a speaker's attitude toward the topic of the conversation while the second type was used to convey a speaker's attitude towards his audience.

Gumperz (1977) has observed five conversational functions from his study, namely:

1. Quotations
2. Addressee Specification
3. Interjections
4. Repetitions
5. Message Qualification.

Another researcher, Poplack (1988, 226-227), on the other hand, has identified a few other functions in her recent study of five Ottawa-Hull neighbourhood. She notes that code-switching provides the speaker with expressions that are often shorter, more succinct and more apt or expensive. Code-switching may also occur when the speaker intends to state proper nouns, known as facility of expressions.

Rayfield (1970) states that code-switching may be used in many ways to emphasize a statement or to create special effects in a speech. He identifies five functions of code-switching as follow:

1. to emphasize a contrast between two clauses when the second clause is coded in the other language;
2. to emphasize a statement which the hearer might not expect;
3. to avoid saying the unpleasant or slightly indelicate matter in the speaker's ethnic language;
4. to emphasize by repeating a statement in two language; and
5. to make a parenthetic remark.

Another view which is taken into account is Kachru's (1983). He states that code-switching is used for role identification when it conveys social information about the speaker, serving to mark him for example as knowledgeable about a specific topic, generally well educated, urban, etc. Kachru (1983) also mentions elucidation and interpretation, register identification and neutralization as motivations for switching.

Current Study

This study was conducted on ten Chinese students, aged between eighteen and twenty four years old. They were selected based on their education and family background and on the basis of bilinguality and the ability to engage in conversations especially in switching between Mandarin and English.

Research Design

The data for this study on code-switching were gathered through transcribing spontaneous conversations of some selected Chinese bilingual students studying English in a private university college in Subang Jaya. The transcribed data were then used to analyse and examine instances of code-switching.

The researcher then interviewed them to gather information about their family background, education level and the language they use in school and at home. These subjects were found to be bilingual in both Mandarin and English. They use both the language freely in their conversations.

Not all the data collected were recorded directly by the researcher or subjects but by the subjects' close friends who acted as informants. This method of data collection was employed to ensure authenticity of the data collected and so that the subjects were less conscious of the language used during their conversations.

The subjects were free to talk about any topics as this study is based on free and spontaneous speeches. I quote Ervin-Tripp who said "Studies conducted in natural setting like those of Labov and Cohen and Mitchell proved to be valuable." (Sampson 1971: 56)

A total of ten sets of oral conversations were collected for analysis. These conversations took place in five formal and five informal situations involving ten subjects. Out of the ten conversations, four conversations were transcribed from male subjects while six conversations were from female subjects.

Let me qualify the meaning of formal situations and informal situations. By formal situation, I mean the students carried out the conversations either with a teacher, an administrative staff in the classroom or registration office whereas in informal situations, students interact freely and informally amongst themselves.

The analysis carried out is based on the concept of conversational functions developed by Gumperz (1982) and supplemented by others like Poplack (1988), Kachru (1983) and Rayfield (1970). The conversational functions form the main frame for analyzing data. By studying these functions, the social meanings and purposes that trigger code-switching among the subjects in specific situations are examined.

Findings and Discussions

A total of fifteen conversational functions were identified as code-switching utterances. However, for the purpose of this research, based on the ten sets of conversations transcribed, only some of the conversational functions discussed above will be referred to. These conversations will be examined in detail and supported with explanations. The matrix language is in ordinary font, whereas the switched code is in italics. The switched code in 'han yin pin yin' will also be translated into English and printed within brackets.

The motivations of code-switching are examined in the light of conversational functions which are interpreted to refer to social meanings. However, it is noted that some of these conversational functions overlap with one another. Thus, the interpretations in this study are only descriptive in nature.

A. Quotations

Speakers switch codes to quote to sound more credible to the listener. Using code-switching for quotation makes the narration more vivid because it makes it 'closer to the real thing'. (Scotton, 1993: 117)

This type of code-switching is used to preserve the authenticity and originality of the message. The example below will illustrate the above:

Situation 8

Student 2: *Ta suo* study everything *ta qiau. Ta suo jiao de na bian hui you liang* parts, *xuan zhe ti* A, B, C, D. *Ta suo* "very easy"

(She said study everything she taught. There'll be two parts, objective, A, B, C, D. She said "very easy.")

From the example above, the speaker quoted the exact words as what the teacher said. Perhaps the speaker felt that the message, which was originally in English would not have the same impact or serves the same purpose on the listener if it had been translated to Mandarin.

B. Interjections

In some instances, code-switching serves to mark an interjection or sentence filler which does not necessary translate well. In cases like this, interjection is used by speaker to express strong or candid feelings. The example below illustrates this function:

Situation 5

Student 3: Aiyoh! *Zoa mo chi dao*! What lah you?
(Aiyoh! Why late?! What lah you?)

'Aiyoh' is a common expression employed to show feeling of disbelief, annoyance or surprise.

C. Repetition

Repetition is used to clarify what was said or to emphasize a certain word or phrase or content of the message. The switches can be made in both languages from English to Mandarin or vice versa.

The few examples below will illustrate this function:

Situation 5

Student 1: Hey! *Dui bu qi. Wo chi dao!*
(Hey! Sorry I'm late!)

Student 2: Jiao tong zhu sai! Traffic jam!
(Bad traffic jam! Traffic Jam!)

Student 3: Aiyoh! *Zoa mo chi dao*! What lah you?
(Aiyoh! Why late?! What lah you?)

Student 2: *Dui bu qi* lah! Sorry!
(Sorry lah, Sorry!)

Situation 6

Student: *Hao de! Xie xie*. Thank you.
(Ok! Thank you.)

Situation 8

Student 1: *Zen yang study*? How to study?
(How to study? How to study?)

Situation 9

Student 1: Very good! *Hen hao! Wo men wan shang qu.*
(Very good! Very good! We go tonight.)

Situation 10

Student: *Jiao tong zhu sai.* Traffic jam.
(Traffic jam. Traffic jam.)

In the above examples the phrases were repeated by a single individual to amplify and emphasize what is being said. Sometimes, it can be seen as to show sincerity as in the phrase 'Sorry' and 'Thank you'.

D. Message Qualification

Sometimes speakers employed switched codes which consist of qualifying constructions such as a sentence or a verb complement following a statement mentioned earlier in the other code. This function helps the user to clarify and reinforce a point for better understanding. To understand this function, a segment of the conversation in Situation 1 is referred.

Situation 1

Student: I don't want to re-sit the paper. *Wo bu yao* fail.
(I don't want to re-sit the paper. I don't want to fail)

In the conversation above, the student qualify the previous message that she does not want to fail the paper, therefore she resorted to copying in the exam.

E. Personalization versus Objectivization

To quote Gumpertz, this function include the speakers' involvement in, or distance from a message or an addressee, whether a statement reflects a personal opinion, feeling or knowledge, or refers to specific instances, or whether it has the status of generally known fact (1982: 80)

Situation 7

Student 2: *Bu yao jiao* Jock Chin. *Wo bu xi huan ta.*
(Don't call Jock Chin. I don't like her.)

Student 1: Why? *Wei shen mo*? She's ok what!
(Why? Why? She's ok what!)

The speaker voiced her opinion about Jock Chin to show her disagreement with the statement made by her friend.

F. Addressee Specification

This type of code-switching can also be picked for the data collected. It serves to direct message to a specific person or to exclude the others from the conversation.

The example below which highlights the use of the term 'hey' is to exemplify this function of code-switching to draw the attention of the addressee to the message.

Situation 5

Student 1: Hey! *Dui bu qi. Wo chi dao!*
(Hey! Sorry I'm late!)

G. Proper Name

Code-switching was frequently made in conversations of the subject for proper names of places, games, countries, topics of subjects, clothes, illness, professions or companies.

Speakers code switch in this manner for three reasons. Firstly, they want to express ideas adequately by maintaining the original language of the terms. Secondly, they do so due to the lack of an equivalent in the other code. The third reason observed is that speakers wish to use the terms in the translated codes.

The following examples explain this function of code-switching:

Situation 2

Student: *You. Wo bu ming bai* terms *zai* in Interchange.
(Yes. I don't understand certain terms used in Interchange.)

Situation 3

Student: *Wo ke yi kan* TV2 *he* TV3 *xin wen?*
(Can I watch news on TV2 and TV3?)

Situation 7

Student 1: *Wo hui dai shi wu. Yi ding yao ji de mai* Coke *he* birthday cake.

(I will bring food. Must remember to buy Coke and birthday cake.)

Situation 9

Student 2: *Zhe ge xing qi* Sunway Pyramid *you zhe kou.*
(Sunway Pyramid got offer this week.)

From the four sets of conversations above, the speakers retain the English words of the proper names, such as:

(i) The title of the book 'Interchange' as the topic of the subject the speakers were discussing.
(ii) TV2 and TV3 as the television stations.
(iii) Coke as the name of a soft drink
(iv) Sunway Pyramid as the shopping centre the students hang out during their free time.

H. Expression to Signify Politeness

This conversational function indicates politeness and respect in addressing a person. It appears that it is only natural to address a person by her seniority or position.

The example below exemplifies this function of code-switching:

Situation 10

Student: (runs into class) *Dui bu qi,* teacher!
(runs into class) Sorry, teacher!

I. Habitual

From the data collected, it is observed that in many occasions, speakers made reference to certain terms only in a particular language. The bilingual speaker does so because for him, those terms have always been expressed in that language and that has become a habit to him.

To understand this function, a few examples are referred, as follows:

Situation 3

Student: *Lau shi, wo bu huizue ni gei wo men de* assignment.
(Teacher, I don't know how to do the assignment you gave us.)

Situation 7

Student 1: No need lah. *Zi shi qu* karaoke.
(No need lah. Just go to karaoke.)

Student 1: *Hao! Lai yi qi ji hua Sandy de* party.
(Ok! Let's plan for Sandy's party.)

Student 1: *Wo hui dai shi wu. Yi ding yao ji de mai* Coke *he* birthday cake.
(I will bring food. Must remember to buy Coke and birthday cake.)

Situation 8

Student 2: *Ta suo* study everything *ta jiao de. Na bian hui you liang* parts, *xuan zhe ti* A, B, C, D. *Ta suo* "very easy"
(She said study everything she taught. There'll be two parts, objective, A, B, C, D. She said "very easy.")

Student 1: *Zen yang study*? How to study?
(How to study? How to study?)

Situation 9

Student 1: *Lai yi qi zai wan shang qu* bowling!
(Let's go bowling tonight!)

From the conversations above, the words such as karaoke, party, birthday cake, assignment, parts, study, assignment and bowling were spoken out of habit.

Use of Innovative Strategies

From the conversations transcribed, it is noted that the subjects also resort to creative strategies to compensate for their limited vocabulary in order to sustain a conversation.

According to a research conducted by Kow Yip Cheng (2000: 187) these creative strategies that were employed by the subjects can be categorized into two categories. The first category refers to strategies related to the communication strategies and second is those related to the subjects' first language (referred to as L1) and second language (referred to as L2).

In this present study, I will only refer to one of the strategies employed, i.e., the use of the particle 'loh' and 'lah' which is categorized under the first category. This can be seen in the following example:

Situation 5

Student 3:	Aiyoh! *Zoa mo chi dao*! What lah you? (Aiyoh! Why late?! What lah you?)
Student 2:	*Dui bu qi* lah! Sorry! (Sorry lah, Sorry!)
Student 1:	*Ni mai wu can gei wo men!* (You buy us lunch!)
Student 3:	*Dui! Ni fu qian. Sui jiao ni chi dao?* (Ya. You pay. Who asked you to be late?)
Student 2:	Ok loh!

Overlap of Functions

The data collected indicate that code-switching serves nine conversational functions and one type of communication strategies that were employed by the subjects of my study. However, the distinction between one function and the other may not be discrete. For example, in one particular conversation, there may be an overlap of functions. The example below explains the overlap of functions.

Situation 7

Student 1:	No need lah. *Zi shi qu* karaoke. (No need lah. Just go to karaoke.)
Student 1:	*Hao! Lai yi qi ji hua Sandy de* party. (Ok! Let's plan for Sandy's party.)
Student 1:	*Wo hui dai shi wu. Yi ding yao ji de mai* Coke *he* birthday cake. (I will bring food. Must remember to buy Coke and birthday cake.)

In the above conversation, the speaker used two conversational functions, namely the proper name as in Coke and habitual as in birthday cake.

On the whole, the data revealed that code-switching serves two broad purposes. Firstly, code-switching were habitually motivated. Secondly, speakers code-switch to compensate their communication deficiency.

Conclusion

This study set out to investigate conversational functions governing code-switching among bilingual Chinese students.

It was found that code-switching was motivated by the use of innovative strategies and the following conversational functions such as:

1. Quotation
2. Interjections
3. Repetition
4. Message qualification
5. Personalization versus objectivization
6. Addressee specification
7. Proper name
8. Expression to signify politeness
9. Habitual

Of the nine conversational functions above, code-switching by my subjects is commonly motivated by repetition, proper name and habitual reason.

By understanding the types of code-switching adopted in the students' conversation, it is hoped that teachers would be able see the positive side of the use of code-switching. This would help teachers to adopt suitable teaching methodologies that would help these students to achieve communication efficiency.

I hope that this study contributes not only to a better understanding of code-switching as a bilingual phenomenon in general, but also to a more accurate view of multi lingual culture in Malaysia as a whole.

REFERENCES

1. Abdullah P. 1979. *Some observations on code-switching among Malay-English bilinguals.* Paper presented at the 14th Regional Seminar, Seameo Regional Centre, Singapore, 16 – 21 April 1979.

2. Asmah, Haji Omar. 1982. *Language and Society in Malaysia.* Kuala Lumpur: Dewan Bahasa and Pustaka.
3. Appel, R. and Muysken, P. 1987. *Language Contact and Bilingualism.* London: Edward Arnold.
4. Ervin-Tripp, S.M. 1964. *An Analysis of the Interaction of Language: Topic and Listener.* American Anthropologists, 66(6) Part 2, 86 - 102.
5. Gumprez, J.J. 1977. *The Sociolinguistic Significance of Conversational Code-Switching.* RELC Journal, 8:2, 1 - 26.
6. —1972. *Verbal Strategies in Multilingual Significance of Conversational Code-Switching.* University of California Working Papers 46. Berkeley: University of California.
7. — 1982. *Discourse Strategies.* Cambridge: Cambridge University Press.
8. Kamwangamalu, Nkonko Mudipanu. 1989. *Code Mixing and Modernization World Englishes.* Volume 8, No. 3. 321 - 32.
9. Kachru, Braj B. 1983. *The Indianization of English: The English Language in India.* Delhi: Oxford University Press.
10. Kow, Y.C. 2000. *The Use of Children's Literature in Malaysian Kindergartens.* National Association for Bilingual Education
11. Noor Azlina Abdullah. 1975. *Code-switching among Bilingual Malays: Some Observations.* An unpublished Sociological Project.
12. Poplack, S. 1988. *Contrasting patterns of Code-Switching in two Communities. Code-switching: Anthropological & Sociological perspectives.* Ed. by Monica Heller, 215 - 44. Berlin: Mouton.
13. Rayfield, J.R. 1970. *The Language of a Bilingual Community.* Paris: Mouton Press.
14. Romaine, S. 1989. *Bilingualism.* London: Basil Blackwell.
15. Scotton, C.M. 1993. *Social Motivations for Code-switching: Evidence from Africa.* Oxford: Clarendon Press.

12
The Current Trends in Technology Enabled Education in India

Malaya Kumar Nayak, London

Trends in Technology Enabled Education

During the three quarters between April and December 1997, India's software exports totaled Rs. 4850 crores (about $ 1.1 billion), a growth of 70 per cent over the same period in the year 1996. It attained an annual rate of $ 5 billion by December 2000. In 2006-07, India's domestic computer software/services market is estimated to be Rs. 37800 crore (US $ 8739.88 million) registering a growth of 27.70 per cent (30.71% in US $ terms) over the year 2005-06 when the domestic software/services industry was estimated at Rs. 29600 crore (US $ 6686.24 million). Whereas software exports totaled Rs. 146000 crore (US $ 33757.23 million) in comparison to a total of Rs. 105000 crore (US $ 23718.09 million) in 2005-06.

Production	*2005-06*		*2006-07*		*% Growth*	
	Rs. Cr.	*US $ Mln.*	*Rs. Cr.*	*US $ Mln.*	*Rs. Term*	*US $ Term*
Domestic	29600	6686.24	37800	8739.88	27.70	30.71
Software for export	105000	23718.09	146000	33757.23	39.05	42.33
Total	**134600**	**30404.34**	**183800**	**42497.11**	**36.55**	**39.77**

Source: http://www.escindia.in/htmlsite/AboutUs.aspx?Id=35

Regardless of these encouraging figures (or perhaps because of them), a number of observers have despaired over the quality of research and teaching at higher educational levels in India. This has been over-shadowed by the huge numbers in education, the academic tradition in a lot of communities and the thoroughness of school and college teaching, which have lead to Indian engineers and software professionals doing well in India as well as abroad. (Bhorat, 2005).

The success stories of Indian engineer-entrepreneurs in the US (in recent times the $ 300 million Hotmail sale to Microsoft) are plentiful. And still it is hard to find a Ph.D. candidate in India. Not that there are not still a multitude of good teachers. The last of the 1950s and 1960s foreign-educated Ph.Ds. are still there, accompanied by a number of enthusiastic younger men-but few students.

Employment is so easily available, and the starting salaries for good B.Es. (graduates with a bachelor of engineering degree) so high (corresponding to the salary of an assistant professor, in the case of software engineers working in India, and many times that for those who get employment on overseas contracts), none of the graduates of top schools wants to go on for an Indian M.Tech. (although they often accept assistantships abroad), let alone a Ph.D.

This was why IBM's decision of setting up a research center in New Delhi, in collaboration with the Indian Institute of Technology, was greeted with real excitement as the center aspired to be staffed "at the Ph.D. level." This follows closely on the decision by Microsoft to have a software development facility operational in Hyderabad in 1998. This center today is Microsoft's largest product development center outside the headquarters in Redmond. This was the second such facility outside the US which concentrates on the interoperability of Win-NT and Back-Office with non-Microsoft products. (http://www.microsoft.com/india/msidc/default.aspx)

These projects, together with the success of a number of small indigenous software ventures started up by (Ph.D.) returnees from overseas, are making Ph.D. programmes look more attractive. And just as environmentalists look at the numbers of tigers to measure the success of their conservation programmes, computer scientists in India analyze this new infusion of brainpower and corporate interest as a healthy indicator for the future of the computer science and informatics disciplines in India. To this date, faculty positions in computer science have been going begging or have been filled by transferring teachers from other departments.

A new phenomenon has been noticed lately, however: Men in their 30s, with five to eight years' working experience in the US following their Ph.D., are returning to the country to accept teaching jobs and Indian salaries. When asked, they say *(a)* they are in a top school (usually the Indian Institute of Technology or the Indian Institute of Science); *(b)* they can afford it since they have built up savings accounts during their time abroad; *(c)* they go back to work overseas in the summers and on sabbaticals; *(d)* they wish to live and to raise their children in India.

The number of overseas organizations setting up software development arms in India keeps on growing. In the last one decade computer vision has scaled down its US software facilities; Baan (the Netherlands maker of enterprise resource planning software) has expanded its India presence fourfold and made its India site the major center for software development; Magic Enterprises (Israel) has set up a joint venture in Pune; Motorola has not only expanded its Bangalore center that provides worldwide support' but has also participated in two Masters-level telecommunications training centers in Bangalore (at the Indian Institute of Science) and Pune (at the Pune Institute of Computer Technology) (Basant and Pankaj, 2005).

IIS Infotech, a $ 20 million global software export company specializing in year 2000 solutions, has also set up a chain of web sites in 10 different cities and is providing a two year web and multimedia course followed by a one year internship in industry. IIS has multilocational office and development centers at Delhi, Mumbai, Banglore and Chennai. (http://www.indiansources.com/iisinfo.htm)

The Centre for Development of Advanced Computing, a government company set up a few years back when the US declined to export Cray supercomputers to India, has developed a six-month postgraduate course in multimedia and advanced computing. Previously, the centre developed some hundred Indian language fonts for the twenty major scripts in India and South-East Asia, in addition to add-on hardware for DOS, and word-processor and database management systems using their scripts.

In the meantime, education using computers or multimedia remains far behind the state of the art. Apart from NIIT, no other group is making major use of multimedia technology, even though the number of new educational CD-ROMs has increased many times. The advertising companies and film industry is absorbing most of the qualified persons in this field. Prices of CD-ROMs must also fall before they become a mass market item. Foreign-produced CD-ROMs are sold for the US retail price plus 75 per cent, whilst local CD-ROMs sell for the equivalent of between $ 25 and $ 50, which is may be twice to three times what a middle-class computerized family might be willing to pay. (Jha, 2006)

A few years back the Department of Electronics floated a scheme for providing a franchised system of privately run multimedia centers all over the country, which was to provide training as well as services. These were intended to operate on the service model of the existing "telephone booths" at every street corner from where one can make local, long distance or intercontinental telephone calls with computerized billing. The Centre for Development of Advanced Computing, which has developed the PARAM series of parallel supercomputers, has also been involved in this effort. They are responsible for developing the curriculum and package of materials for the multimedia centers under the Department of Electronics Programme.

Issues and Solutions

This information brings us to the primary issue of overcoming India's major weakness in the age of technology. India has a population of 950 millions plus and 30 per cent are below the poverty line. 'What is more important is that 48 per cent of the people are illiterate. Indians live mentally in different times. India is like a snake whose head is in the 20th century and the tail is in the 17th century. This two speed India symbolizes a structural weakness in making India into an economic super power. What is important is to make India into a single speed India, and this will be possible if India is able to use information technology to overcome the problem of illiteracy and poor health.

The irony of a two-speed India is striking. At one level, bright technocrats are making their mark in technology. At another level, 97 per cent of the population in India does not speak English. India still lives in 600,000 villages with only 30 per cent population in urban areas. 80 per cent of the people do not have access to a toilet.

Looking to the potential of Information Technology (IT), can it be used as a lever to move India from the two speed condition to a single speed developed nation? I think it is possible.

The first step is to make computers operate in Indian languages. At present, to make this happen, technologies like Graphic

Intelligence Based Script Technology (GIST) developed by Center for Development of Advanced Computing (CDAC) and computer software solutions developed by National Center for Software Technology (NCST) are already available.

The second step is developing total literacy. While India may produce world class professionals and technocrats, only 52 per cent of Indians are literate. One common trait behind the success of the Asian Tigers is education. Initiative has been taken for a 100 per cent literacy programme in India. Computers and interactive television facility must be used for removing illiteracy within a short period. Software like the one developed by Dr. Thirumurthy of Vallabh Vidyanagar that helps adult illiterates to learn the Gujarati alphabet in 1/10th time it takes to learn from a human teacher is the need of the time. IT can also be used for multiplying manifold the potential of the human teacher. In Mahabharata, Drona refused to teach Ekalavya, who went on to master archery in front of Drona's statue, to the extent of rivaling Arjuna. Today Ekalavyas do not need such statues because interactive television technology is available. Indira Gandhi National Open University is using this technology in their long distance learning programmes for certain subjects and short courses on management and so on.

India should have rugged computers in all the schools. One may wonder how, when there are not even blackboards in Indian schools, can we talk about computers? Moreover, electricity may not be available in all schools. This invites attention to an interesting experiment to generate electric power using bullocks by Shri Kantisen Shroff of the Shroff Foundation Trust at Kalali, near Baroda in Gujarat. Shri Shroff calls Nandi Urja. After all, the bovine sight that Gates had in Delhi can also help in solving the problem of electricity in rural areas.

If there are computers in school, educational material in the digital form is also needed. A massive effort at putting all educational material in different Indian languages into a computer readable form must be made. Incidently, this will provide tremendous employment opportunities for the educated young men and women. Computers with CDROMs will bring a new world of knowledge to every school even in the remotest village of India. This may sound unrealistic to many but it is high time for India to have a vision to break away from the vicious cycle of illiteracy, poverty and backwardness. However, the question arises: Where is the money for all this to come from? This is the third step for building a single speed India.

Every Member of Parliament gets a grant of more than Rs. 10 million each year to be spent on development work in his constituency. This is called the Members of Parliament Local Area Development (MPLAD) Programme. The Department of Electronics (DOE) got five schemes approved under this programme for Members of Parliament for developing the culture of IT in their constituency. The MPLAD funds can be used to achieve this objective. (Momaya, 2003).

The first scheme relates to putting computers in schools. There are more than 600,000 primary schools, 75,000 high schools and 8,000 colleges in India. The idea is to put computers in schools so that the next generation coming out from the schools will not only be literate but computer literate. The second scheme is to place a computer, modem and a printer in every college and link it with the Education and Research Network (ERNEST) of the DOE and therefore create an "information footpath." The intention is that, in spite of the library budget or the physical location of the college, students can access databases and the latest technical literature and the facility of E-mail. A third scheme provides for starting HAM (amateur radio) clubs in high schools, so that children can become technology minded in electronics and communication. The fourth scheme visualizes provision of a Citizen Band (CB) radio particularly in public transport vehicles and in hospitals, so that, in case of an accident, the nearest hospital could be contacted and valuable lives saved. The fifth scheme is an employment generation scheme through setting up of very Small Aperture Terminals (VSATs) so that bibliographic databases industry can be given a boost. Dr. Viswanathan, Director of Indian National Science Documentation Centre (INSDOC) mentions that the potential for employment is anywhere between three lacs and thirty lacs.

There seems to be a ray of hope under the MPLAD programme. Shri Shrikant Jichkar, the then MP, a HAM enthusiast himself, has used the funds for setting up HAM clubs. Dr. Aram, the then MP made a VSAT available to the Bharathiar University, so that they can avail the advantage of high speed data communication. May be there are other MPs in the current government who have taken a similar initiative.

For employment generation in the database industry or translation of educational material into computer readable form in the different languages, funds from Prime Minister's Rozgar Yojana and Jawahar Rozgar Yojana can be used, apart from the MPLAD funds. The industry also can be given tax incentives by the state and the central governments to fund some of these activities (IFC 2005).

In the ultimate analysis, technology depends on developing the right type of scientific and technological manpower. Here India faces a lot of problems. There are five dangers that the country seemingly faces, and perhaps a Panchasheel strategy can be followed to overcome those five dangers.

The first problem is a cancer eating up the Indian education system for developing scientific manpower. For the last nearly 15 years, the number of students who are taking regular graduate science courses is going down. It is the science graduate students who provide the foundation for pure research and break-throughs. This creeping cancer in our science education is a reality, since a science career is unattractive to the youth of the times.

Even if the technical courses like engineering or medicine, which are popular, are considered there is another problem that is faced in the country owing to the process of social development. This is the second problem. For years, India had a very imbalanced and dictatorial society. Consequently, certain communities came to be known as forward communities and exploited the weaker segments of the society. At present, the political environment and growing awareness of the oppressed classes have moved the Government to formulate policies in order that these classes get an opportunity to draw level with the backlog. The policy of quota system in professional courses is designed to promote the weaker sections. This is a very significant and welcome development.

But like all things it is not an unmixed blessing. One consequence of this policy of quota system is that the communities which do not get the advantage of quota system may have brilliant students, however only a small number of them would be able to get into the type of technical courses that they like. A major portion of bright student manpower is therefore left out in pursuing their career in engineering or medicine. A solution to this problem must be found.

The third problem relates to nurturing and encouraging creativity which is the sine qua non for the development of technology. Technology develops in an environment where creativity is nurtured, which in turn encourages scientific research, and once someone invents anything or makes a break-through, there is encouragement provided for him to develop his Intellectual Property Rights (IPR).

In the context of WTO and discussions on IPRs, patents have become a live issue. India, the patent regime acts as a wet blanket for creativity. It is nearly anti-creativity and research. For instance, Sam Pitroda studied in Baroda in India and then went to the USA, got a number of patents, became a multimillionaire, came back and launched a telecom revolution for his country. If Pitroda had remained in India, he would never have got the patents. It takes 6 years to get a patent in India, whereas it takes 22 months in USA.

That brings the discussion to the fourth problem. A strategy is needed to get the right faculty to teach in Indian institutions. Competent faculty may not be easily available. Teaching has to be made into an attractive career.

The fifth problem which is faced today in India is the difficulty of getting bright creative youth for research and development. The attractions available without delay for working for MNCs or private sector in the country or abroad are too tempting (Mitra, 2006b). The country will face a severe manpower problem at the very fountain spring of technology, the research and development laboratories.

These five problems must be dealt with by a package of five solutions. In brief, a panchasheel strategy for development of technical manpower in India. Here are the five ideas of the panchasheel.

The first is related to the B.Sc. science courses. This article makes two suggestions with regard to this. The first is that a computer course module must be made a part of the input of every B.Sc. course all through the country, regardless of the main course, be it chemistry, physics, geology or geography. This means everyone who comes out of the college would have been trained in computer science and IT. At present, the need for the computer courses is being recognized widely. A couple of decades ago the students after doing the 12th standard were going for learning typing. Nowadays they go for computer courses where they are forced to pay enormous fees by the rapidly increasing teaching shops. The standards are also not homogeneous in the burgeoning computer teaching shops. If computer science becomes a part of the education of all students' who get a B.Sc. degree, the whole perception of the B.Sc. course will change. More importantly, the country will have a vast number of students' trained in computer science. An added benefit will be the domain knowledge of the different branches of science. India will therefore be able to build a vast army of foot soldiers of technology in the up-and-coming information age. India can as a result provide for an explosive growth of IT that can take place in this country. Moreover, the students will be saved from being exploited by countless private teaching shops which are charging exorbitant fees. This is not to condemn the private companies wholesale. There are many good ones which are providing the manpower required by Indian industry in the present day. However, when thinking of a national strategy for scientific manpower, it should be recognized that IT is going to be the key technology of the future. This truth is recognized even by the political groups.

The second suggestion is to have, like the National Science Foundation of USA, a well funded program, so that a brilliant student can think of taking science as a career and also become interested in research and development. This will tackle the problem about attracting bright youngsters to research and development as well as attracting bright faculty for teaching (Mitra, 2006a).

The second major problem is the problem of the brilliant students' from the non-reserved communities losing the prospect to learn technology. There is the formal education system of universities. There are private initiatives, private institutions which are almost run on commercial lines, there is in-company training. These three form the three streams of education today. It is suggested that there should be a fourth stream of education. This is the third idea. What is meant by the fourth stream is a stream of institutions set up by the industry to meet the particular needs of the industry. They must have full freedom in designing their curriculum which will be up-to-date and as per the market demand. They can charge profitable rates for fees. However, to enable the middle class and the poor students, who may not be belonging to the reserved communities and who may like to take professional careers, banks and education trusts should come forward to give economical study loans. As these courses will be so industry specific, once a person gets into these courses, he is bound to have an excellent well paying career. The entire operation of running educational institutions will become a bankable proposal.

The fourth set of ideas deal with the third problem about creativity and encouragement of talent by IPRs. Without any further faltering, the patent act should be amended so that it is in tune with law in developed countries, so that the patent has the same credibility as those in developed countries in the global market. Till this is done, it is suggested that we should at least improve the speed of giving patents. We must reduce the time taken for issuing a patent from the current six years to less than a year.

Secondly a venture capital fund must be set up. Any promising technology by an Indian inventor needs to be assisted by this venture fund to take patents in the US and other developed countries. It costs more than five lacs for a US patent and more than Rs. 50 lacs for the rest. In this fashion, Indian scientists and technocrats will be encouraged and there will be full IPR protection. This will mean outstanding returns in financial terms to the Indian scientist. This is one method of eventually getting the right manpower.

The fourth problem is the issue of getting good teaching staff. The fifth set of ideas deal with these problems. It has already been mentioned that if India can have something like the National Science Foundation and have programs and funding schemes to encourage bright people to take to teaching as career, it will be very much helpful. At the same time, the fourth stream also will assist in providing better faculty as the industry executives can be convinced to come and teach in these institutions and on deputation. There should be a culture of the faculty from the education institutions going on deputation to industry to get their financial rewards and also getting hands on exposure to the industry. Such flexibility at the moment is not possible in the current system.

Indians will have to think of these innovative methods, if they want to deal with the problems of scientific and technical nature they are facing in a pragmatic manner.

Conclusion

This article has placed before you some concepts about how India can by adopting a conscious strategy of choosing the western model of technology based development, overcome the problems of a two speed India, and simultaneously emerge as an economic and technological super power. This means giving up many of the traditional approaches and mind set.

REFERENCES

Basant, Rakesh, and Pankaj Chandra (2005). "Role of Educational and R&D Institutions in City Clusters: An Exploratory Study of Bangalore and Pune Regions in India." Unpublished, Indian Institute of Management, Ahmedabad.

Bhorat, H. (2005). "Links between Education and the Labor Market." In *Skill Formation and Globalization*, ed. M. Powell. Aldershot, UK: Ashgate.

http://www.escindia.in/htmlsite/AboutUs.aspx?Id=35 Retrieved on June 23, 2008.

http://www.indiansources.com/iisinfo.htm Retrieved on June 23, 2008.

http://www.microsoft.com/india/msidc/default.aspx Retrieved on June 23, 2008.

IFC (International Finance Corporation) (2005). "India's Issues and Challenges for Future Private Investment in Higher Education." Unpublished presentation, IFC, Washington, DC.

Jha, C. S. (2006). "Higher Education in India: Restructuring for Increased Innovation." South Asia Finance and Private Sector Development, World Bank, Washington, DC.

Mitra, Raja (2006)a. "India's Emergence as a Global R&D Center." Unpublished, Swedish Institute for Growth Policy Studies, Stockholm.

Mitra, Raja (2006b). "India's Potential as a Global R&D Power." In *The Internationalization of Corporate R&D: Leveraging the Changing Geography of Innovation*, ed. Magnus Karlsson. Stockholm: Institute for Growth Policy Studies.

Momaya, K. (2003). "Sources of Funding for Startups in India." Indian Institute of Technology, Foundation of Innovation and Technology Transfer, New Delhi, and ICICI Knowledge Park, Hyderabad.

BIBLIOGRAPHY

Sahlberg, P. (2006). "Education Reform for Raising Economic Competitiveness." *Journal of Educational Change* 7 (4): 259–87.

Sengupta, S. (2006). "Skills Gap Hurts Technology Boom in India." *New York Times*, October 17.

13
Learning in the Twenty First Century

Dr. Meenu Agrawal, India
Dr. Nadia Yusuf, Dubai

The 21st Century Learning Initiative was established in 1995 by a group of English and American businessmen and organizations to make sense of research on learning and learning processes that were fragmented in many different disciplines, and embedded in many different universities, research institutions and businesses around the world.

The 21st Century Learning Initiative's essential purpose is to facilitate the emergence of new approaches to learning that draw upon a range of insights into the human brain, the functioning of human societies, and learning as a community-wide activity. One believes this will release human potential in ways that nurture and form local democratic communities worldwide, and will help reclaim and sustain a world supportive of human endeavour.

The 21st century was ushered in by the greatest technological revolution in history.[1] Technological advances, immigration, globalization and a ubiquitous media culture define the landscape of the new millennium.

Environments in which students develop models, collect data, and evaluate alternative designs help them develop vital skills needed by practicing engineers. Student learning improves when students actively participate in knowledge construction and in assessment of their own learning. The new millennium was ushered in by a dramatic technological revolution. We now live in an increasingly diverse, globalized, and complex, media-saturated society. According to Dr. Douglas Kellner "this technological revolution will have a greater impact on society than the transition from an oral to a print culture."

When we are born we need to be alive, a natural process of our entity to survive motivates us to carry activities in its protection. General lessons are selection and sourcing of food, defense against risk, expansion of own species or gene, dominion to live healthy and strong, etc; Learning begins from the birth of an infant, the amusing actions are in fact the learning lessons of basics of requirements for survival. Perfection in lessons depends on the quality of character we are, some become master who dominate in the group and some merely succeed to achieve bare needs.

The goal of education is not mastery of subject matter, but of one's person. Subject matter is simply the tool. Much as one would use a hammer and chisel to carve a block of marble, one uses ideas and knowledge to forget one's own personhood.

Education is future-oriented—it is about development and growth, even when we are studying the past. Thus, as educators, the aspect of thinking we tend to focus upon is learning. As we have stressed, much thinking is commonplace—it goes on all the time, often without our being aware of it. Education takes us into the conscious world. It involves activities that are intended to stimulate thinking, to foster learning. We set out to help another person to learn, or to learn something ourselves (a process of self-education). Both can take place at the same time. One learns as one teaches. In conversation one learns about people and communities and also learn the craft of informal education.

Thomas Edison, Henry Ford and many other super achievers never finished grade school. They succeeded because they knew how to research, collect information for a selected project and process knowledge. Classroom environment does not work that way, it focuses on the collection of knowledge without a clear purpose, other than high-class grades. If the purpose does not motivate, other than to please the teacher, then there is nothing to process outside of memorizing answers for test. The typical student is academic challenged while being motivation starved. Lack of motivation is lack of knowledge processing skills.

What can be considered a quality education? A quality education is custom design that addresses the unique abilities of each student and has a positive emotional experience. Custom education evaluates natural talent and how the student learns. This is why home schooled students out perform classroom students. Parents learn what works and does not work, then focus on what works. With this method, students develop a love to learn and learning becomes a lifelong process.

Swami Vivekananda Youth Movement is a development organization, engaged in building a new civil society in India through its grassroots to policy-level action in health, education and community development sectors. Acting as a key promoter-faciliator in the community's efforts towards self-reliance and empowerment, Swami Vivekananda Youth Movement (SVYM) is developing local, innovative and cost-effective solutions to sustain community-driven progress. Swami Vivekananda Youth Movement is also rooted to its values of Satya, Ahinsa, Seva and Tyaga, which is reflected in its programme design and delivery, transactions with like-minded organizations have been the hallmark of SVYM's evolution over the twenty four years.

It would not be a sign of health if such an important social interest as education were not also an arena of struggles, practical and theoretical. It is the business of an intelligent theory of education to ascertain the causes for the conflicts that exist and then, instead of taking one side or the other, to indicate a plan of operations proceeding from a level deeper and more inclusive than is represented by the practices and ideas of the contending parties.... It means the necessity of the introduction of a new order of conceptions leading to new modes of practice. For over a century, mechanical factory models of teaching and learning have been at war with critical, interactive education.

This paper will take the position that the purpose of education is to enable individuals to reach their full potential as human beings, individually and as members of a society; this means that these individuals will receive an education which will enable them to think and act intelligently and purposefully in exercising and protecting the Rights and Responsibilities claimed by the Declaration of Independence.

Technology Teaching

G.L. Shekar, Special Officer, e-Learning Centre, Visveswaraya Technological University (VTU), Mysore, was inaugurating a three week virtual training programme for teachers, on using multimedia and developing electronic content said "We cannot escape from technology, so the best thing is to adopt it like the mobile phone and the Internet. By doing so we are not replacing teachers, only supplementing them." He said, adding that there should be no distinction between "teachers" and "students," because both were learners."

India is a country of villages. In village, students do not have good and intelligent teachers but now new methods of learning can help for these types of burning issues. In modern age, the material could be collected at the data centre from where learners could access video lessons through learning management systems. Distance learning could be enhanced through the use of multimedia and those who wanted lecture notes should be able to obtain them.

According to Mr. G.L. Shekar "India is the only country that has launched a satellite exclusively for educational purpose," he said, explaining how the Edusat network provided direct interaction through audio and video through the use of a satellite rather than a telephone. He said that the Visveswaraya Technological University that was affiliated to 122 engineering institutions was keen on "It is a virtual world now," technology.

Besides offering examination revision service, technology-specific classes, soft skill lessons, campus recruitment programmes, full semester and supplementary programmes, the University invited industry leaders to interact with a large numbers of students over its studio network.

Students had access to preparatory material, archived content, live seminars, electronic learning content and interactive forums. "When we improve the productivity component of teachers, the quality of education goes up," he observed there would be both theoretical and practical sessions, including evaluation. The Consortium of Educational Communication (CEC) had chosen the college to conduct the programme because it possessed a satellite interactive terminal of Edusat, besides video conferencing facility. G.D. Sharma, Director of the Consortium, in a videoconferencing session from New Delhi, said "It is a virtual world now,"

A study of technology, which provides an opportunity for students to learn about the processes and knowledge related to technology that are needed to solve problems and extend human capabilities.

Technology is how people modify the natural world to suit their own purposes... generally it refers to the diverse collection of processes and knowledge that people use to extend human abilities and to satisfy human needs and wants.

The role and impact of technology in both our personal and working lives is ever growing. Understanding how people shape technology and how technology shapes people's interactions with each other and the natural world is important not only for those who research, develop and implement new technologies but also for all those people and organizations that have to use those technologies in their working and personal lives.

The Nature of Technology Education

Technology has a number of distinct characteristics:

1. *It Involves Design:* At the centre of technology lies design. That "design is the very core of engineering" is affirmed by the requirement that all degree engineering courses should embody it. *The design process* in technology is a sequential process which bègins with the perception of a need, continues with the formulation of a specification, the generation of ideas and a final solution, and ends with an evaluation of the solution.
2. *It Involves Making*: The motivating factor behind all technological activity is the desire to fulfill a need. For this reason all designs should be made or realized-whether that is through prototype, batch-or mass-production or some form of three-dimensional or computer model-if the need is to be truly fulfilled, the design is to be legitimately evaluated, and the design activity is to have been purposeful and worthwhile.
3. *It is Multi-Dimensional:* Not only may design and production involve co-operation between different specialism's (between, for example, designer, production engineer and materials scientist), but may involve "technologists" in performing a multitude of functions, such as working with others, operating within budgets, persuading decision makers, communicating to clients and working to deadlines.
4. *It is Concerned with Values*: Technology is informed by values at every point. Value decisions may be called for not only in relation to the specific design criteria (i.e., aesthetic, ergonomic and economic judgments, suitability for purpose and ease of manufacture) but also in relation to the rightness or wrongness of a particular solution in ethical terms.

Technology is about taking action to meet a human need rather than merely understanding the workings of the natural world, which is the goal of science. The invention of the microscope was driven by a need to explore the world of the small, beyond our unaided vision. It uses much more than scientific knowledge and includes values as much as facts, practical craft knowledge as much as theoretical knowledge. The iPod is an example of where the physics of making a small device carry so much music is married with creative design to make an iconic must have accessory. It involves organized ways of doing things. It covers the intended and unintended interactions between products (machines, devices, artifacts) and the people and systems that make them, use them or are affected by them through various processes.

Technology is a hand on, can do profession where people have to be skilled in many of the following: engineering, communicating, designing, developing, innovating, managing, manufacturing, modeling, and systems thinking. But technology also gives us various products which can be used for good or ill or where the benefits are disputed and similarly the processes involved in producing and using technology means that we should all take an interest in whether it provides us and everyone else with a sustainable future.

Therefore, instructors have had to become instructional designers conscious of how technology works and what it can offer to the teaching and learning process. Current mobile technology challenges that design even further as it demands a totally different approach to instructional design and also teaching methodology. It requires fluidity never before seen and new skills from both teacher and student. In fact, one would argue that while we focus on the skills needed for students in the 21st century.

Last but not the least; we would like to conclude that the public is keeping abreast with the technology changes. More than ever, individuals value the importance of technology changes in education.

"A simple question to ask is, 'How has the world of a child changed in the last 150 years?" And the answer is, "It's hard to imagine any way in which it hasn't changed! But if you look at school today versus 100 years ago, it is more similar than dissimilar." **— Peter Senge, Senior Lecturer Massachusetts Institute of Technology.**

REFERENCES

1. http://atschool.eduweb.co.uk/trinity/watisted.html
2. http://www.open2.net/sciencetechnologynature/worldaroundus/whatistechnology.html
3. http://www.zwire.com/site/news
4. Innovations in Science, Technology, Engineering, and Mathematics Learning and Teaching By Anthony Eamonn Kelly, Richard A. Lesh, John Y. Baek.
5. A Definition with Commentary, by Al Januszewski, Michael Molenda.
6. Technology for active learning by Yehudit Judy Dori, John Belcher, Mark Bessette, Michael Danziger, Andrew McKinney, and Erin Hult (PDF).
7. How Does Technology-Enabled Active Learning Affect Undergraduate Students' Understanding of Electromagnetism Concepts? by Yehudit Judy Dori and John Belcher (PDF).
8. Wells, M., Hestenes, D. & Swackhamer, G., "A modeling method for high school physics instruction," Am. J. Phys. 63: 606-619, 1995.
9. Wilson, J. and W. Jennings, "Studio Courses: How Information Technology is Changing the Way We Teach, On Campus and Off," Proceedings of the IEEE, Vol. 88, No. 1, January 2000, pp. 72-80.
10. Kiaer L., D. Mutchler, and J. Froyd, "Laptop Computers and the Integrated First-Year Curriculum at Rose-Hulman Institute of Technology", CACM, 41(1), January 1988, pp. 45-49.
11. Kolb, D.A., Experiential Learning: Experience as the Source of Learning and Development. Englewood Cliffs, New Jersey: Prentice-Hall, 1984.
12. Harb, J., S. Durrant, and R. Terry, "Use of the Kolb Learning Cycle and the 4MAT System in Engineering Education," J. Eng. Ed., 83(2), April 1993, pp. 70-77.
13. Chen, J., M. Ellis, J. Lockhart, S. Hamoush, C. Brawner and J. Tront, "Technology in Engineering Education: What Do the Faculty Know and Want?" J. Eng. Ed. 89(3), July 2000, pp. 279-283.
14. Prenksy, Marc (2005). Listen to the Natives, Educational Leadership, December 2005/January 2006, Vol., No. 4, Learning in the Digital Age.
15. Scardamalia, M., & Bereiter, C. (1999). Schools as knowledge building organizations. In D. Keating & C. Hertzman (Eds.), Today's children, tomorrow's society: The developmental health and wealth of nations.
16. Vanderbilt Cognition and Technology Group: http://www.nscc.edu/
17. Kellner, Douglas. New Technologies/New Literacies: Restructuring Education for the New Millennium. http://logosonline.home.igc.org/kellner.htm
18. Schlechty, Phillip. (1991) *Schools for the 21st Century – Leadership Imperatives for Educational Reform*. Jossey-Bass Inc., Publishers.
19. Kellner, Douglas. New Technologies/New Literacies: Restructuring Education for the New Millennium. http://logosonline.home.igc.org/kellner.htm

14

Alliances Between Industries and Educational Institutions in Information Technology (IT) Advancement in Nigeria, West Africa

P.C. Okwelle, Nigeria

Introduction

The world is rapidly becoming a global digital society. At the heart of today's globalization is the ease with which information moves around the world, providing opportunities for ideas, innovations and life styles to get easily spread to different places and people on the globe and central to this is Information Technology (IT) (Ola, 2004).

The increasing adoption of IT in almost all aspects of human activity poses great challenges to Nigerian's development. Indeed, virtually every country of the world has recognized the importance of ICT with regard to development. Ukwungwu (2004) defined ICT as the means of acquisition, processing, storage and dissemination of data by a combination of computers and telecommunication accessories. This definition implies that ICT refers to whole range of facilities or technologies involved in information processing and electronic communications, to be handled by Information Technology (IT) experts, who are equipped with capabilities that wi'l maximally utilize ICT for the improvement of society.

The importance of ICT to national development was underscored by the report of Commission of the European communities (EC) (2000) which states that the success of some developed countries with regard to maintaining high gross domestic product (GDP) growth per capital and high labour productivity over the past decade has been associated with high levels of investment in ICT. It is possible therefore, that the ICT revolution will plunge many developing countries into a period of turbulent changes: a period in which both challenges and opportunities will materialize. Countries that fail to keep up with the transformation engendered by this process, whether as a result of ill-conceived policies or inadequate resources, will suffer a number of negative consequences, including the serious curtailment of development efforts. Such countries will inevitably occupy a weaker position within the knowledge-based global market (United Nations Economic and Social Commission for Western Asia [ESCWA], 2003).

Osuji (2005) describing Nigeria's position in the global technology arena said that there is a big gap between the average Nigerian's computer skills and the skills of citizens of other countries around the world. This technology, deficit he continued, translates into a major handicap in efforts to bridge Nigeria's digital divide. In the view of Adebayo, Nigerian's Communication Minister, quoted by Aragba -Akpore (2005), Nigerians were steadily adopting the technology on ground, but was worried that not much progress has been made in their understanding of the tool.

For Nigerian economy to remain relevant and competitive in a world with a new technology order, they must not only embrace IT but must adapt to changes that are daily being created by IT. Ekeh (2004) posits that it would be frightening to imagine the consequences of Nigeria failing to join the current advances in IT. Some of the frightening possibilities, according to Ekeh, include the fact that our graduates would come out of school still unemployable, our doctors will not keep pace with modern diagnostic trends, justice would continue to be delayed in our judiciary and the overall impact will be the continued stagnation of Nigerian economy.

Advancements in ICT are taking place very rapidly each passing day. The rapid changes in technology create a situation where we find new models of computers being introduced almost every month. System design methodologies and software development tools are also changing rapidly. Nsikak-Abasi (2004) maintained that certainly, at the present rate of world ICT growth, new entrants will very soon flood the market rendering the present ones archaic. According to Anumihe (2004) the revolution in products, process, markets and regulation created by IT was not about to stop or even slow down. The only option is to adopt, change and evolve.

This trend poses challenges to industries and educational sectors. It is the educational institutions that provide knowledge and skill needed to help students quickly acclimate into the work force with computer literacy, knowledge about software applications, programming and operating systems. The industrial organization benefit by gaining access to the best students for potential hire and to innovations that leads to new products. Thus, collaboration between industry and academic can be mutually beneficial.

To meet the challenges of the future brought about by IT innovations, industry and academia connections must be revisited often. The problem of this present study therefore, is to identify obstacles and possible areas of shared solutions between Nigeria's industries and educational institutions in meeting the global technology revolution.

To guide this study, the following research questions were posed:

1. What are the obstacles facing industries and educational institutions in keeping current with IT advancement in Nigeria?
2. What solutions to these obstacles can be shared through alliances between industries and educational institutions in Nigeria?

The study also tested the following hypotheses at 0.05 level of confidence:

Ho_1 There is no significant difference between the mean responses of IT Practitioners in industries and educational institutions on the obstacles facing IT advancement in Nigeria.

Ho_2 There is no significant difference between the mean responses of IT Practitioners in industries and educational institutions on the shared solutions to the obstacles with IT advancement in Nigeria.

Method

The study was a descriptive survey design, carried out in the Niger Delta region of Nigeria. The Niger Delta region, which plays host to oil and gas activities, was used because of a good number of industries and institutions of higher learning located in this area, presumed to embrace IT innovations.

The population of the study consisted of all IT lecturers/ instructors in higher institutions and Heads of IT units in major industries in the seven (7) states of the Niger Delta namely: Akwa Ibom, Bayelsa, Cross Rivers, Delta, Edo, Ondo and Rivers. From each state, three (3) lecturers/instructors each from a University, Polytechnic and College of Education as well as one head of IT unit from 10 industries, totaling 63 lecturers/instructors and 70 IT heads of units, consisted the sample of the study. In all, a total of 133 IT Practitioners formed the sample of the study.

The instrument was face validated by five IT Practitioners and was pilot-tested on 25 subjects to determine its reliability. A split-half method was applied to their responses and a reliability coefficient of 0.89 was obtained using Spearman Brown prophecy formula. The researcher administered the final version of the instrument directly to the respondents and a 100 per cent return was obtained. Statistical mean was employed to answer the research questions. Any response with a mean value of 3.50 and above was accepted and below was rejected. The t-test for large independent samples where N is greater than 30, (Denga, 1987 and Nworgu, 1991) was used to analyze the hypotheses.

Results

The findings of the study based on the analyses of data to the research questions and hypotheses are summarized in Tables 1 and 2 below.

Table–1
Mean, Standard Deviation and t-Test Values Subjects' Responses on the Obstacles Facing Industry and Academia in IT Advancement

S.No.	*Items*	*Industry IT Practitioner*		*School IT Practitioner*		*Cal t-value*
		X_1	SD_1	X_2	SD_2	
1.	Design of curriculum that emphasizes current practices in IT	3.51	1.40	3.80	1.10	0.69
2.	Proliferation of new course topics in IT	3.63	1.40	4.20	1.02	0.19
3.	Modification of course content to include the use of new technology	3.56	1.39	4.30	0.73	*2.87
4.	Lengthy curriculum review cycle	3.74	1.50	4.10	1.01	*4.00
5.	High cost of upgrading IT systems	3.68	1.49	3.66	1.03	0.14
6.	Limited fund to procure IT infrastructures for training	3.51	1.02	3.70	1.50	1.40
7.	Obsolete hardware and software for training	3.66	1.40	3.81	1.14	1.50

Contd...

S.No.	Items	Industry IT Practitioner		School IT Practitioner		Cal t-value
		X_1	SD_1	X_2	SD_2	
8.	Re-training personnel to be up-to-date with current practices in IT advancement	3.70	1.50	3.90	1.21	0.57
9.	Retaining personnel knowledge-able in the use of latest IT systems	3.58	1.40	3.62	1.42	0.11
10.	Hiring personnel knowledgeable in latest IT systems	3.74	1.50	4.10	1.00	1.20
11.	Provision of up-to-date instruc-tional materials	3.53	1.44	4.60	0.25	0.34

Critical value of t = 1.96; *df* = 131; number of IT unit heads (N_1 = 70); Number of IT lecturers/instructors (N_2 = 63); X_1 = mean of IT unit heads; X_2 = mean of IT lecturers/instructors (*) significant difference between means at 0.05 level.

Table–2
Mean, Standard Deviation and t-Test Values of Subjects' Responses on Shared Solutions to IT Advancement

S.No.	Items	Industry IT Practitioner		School IT Practitioner		Cal t-value
		X_1	SD_1	X_2	SD_2	
1.	**Industry advisory committees** A body of IT managers and rec-ruiters of technology-based disciplines, to advise academia on latest IT advancement necessary for curricula modification	3.69	1.50	3.82	1.20	1.50
2.	**Alumni/school relationship**. Alumni of the school IT-based programmes who work in industry helping in providing input regar-ding the relevancy of the content of individual courses and the curriculum as a whole	2.72	1.40	4.62	0.30	0.35
3.	**Instructors internship** Involving fulltime employment of IT lecturers/instructors during long vacations or sabbatical leave	3.6	1.39	3.78	1.02	0.19

Contd...

S.No.	Items	Industry IT Practitioner		School IT Practitioner		Cal t-value
		X_1	SD_1	X_2	SD_2	
4.	**Students internship** Allowing students of Technology oriented disciplines to work part-time in industry while continuing to make progress toward their graduation	3.54	1.10	3.74	1.45	1.41
5.	**School/industry exchange programme** A loan programme where an IT lecturer is assigned to work for the cooperating organization while an employee of that organization is scheduled to work for the school	3.61	1.39	3.84	1.10	0.70
6.	**School training/updating** Providing training for industry personnel or IT lecturer on latest technology by hiring a professional trainer and holding training programme at the local place of business	3.63	1.40	4.10	1.01	0.20
7.	**Industry projects for schools** Industry occasionally allowing schools to execute real projects or case study	3.73	1.45	4.13	1.01	1.20
8.	**Research sharing** Industry sharing valuable resources (latest software) with school via networks	3.52	1.40	4.50	0.30	1.20
9.	**Donations to schools** Industry donating money, up-to-day computers (Hardware/software), IT infrastructures or even employee time to schools.	3.50	1.02	3.71	1.45	1.41
10.	**Research grants to schools** Industry funding school research and development efforts in technology-oriented discipline.	3.62	1.40	3.78	1.10	1.51

The data in Table 2 shows that all he item statements received mean ratings above 3.50. No significant differences existed between means at 0.05 levels.

Discussion

The result shown in Table 1 reveal that all the Information Technology Practitioners sampled perceived all the 11 obstacles as facing industry and academia in IT advancement in the new global economy. Though, significant differences existed between the mean scores of both groups of IT Practitioners in items 3 and 4, each skill rated the items above 3.50. These findings are important because they provide empirical bases for building partnerships among stakeholders, particularly between industries and educational institutions for the development of vertical ICT sector in Nigeria.

The importance of industry/school cooperation in IT advancement was highlighted by ESCWA (2003) when it reported that some of the obstacles faced by business in Arab countries in developing and implementing ICT innovations are related to the weak link between industry and academic institutions. For Nigeria to be part of the global IT driven society, the spirit of partnership between industry and institutions of learning must be given broad latitude.

Table 2 shows that all the respondents were in agreement with the suggested ways in which partnership can be formed between industry and educational institutions in order to cope with IT advancement. There was not significant difference between the mean scores of both groups of respondents. Indeed efforts aimed at successfully establishing cooperation between these two important sectors in the direction of IT advancement should be considered as a matter of urgency if Nigeria wants to integrate her economy into the global economy.

Many companies and organizations should see funding school research and development efforts in the area of technology-oriented disciplines that incorporate IT systems as a valuable way to invest in the future. Such aids must be encouraged, provided there are few or no strings attached. Spering (2004) agrees that it is in the interest of co-operate bodies to support education if they want a secure business environment. On the other hand, higher institutions should be ready to explore every opportunity offered by companies in improving their IT infrastructures.

Conclusion

The present study has been able to identify some problems facing both industries and educational institutions in coping with IT innovations. Also few ways to which both sectors can be in alliance to overcome some of their problems and achieve their objectives were addressed. It is recommended that these suggested areas of partnerships should be considered for implementation. The author believes that the benefits that can be attained far exceed any costs that may be involved in the implementation of any of these suggestions.

REFERENCES

Anumihe, H. (2004, March 22). Embrace new technology trends. *The Punch* p. 47.

Aragba-Akpore, S (2005, March 22) Nigerians yet to fully exploit ICT potentials. *The Guardian* p. 23.

Commission of the European Communities (EC) (2000). Better, but not yet the best: Enterprise policy action to improve Europe's competitiveness. *Commission staff working paper (Brussels, EC).*

Denga, D.I. (1987). Educational measurement continuous assessment and psychological testing. Calabar, Nigeria: *Rapid Educational Publishers Limited.*

Ekeh, L.S. (2004, March 22). IT is 21st Century wealth creator. *The Punch* p.45.

Nsikak-Abasi, U. (2004). Integrating ICT into the university course lecture. *Nigerian Journal of Curriculum Studies*. Vol. 11. No. 1, pp. 221-225.

Nworgu, B.G. (1991). *Educational research basic issues and methodology*. Ibadan, Nigeria: Wisdom Publishers Limited.

Ola, V. (2004, March 22). Embrace New technology trends, ex-CBN governor urges banks. *The Punch.* p. 47.

Osuji, F. (2005, January 19). New role for ICT in the country's education. *Vanguard,* pp. 26-29.

Spiering, T. (2004, November 25) WAMCO boss urges private sector to support education. *Vanguard,* p. 34.

Ukwugwu, J.O. (2004). Integrating ICT in curriculum for human resource development. *Nigerian Journal of Curriculum Studies*. Vol. 11. No. 1, pp. 192-194.

United Nations Economic and Social Commission for Western Asia (ESCWA) (2003). *Review of information and communications technology and development.* New York. Issue No. 1, p. 20+.

15

Contextual Factors Influencing Lecturer use of E-Learning

Dr. Paul TJ James, Thailand

Introduction

Much research has been carried on in the area of e-learning which continues to be one of the hottest research topics in higher education today (Chan, Chow, and Jia, 2003) and as such the popularity of e-learning *may pose one of the greatest challenges currently facing traditional educational institutions* (Wong, 2007) as the Internet and other developing ICT technologies brings new possibilities and opportunities for the development and use of e-learning in Thai higher education.

Information and Communications Technology (ICT) has become the "*do all*" icon in education, as it is perceived to embody a dominant ideology that reflects a political (and therefore funding) bias that appears to *favour technology as meaning innovation* (James, 2008).

Kember and Kwan (2000) found that conceptions of teaching practice were related to lecturers' approaches to teaching, mirroring (Cox et al., 1999) who suggested that lecturer perceptions about the usefulness of ICT in aiding classroom work were influential in terms of ICT use and availability for students. For example, lecturers who had perceptions related to the 'teacher-centred/content-oriented' orientation were more likely to take a 'content-centred' approach; while those holding conceptions related to the 'student-centred/learning-oriented' orientation were more likely to take a 'learning-centred' approach (James, 2008). Further, increasing access to students of all ages rather than just young students out of school and pedagogically modularising programmes so that educational programmes can be managed in a more student-oriented manner would appear to help develop more effective use of expensive resources (Chan, Chow, and Jia, 2003). These contextual factors therefore influence the approach that lecturers finally adopt in their teaching pattern and behaviours.

However, the lecturer is not the only factor in the application of ICT and e-learning practices in the classroom and Figure 1, below illustrates the relationship between the major contextual factors imposing on the lecturer arena.

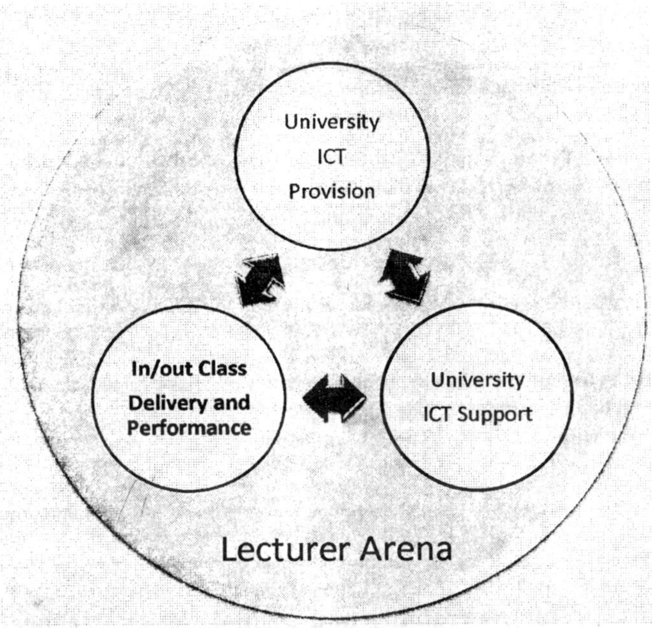

Figure 1 : Lecturer Arena

The outline of the research framework for this study is shown in Figure 1 above. The framework consists of three major components, namely University ICT Provision; University ICT Support; In-Out Class Programme Delivery and Performance. as *...technology and the Internet are not only changing modes of lesson delivery but also reshaping the rhetorical space in which literacy and learning occur* (Andrews and Haythornthwaite, (2007); Collis, (1998); and Faculty - Mitchell and Honore (2007)). There would appear to be a number of contextual factors in the literature imposing on the lecturer arena, as depicted in Table 1, below:

Table–1
Contextual Factors in the Literature Imposing on the Lecturer Arena

Component and Example Research Question	*Literature*	*Aspect*
University ICT Provision	Deband (2004)	Management and implementation
How useful is the level	Legris *et al.* (2003)	Technology acceptance
of ICT provision at this university?	Laurillard (1993)	ICT use
Programme Delivery and Performance	Chen and Hsiang (2007) Little (2001)	ICT implementation
In what ways do the university CMS provision affect student/staff abilities to engage in e-Learning practices at this university?	Rovai and Barnum (2003) Sehoole and Moja (2003)	E-learning provision E-learning operationalization E-learning interaction
	Visscher (1996)	ICT implementation
CMS University ICT Support	Deband (2004)	ICT management
How effective are the CMS support mechanisms at this university?	Resta and Laferrière (2007)	Support technology
	Tijdens and Steijn (2005)	ICT use
	Visscher and Wild (1997)	ICT support mechanism

However, of increasing concern would be the human elements such as lecturer capability and administration/management changes supporting ICT developments as a consequence of increased e-learning strategic orientations in Thai universities. Consequently, technology itself could provide a more flexible and much more adaptable approach to e-learning involvement in pedagogic developments. The growth in *virtual* university activities (first mooted in the mid 1980s), allows traditional universities to expand their reach and increase the flexibility of the educational offering. Through this, blended learning – a combination of traditional classroom and on-line study-offers new learning methods and pedagogy, while open source software and courseware facilitate sharing of resources and reduces costly duplication of effort through information technology which has been viewed as a solution to universities' cost and quality problems (Selim, 2007). On-line technologies, and more specifically web-based applications referred to above, are increasingly being utilised to aid in the delivery mechanism in higher education to address issues of cooperative learning and peer teaching (Lockyer, Patterson and Harper, 2001).

These changes promote the more important learner-centred pedagogy that appear to be deemed appropriate today by many researchers (Harvey and Knight, 1996) and indicate that web-based platforms operate more effectively (Lockyer, Patterson and Harper, 2001). However, while the use of ICT across educational organisations has been established, integration into the teaching and learning process has been slow to establish (Harrison *et al.*, 2002).

Methodology

The empirical data for the analysis was collected through an on-line synchronous web-based survey using a self-administered open-ended questionnaire was used to collect data for this study (Kehoe *et al.*, 1997) as web-based surveys are becoming increasingly common for reasons of efficiency (Lazar and Preece, 1999); Sheehan and Hoy (1999) and Weible and Wallace (1998). The on-line survey was initiated using targeted e-mails to all Masters Degree lecturers of international programmes at one university (Comley, 2000) stating the survey rationale, strategy and process. The survey was supplemented with data resulting from an assessment of appropriate freely available documents located on the university website (in English).

A number of open-questions in the survey asked the participants their views regarding the use e-learning at the university; how they conduct assessment and implementation strategies for courses; as well as what challenges and issues, they had experienced from engaging in and utilising the available e-learning technologies.

The survey was administered intentionally through a pop-up boxes which ensured that every targeted manager who logged into their account was given the opportunity to participate. In this respect, there were no random possibilities to capturing the opinions of the targeted managerial population. The number of individuals exposed to the pop-up boxes accounted for 100 per cent of the target group for the survey – 55 in total. The survey responses (29/55-53.13%) were automatically verified and stored using database technology.

This project sought to engage an appropriate number of respondents as were employed in such studies as Kember and Kwan (2000) (17 lecturers); Gonzalez (2008) (7 lecturers) and Roberts (2003) (7 lecturers).

The methodology considered, follows on from Hodgson *et al.*, (2001) question as to whether *the adoption of research methods designed for face-to-face settings are appropriate* for use on-line? The major objective in this research was to explore lecturer views whilst using e-learning techniques although this was not the first attempt at this, it was considered appropriate to the type of data acquisition and the contextual environment in which those data could be ascertained – given that there has been a structural and naturalistic change in accepted research orientation since Issroff (1993).

Findings

The main research outcomes (based on Figure1: Lecturer Arena) are contained in Figure 2, below, and are further discussed in each respective section. The significance of each factor identified is further enhanced by the engaged literature as contained in Figures 3-5 following

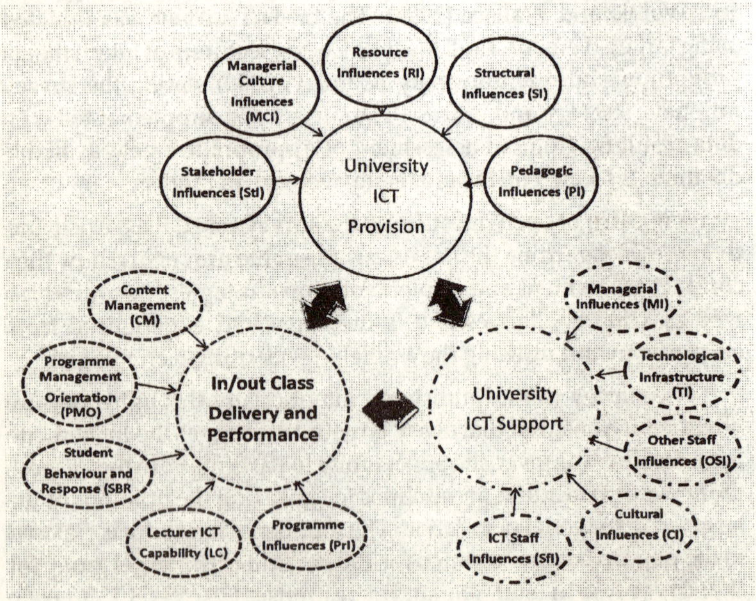

Figure 2 : Lecturer Arena Research Outcomes

University ICT Provision

All (100%) of the curriculum has some form of ICT involvement – however, reports of e-learning use (93.1%) had no involvement beyond e-mail or digital lecture presentations (StI).

Lecturer-engaged approaches to the implementation of e-learning practices are not considered practical (89.7%) (PI and RI); and therefore was not considered widespread (70.6%) (RI); nor was this seen by many lecturers as a useful development (75.9%) (SI) as it was perceived to put pressure on their ICT skill developments (82.8%) (MCI and StI).

When lecturers did engage with ICT for classes, it appeared that many underestimated the time it took to develop a useful programme (75.9%) (SI); were overwhelmed with the planning requirements (89.7%) (MCI); and could not continue from one programme to the next (65.5%) (RI) as different classroom allocations utilised different technical problems that needed to be overcome (93.1%) (RI).

Lecturers did not have a task or responsibility to provide full on-line access for any normal programmes (100%) (MCI and PI), but lecturers were aware that students could access specialised self-study teaching modules (89.7%) (RI) offered independently by the university. However, most lecturers (82.75%) (MCI and PI) considered that these were ICT related, rather than specific teaching programme related. This aspect of the research project corroborates the results of other research into the factors signalled as seen in Figure 3, below:

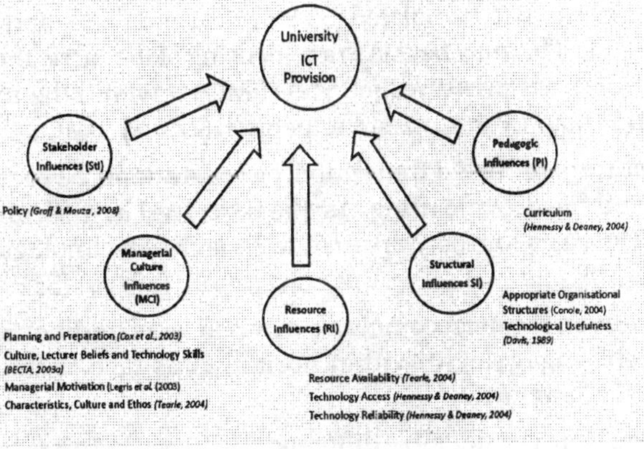

Figure 3 : University ICT Provision

Only 15 per cent of the specific programmes available have a Fprescribed approach to the implementation of e-learning practices as the university had adopted a partial-blended approach to e-learning which involved the integration of e-learning with traditional media and methods in line with course content, level and students (Hanna, 1998). Thus, the university-wide systems are not effectively integrated into the learning sphere and this creates increasing pressures on the university quality system due to the disparity between the pedagogic needs of the student, lecturer requirements and the present scope of the university's managerial strategic intent. Figure 3, above, corroborates the results of other research into the factors highlighted through this research project.

Lecturers appeared to give greater importance to stakeholder issues (management), as this was deemed to have a profound effect on ICT provision throughout the university. This coupled with pedagogic and resource issues were raised as the primary factors influencing ICT provision.

In/Out Class Delivery and Performance

Only (6.9%) (CM and PrI) of lecturers have offered an e-learning aspect to an offered course beyond e-mail and digital presentations which included collaborative efforts such as on-line Chats and interactive media files.

When considering lecturer skills and access to ICT; perceived knowledge of ICT; and the deployment of e-learning has not been well positioned (75.9%) (LC) or utilised (79.3%) (PrI). Blended-learning activity appeared to be isolated (65.5%) (CM and PMO) and localised (51.7%) (PrI). This may be due to a refocusing of the curriculum due to adverse external pressures (68.9%) (PMO) – within the university (44.8%) (RI) and from outside competition (27.6%) (PMO).

Lecturers reported that practices for students beyond simple e-mail and file downloading may be perceived as difficult (51.7%) (SBR). The basis for this appeared to be lack of technological skills (58.8%) (SBR and LC), as well as behavioural (69.0%) (SBR and LC).

However, the most commonly advised were traditional models of student engagement within normal class face-to-face events (75.9%) (PrI and PMO).

There were considerable differences between lecturers in relation to their approach and knowledge of ICT (LC). For example, some lecturers have either not considered e-learning yet (86.2%) (LC) or have considered it but not taken it forward (10.3%) (LC). Various reasons were advanced such as the lack of skills (24.1%) (LC), but the most prevalent reason was the perceived complexity of developing material through ICT (75.9%) (CM) and the perception that students may not have sufficient skills to effectively handle the new e-learning requirements (51.7%) (SBR).

If e-learning activities were used lecturer perceptions varied greatly, and suggested the on-line delivery of specialist software driven course materials (79.3%) (LC); on-line management of course literature (65.5%) (PrI; PMO and TI); bulletin/discussion boards (17.2%) (RI and TI); on-line formative-assessment (6.9%) (LC and PrI); on-line submission of student assignments (68.9%) (SBR; LC and PMO).

Lecturer perceived reasons for the university use of e-learning practices were stated as cost-reduction (82.7%) (RI; PMO and MI); managing increased student numbers (17.2%) (MI); improved teaching focus and capability (44.8%) (LC and SBR); and encouragement of student-centred learning (34.5%) (SBR; CI and MCI).

However, when using e-learning, the dominant model the university uses is a low-level 'blended' approach, combining ICT and traditional methods to deliver classroom learning after Hanna (1998).

There is also the potential to establish a collaborative teaching and learning community (Bates, 2005), which—from the data—appears ineffective in practice. This is possibly not a result of strategic deference, but as a consequence of managerial disengagement and perceived low level of enthusiasm or interest relating to ICT developments.

However, the most commonly advised were traditional models of student development based on close *delivery* of technical skills in which current research suggests is not the most effective approach for the development of important e-learning outcomes (Hiebert *et al.*, 2002). Further, the perception of inadequate e-learning engagement from lecturing staff may result in consequential low-levels of participation from students (Chan, Chow and Jia, 2003).

These findings also corroborate the outcomes of Maki and Maki (2002) suggesting that in the short-term there is little constructive development in e-learning policy at this university which may give rise to important operational concerns in the long-term. This aspect of the research project corroborates the results of other research into the factors signalled as seen in Figure 4, below:

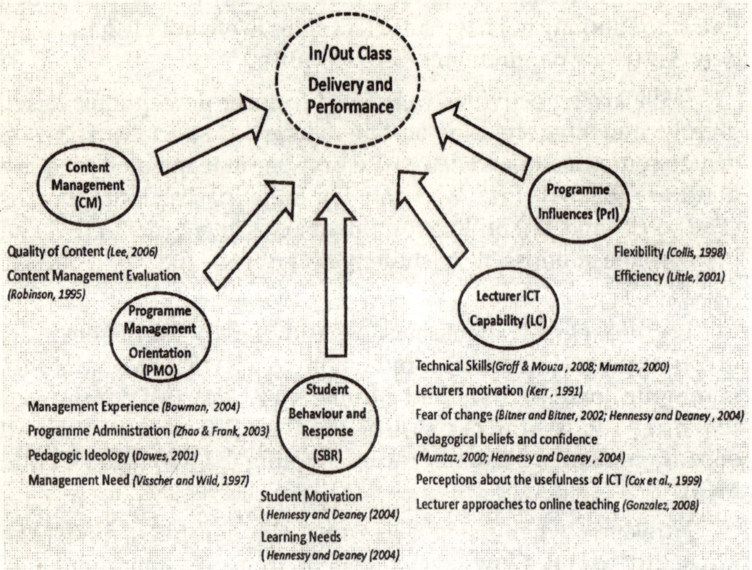

Figure 4 : In/Out Class Delivery and Performance

University ICT Support

New ICT programmes for lecturers along with pedagogical and technical support were being continuously developed and provided (TI and SfI). However, lecturers were not encouraged to introduce (31.0%) (TI and MI) or utilise (41.4%) (RI; PI and SBR) e-learning practices in classroom.

This was perceived by lecturers as being due to lack of interest of technical support (55.2%) (SfI; CI and MI); unskilled technical support staff (68.9%) (SfI); and lack of an ICT centre management mandate (48.3%) (MI and OSI)—which in itself indicates the university orientation (StI and MCI).

The gap between lecturers' skills in their personal use of ICT and their skills in using ICT with learners has not been bridged which may reflect a lack of lecturer confidence in their use of ICT in public (51.7%) (MCI; LC and CI) or the lack of availability of ICT support services (62.1%) (MI; SfI and MCI). This aspect of the research project corroborates the results of other research into the factors signalled as seen in Figure 5, below:

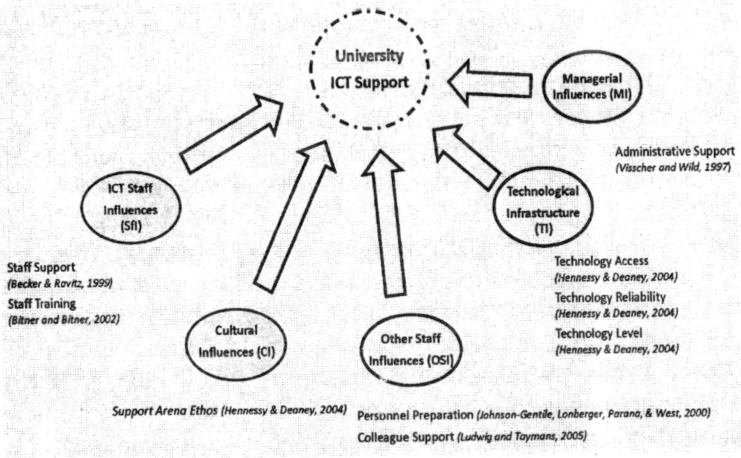

Figure 5: University ICT Support

The lack of effective engagement by support services in this study signifies a particularly important issue raised by Collis and Moonen (2001), and does little to address the very necessary requirements of support in the development of university-wide e-learning practices which would represent the need for a significant change in teaching and administrative practices (McPherson, 2003b).

It would appear that the university is testing possible low-level future technological and pedagogic options following Bates (2001); and that this testing is viewed as unsympathetic by many students to their pedagogic needs as it is perceived as a cost-cutting measure (Mitchell and Honore, 2007) as the support mechanisms remained unclear. Staff were not actively trained in the use and application of e-learning practices (100%) leading to speculation regarding the efficacy of the role and responsibility of management (Trinidad, 2005); nor were they helped to engage effectively with support practices integrated into a wider system of ICT management following Sehoole and Moja (2003) or sustaining the level of lecturer confidence in ICT use (Collis and Moonen, 2001). Consequently, there appears to be little managerial support for widespread staff or student e-learning engagement or *technology-enhanced learning* (Fox and Trinidad, 2006).

Conclusion

The findings of this small-scale study corroborate the outcomes of Collis and van der Wende (2002) in that *change in relation to the use of ICT has been gradual and unsystematic* which in practice reflects a combination of specific and unrelated environmental parameters such as strategic intent and resource feasibility. Clearly, changing teaching patterns and their impact on developing lecturer skills and attitudes advanced through ICT create on-going issues in the classroom in order to get the maximum benefit from the e-learning environment (McFadzean, 2001). The data would indicate the importance of exploiting lecturer e-learning practices in ICT (Begicevic *et al.*, 2007) - corroborating Zhang (2007) and Fredriksson *et al.* (2008) - in terms of the need for a clear vision for the overall management of ICT. Support ICT services linking e-learning developments to the wider university community through more effective measures designed to enhance and improve present practices and attitudes may result in greater overall confidence in its use and more importantly – its take-up.

Acknowledgements

Many thanks should be given to the individuals who responded to the survey and to my internal Bangkok University reviewing panel.

REFERENCES

Andrews, R. & Haythornthwaite, C. (2007). *The SAGE Handbook of E-learning Research*, Sage, UK.

Bates, A.W. (2001). National Strategies for E-Learning in Post-secondary Education and Training. Paris: International Institute for Educational Planning, UNESCO.

Bates, A.W. (2005). *Technology, E-learning and distance education*. London: Routledge Falmer.

Becker, H. & Ravitz, J. (1999). The influence of computer and internet use on teachers' pedagogical practices and perceptions. *Journal of Research on Computing in Education*, Vol. 31(4), 356-384.

BECTA, (2003a). *What the research says about barriers to the use of ICT in teaching*. British Educational Communications and Technology Agency, UK.

Begicevic, N., Divjak, B. & Hunjak, T. (2007). Prioritization of e-learning forms: a multi-criteria methodology. *CEJOR*, Vol. 15, 405–419.

Bitner, N. & Bitner, J. (2002). Integrating technology into the classroom: Eight keys to success. *Journal of Technology and Teacher Education*, Vol. 10, 95-101.

Bowman, D. (2004). Thinking through the technology puzzle. *The Educational Technology Journal*, 14(1).

Chan, A.Y.K; Chow, K.O. & Jia, W. (2003). A Framework for Evaluation of Learning Effectiveness in On-line Courses. In W. Zhou *et al.*, (Eds.): *ICWL 2003*, LNCS 2783, 383–395.

Chen, R.S. & Hsiang, C.H. (2007). A study on the critical success factors for corporations embarking on knowledge community-based e-Learning. *Information Sciences*, Vol. 177, 570–586.

Collis, B. (1998). New didactics for university instruction: why and how? *Computers and Education*, Vol. 31, 373-393.

Collis, B. & Moonen, J. (2001). *Flexible Learning in a Digital World: Experience and Expectations*. London: Kogan Page.

Collis, B. and van der Wende, M. (2002). *Models of Technology and Change in Higher Education: An International Comparative Survey on the Current and Future Uses of ICT in Higher Education*, CHEPS University of Twente.

Comley, P. (2000, 10-12 April). Pop-up Surveys - What works, what doesn't work and what will work in the future, 237. http://www.virtualsurveys.com/papers/paper_4.asp. [viewed 10 August 2007].

Conole, G. (2004). E-learning: the hype and the reality. *Journal of Interactive Media in Education*, Vol. 12, available at: www-jime.open.ac.uk/2004/11/ [viewed 23 January 2007].

Cox, M., Preston, C. & Cox, K. (1999). What Factors Support or Prevent Teachers from Using ICT in their Classrooms?, *British Educational Research Association Annual Conference*, UK.

Cox, M., Webb, M., Abbott, C., Blakely, B., Beauchamp, T. & Rhodes V. (2003). *ICT and pedagogy: A review of the research literature* (London: DfES and Becta).

Davis, F. D. (1989). Perceived usefulness, perceived ease of use, and user acceptance of information technology. *MIS Quarterly*, Vol.13(3), 319–340.

Dawes, L. (2001). What stops teachers using new technology? In, M. Leask (ed.), *Issues in Teaching using ICT*, 61-79. London:Routledge, UK.

Deband, O. (2004). ICTs and the Development of eLearning in Europe: the role of the public and private sectors. *European Journal of Education*, Vol. 39, No. 2, 191-208.

Fox, R. & Trinidad, S. (2006). Technology's role in leveraging curriculum reform. Paper presented at the *Conference on ICT in Teaching and Learning*, ICT 2006, July 7-10, Hong Kong.

Fredriksson, U., Jedeskog, G. & Plomp, T. (2008). Innovative use of ICT in schools based on the findings in ELFE project. *Educational Information Technology*, Vol. 13, 83–101.

Gonzalez, C. (2008). Conceptions of, and approaches to, teaching online: a study of lecturers teaching postgraduate distance courses. *Higher Education*, May. DOI 10.1007/s10734-008-9145-1.

Groff, J., & Mouza, C. (2008). A framework for addressing challenges to classroom technology use. *AACE Journal*, Vol. 16(1), 21-46.

Groth, L.A., Dunlap, K.L. & Kidd, J.K. (2007). Becoming Technologically Literate

Through Technology Integration in PK-12 Preservice Literacy Courses: Three Case Studies. *Reading Research and Instruction*, Volume 46, No. 4 , Summer, 363-386.

Hanna, D.E. (1998). *Higher* education in an era of digital competition: Emerging organizational models. *Journal of Asynchronous Learning*, 2(1).

Harrison, C; Comber, C; Fisher, T; Haw, K; Lewin, C; Lunzer, E; McFarlane, A; Mavers, D; Scrimshaw, P; Somekh, B; & Watling, R. (2002). ImpacT2: The Impact of Information and Communication Technologies on Pupil Learning and Attainment. *ICT in Schools Research and Evaluation Series, No. 7*, London: DfES/BECTa. http://www.becta.org.uk/page documents/research/ImpaCT2 strand2 report.pdf. [viewed 14 August 2007].

Harvey, L. & Knight, P. (1996). *Transforming Higher Education*, The Society for Research into Higher Education & the Open University Press, UK.

Hiebert, J; Gallimore, R. & Stigler, J.W. (2002). A knowledge base for the teaching profession: What would it look like and how can we get one? *Educational Researcher*, Vol. 31(5), 3–15.

Hennessy, S. and Deaney, R. (2004). *Sustainability and Evolution of ICT-Supported Classroom Practice. Becta/DfES, UK.*

Hodgson, V., Watland, P. & Asensio, M. (2001). Researching Networked Learning. In Rust, C. (Ed), Proceedings of the_*2001 9th International Symposium, Improving Student Learning*, 336-347.

Issroff, K. (1993). Methodology for research in computer-supported cooperative learning. In *PEG 93: AI Tools and the Classroom: Theory into Practice*, Moray House Institute of Education, Scotland, UK.

James, P.T.J. (2008). *ICT in Schools*, Educational Technology Books, UK.

Johnson-Gentile, K., Lonberger, R., Parana, J., & West, A. (2000). Preparing pre-service teachers for the technological classroom: A school-college partnership. *Journal of Technology and Teacher Education*, Vol. 8, 97-109.

Jones, N. & O'Shea, J. (2004). Challenging hierarchies: The impact of e-learning. *Higher Education*, Vol. 48, 379–395.

Kehoe, C.M; Pitkow, J.E. & Morton, K. (1997). *Eighth WWW user survey*. http://www.gvu.gatech.edu/user_surveys/survey-1997-10. [viewed 6 October 2007].

Kember, D. & Kwan, K. (2000). Lecturers' approaches to teaching and their relationship to conceptions of good teaching. *Instructional Science*, Vol. 28(5), 469–490.

Kerr, S.T. (1991). Lever and fulcrum: educational technology in teachers' thought and practice. *Teachers College Record*, Vol. 93 (1), 114-136.

Kim, J-H., & Kwon, J-M. (2002). *Research on establishing e-Campus VISION* (RR 2002-1). Seoul: KERIS.

Laurillard, D. (1993). *Rethinking university teaching: A framework for the effective use of educational technology*, Routledge, UK.

Lazar, J. & Preece, J. (1999). Designing and implementing web-based surveys. *Journal of Computer Information Systems*, xxxix (4), 63-67.

Lee, I. (2006). Korean Content Management in e-Higher Education: Here and Hereafter. *Educational Technology Research and Development*, Vol. 54, No. 2, 209-219.

Legris, P; Ingham, J. & Collerette, P. (2003). Why do people use information technology? A critical review of the technology acceptance model. *Information and Management*, Vol. 40(3), 191–204.

Little, B. (2001). Achieving high performance through e-learning. *Industrial and Commercial Training*, Vol. 33, No. 6, 203-207.

Lockyer, L; Patterson, J; & Harper, B. (2001). ICT in higher education: evaluating outcomes for health education. *Journal of Computer Assisted Learning*, Vol. 17, 275-283.

Ludwig, M. & Taymans, J. (2005). Teaming: Constructing high-quality faculty development in a PT3 project. *Journal of Technology and Teacher Education*, Vol. 13, 357-372.

McFadzean, E. (2001). Supporting virtual learning groups. Part 1: A pedagogical perspective. *Team Performance Management*, Vol. 7 (3,4), 53-62.

Maki, W.S & Maki, R.H. (2002). Multimedia comprehension skills predicts differential outcomes of web-based and lecture courses. *Journal of Experimental Psychology: Applied*, Vol. 8(2), 85–98.

McPherson, M.A. (2003b). In McPherson M.A., Henderson L. and Kinshuk L. (Eds), **Organisational critical success factors for managing the implementation of e-learning in higher education**, in Proceedings of the Workshop on The Changing Face of HE in the 21st Century, 8-14. Massey University, New Zealand.

Mitchell, M. & Honore S., (2007). Criteria for successful blended learning. *Industrial and Commercial Training*, Vol. 39 No. 3, 143-149.

Mumtaz, S. (2000). Factors affecting teachers' use of information and communications technology: a review of the literature. *Journal of Information Technology for Teacher Education*, Vol. 9 (3), 319-341.

Rovai, A.P. & Barnum, K.T. (2003). On-line course effectiveness: An analysis of student interactions and perceptions of learning. *Journal of Distance Education*, Vol. 18(1), 57–73.

Resta, P. & Laferrière, T. (2007). Technology in Support of Collaborative Learning. *Educational Psychology Review*, Vol. 19, 65–83.

Roberts, G. (2003). Teaching using the web: Conceptions and approaches from a phenomenographic perspective. *Instructional Science*, Vol. 31(1–2), 127–150.

Robinson, B. (1995). The management of quality in open and distance learning. Proceedings of the *5th annual conference of the AAOU*, 95–109.

Sehoole, C.T. & Moja, T. (2003). *Pedagogical Issues and Gender in Cyberspace* Education:Distance Education in South Africa. *African and Asian Studies*, Vol. 2, No. 4, 475-496.

Selim, H.M. (2007). Critical success factors for eLearning acceptance: Confirmatory factor models. *Computers and Education*, Vol. 49, 396–41.

Sheehan, K.B. & Hoy, M.B. (1999). Using e-mail to survey internet users in the United States: ethodology and assessment. *Journal of Computer Mediated Communication,* March.

Tearle, P. (2004). Implementation of ICT in UK secondary schools. *Becta Research Conference,* UK.

Tijdens, K. & Steijn, B. (2005). The determinants of ICT competencies among employees, *New Technology, Work and Employment,* Vol. 20:1, 60-73.

Trinidad, S. (2005). Taking the next step in using technology. In S. Trinidad & J. Pearson (Eds.), *Using information and communication technologies in education,* (1-15). Singapore: Prentice Hall.

Visscher, A.J. (1996). Information technology in educational management as an emerging discipline, *International Journal of Educational Research,* Vol. 25(4), 291–296.

Visscher, A.J. and Wild, P. (1997). The potential of information technology in support of teachers and educational managers managing their work environment. *Education and Information Technologies,* Vol. 2(4), 263–274.

Weible, R. & Wallace, J. (1998). The impact of the Internet on data collection. *Marketing Research,* Vol. 10(3), 19-23.

Wong, A.L. (2007). Cross-Cultural Delivery of e-Learning Programmes: Perspectives from Hong Kong, *International Review of Research in Open and Distance Learning,* Vol. 8, Number 3.

Zhang, J. (2007). A cultural look at information and communication technologies in Eastern education, *Education Tech Research Dev,* Vol. 55, 301–314.

Zhao, Y. & Frank, K. (2003). Factors affecting technology uses in schools: An ecological perspective, *American Educational Research Journal,* Vol. 40(4), 807-840.

Zhao, Y., Pugh, K., Sheldon, S. & Byers, J. (2002). Conditions for classroom technology innovations, *Teachers College Record,* Vol. 104 (3), 482-515.

16

E-Learning: A Perspective

Sachidanand Menon, India
Swaraj Chakraborty, India

A drop of ink can make a million think. But with rapid technology strides in Silicon Valley, the drops of ink have slowly but surely dried up to be replaced by mice clicks. This tech transition has taken millions more across the information superhighway of academic learning. Powered by advances in computing power and communications technology, modern e-learning has truly erased geographic and social divides, bridging the gap between knowledge givers and seekers.

Besides real-time sharing of knowledge, which is the essence of e-learning, technology today has become an enabler for a host of other initiatives like online performance assessment, training and analytical tools, just-in-time scheduling and other promising features. Before we get to the crux of the matter, however, let's take a look at the basic framework under which e-learning operates.

Market Potential and Trends

The global e-learning market is set to generate a whopping $ 56 billion by the year 2010.[1] Back home in India, low Internet penetration at a mere 3.7 per cent[2] is proving to be a stumbling block for e-learning initiatives. Despite that, the Indian market has been pegged at about Rs. 105 crores, with a predicted quantum leap to Rs. 1,092 crores in another five years.

The rural-urban divide is another challenge that the e-learning domain in India is yet to surmount. A major contributing factor to this divide has been the dismal state of information technology infrastructure. Besides the low Internet penetration, broadband lines are not really cost-effective while dial-up connections, though relatively cheaper, continue to be unreliable.

With telecom tariffs spiraling down, however, and an emerging market in cheap second-hand computers, the economics may be more supportive to envelope a larger section of the masses in the near future.

Technology and Implementation

The technology backbone of e-learning comes from Information Technology, with hardware devices like personal computers, projectors and printers being the physical interfacing platforms. The transfer of knowledge is enabled in the virtual world through various software applications that follow established compliance protocols like SCORM (Sharable Content Object Reference Model, which is a collection of standards and specifications for web-based e-learning).

E-learning technologies can be classified into two delivery modes-synchronous and asynchronous.[3] As the name suggests, synchronous technologies aim at real-time dissemination of knowledge while asynchronous technologies are tuned to "delayed response". Both have their disadvantages and benefits. For example, a school examination requires synchronous mode while subject workshops can potentially use the asynchronous mode to save teaching time and repetition.

A few synchronous technologies are listed below:

- VoIP
- Webex
- Videoconferencing
- Chatrooms.

The asynchronous technologies span

- E-mail
- Printed courseware
- Compact Discs.

The typical e-learning life cycle can be captured graphically as given in the illustration below, which splits the growth curve into three phases:

Advantages

- E-learning offers huge potential for economies of scale. It would take only a dozen or so qualified and dedicated

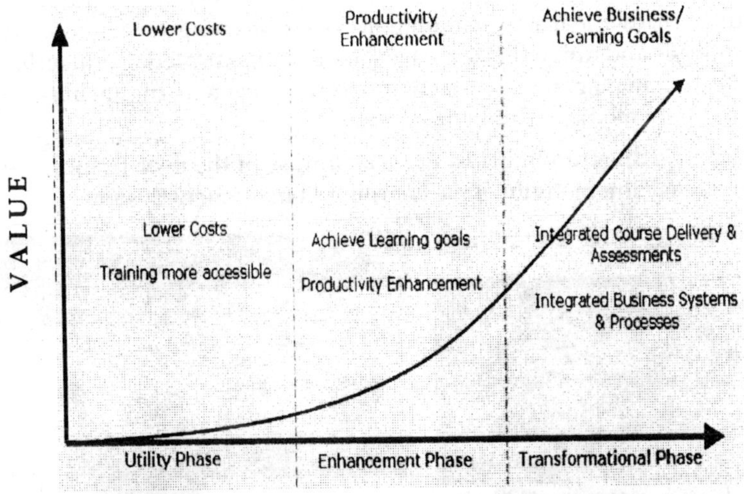

educationists to theoretically reach across to thousands, even millions, of knowledge seekers.

- The Gartner Group reports that the retention of e-learning is twice as high as that of traditional classroom instruction, at half the cost.[4]
- In a country like India, e-learning has the potential to transcend barriers like gender, religion and caste.
- E-learning lends itself to easy repetition and being a time-independent mode of learning, offers tailor-made consumption modules.
- Since geographical barriers are erased, small towns in rural India can benefit from quality education being imparted from the metros and Tier 1 towns by the best of the teaching fraternity.

The HCL Experience

HCL's E-learning practice keeps up with the latest market trends and aims at providing a wide range of end to end solutions. Our primary objective is to facilitate learning and training initiatives and Learning Management Systems (LMS). In fact, we have structured our customer base into two major segments: the corporate segment.

Our second segment is the academic segment–typically consisting of K-12, colleges and universities and publishers catering to these. The K-12 segment oversees some characteristic solutions like child development and reading intervention programmes, prescriptive learning, simulation-based learning and so on. For colleges and universities, we have more sophisticated solutions like student management system, campus card system, digital libraries and new media learning like podcasting.

The illustration below gives a glimpse of the user-friendliness and easy interactivity of the Learning Management System.

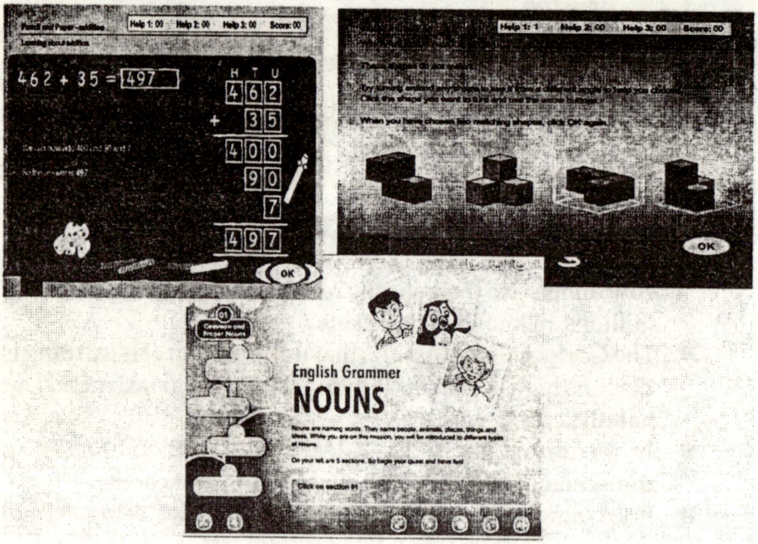

As is evident, the LMS takes a fun approach to learning, with graphical content and interactive puzzles to enhance knowledge retention.

An important component of every education initiative is the assessment module. HCL Technologies has set up a comprehensive framework for effective assessment, as shown in the illustration below. The process flow spans all the important components required for rigorous assessment, enabled by technology to make it accurate, timely and ready-to-implement on a large scale.

Future Roadmap

With technology being in a constant state of innovation, activists in the field of e-learning can look forward to improved services and greater reach. The most promising of the developments centers around e-learning 2.0 , which has seen grown parallel to **Web 2.0.**

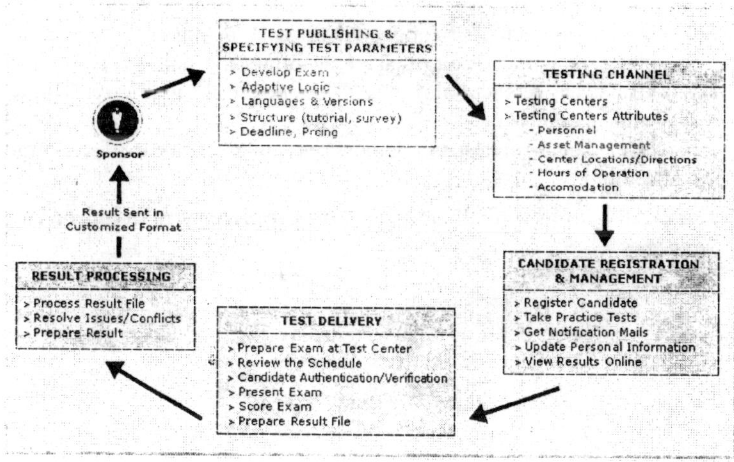

The goal of e-learning 2.0 is to blur the lines between the teaching and student community by facilitating collaborative learning through social software like blogs, wikis and podcasts.[5]

The revolution here would center around changing from the traditional "one-way" flow of instruction to "multi-channel, multi-source" teaching, with the added advantage of highly interactive environment for students and teachers. In fact, e-learning 2.0 has the potential make teachers out of students and vice versa.

Concluding Remarks

- The Indian e-learning is slated to grow to Rs. 1,092 crores by 2012.
- Low Internet penetration and relatively higher IT costs have contributed to a rural-urban divide.
- The government's focus area should be to shore up IT infrastructure in rural areas, while at the same time bringing service costs down. This will help in the flow of knowledge from qualified urban academicians to needy rural knowledge seekers.
- Future technologies like **e-learning 2.0** have the potential to transform the learning environment from the prevalent "instructional" mode to more interactive and participative.

REFERENCES

1. *Source: CLSA Asia Pacific Markets.* http://www.alootechie.com/content/e-learning-market-may-grow-27-million-280-million-2012.

2. http://www.internetworldstats.com/asia/in.htm
3. http://en.wikipedia.org/wiki/E_learning#cite_note-13
4. http://www.isodynamic.com/web/pdf/IsoDynamic_ elearning_white_paper.pdf
5. http://elearningtech.blogspot.com/2006/02/what-is-elearning-20.html

Remark: All graphs and illustrations are proprietary material of HCL Technologies.

17

Drop Out Prevention Using E-Learning and Homeschooling: Well Educated People without Schools

Dr. Shobana Nelasco, India
Andreas Becker, Thailand

'Everyone has the right to education. Education shall be free, at least in the elementary and fundamental stages. Elementary education shall be compulsory.'

Universal Declaration of Human Rights, Art. 26. United Nations, 1948.

The US promotes their "No One Left Behind" policy, Hamburg in Germany changes its multi-graded-school-system to only ONE school for all and UNESCO discusses since years an "Education for All". All are good starting points but especially in western cultures an increasing rate of school drop-outs and in Asian cultures an increasing rate of juvenile self murders draw an alarming picture of our future - Our Children!

What causes children which have an educational perspective to drop out or even self murder them?

How can modern educational concepts like e/b-learning help to prevent it?

A student's motivation is much higher when he is able to find himself back in lessons—when he is a vital part of his own daily schooling experiences. E-learning and home schooling as well as learning in small flexible family style groups offer all this. Beyond strict time and place boundaries there is a place for children - an individual educational place for everyone. The Internet and Computers offer us new dimensions and a good perspective for our children, even in rural areas with less or no schooling ability.

Looking back in history shows us, that many great discoverers and developers often faced the same problems like modern school dropouts. First when they were able to live beyond strict school boundaries they developed their real potential (i.e., Albert Einstein).

We don't need sterile school buildings, made to control people instead of giving them their self-confidence. We need flexible educational institutions and teachers which are much more partners of a student self-determined learning process then selfish directors of a official determined learning process.

Drop Out and Self Murdering

Facts

In 2003 a survey within the World Bank stated about 3 times as much countries with a constitutional guarantee of education then without (Tomaševski 2005).

Even then there are an increasing number of students not practicing these rights.

Causes

Poverty is the main reason on dropout. A 2004 UNICEF survey estimates about 14 million children out of 44 million in former communist countries are living below national poverty lines (UNICEF-ICDC 2004). The rate in Central Asia is even higher. Especially poorer countries aren't able to keep their under-funded school system free even its guaranteed by their constitution.

> Dear Teacher,
>
> My son is slow in learning and thus it is impossible to force him to learn. So, I'm taking my son off with me. We live in a rural area and look after other's livestock for a living. It's hard to take my son to the school all the time. Bye.
>
> Quote from a mother's note to the school administration in Bayan-tumen soum, Dornog aimag, Mongolia.

Lack of motivation is a growing factor also in high developed and well situated industrial states like Germany, Belgium, US, Canada ... About half of the students measured by the OECD Pisa study were bored by the traditional schools in their countries (OECD 2008). School is for them a place where they don't want to be. It leads to bad academic performance, but also to disruptive behaviors'. Teachers mostly react inadequate to these problems with punitive and repressive attitudes which leads even to horror scenario like happened in Germany and the US where students kill their teachers and classmates.

Disappearance is a factor in each society regardless of their social status. Even in Great Britain Ofsted reported in 2004 about 10.000 students which were lost by the system. It might be that they are still in an educational surrounding like homeschooling or e- learning but nobody kept track about this.

Tokokyohi (like it's called in Japan) is a synonym for the existing school phobia or even refusal. Since the 80's it's an incredible growing factor especially in Far East country like Korea and Japan. Students get burned out by the extremely demanding and alienating school system (div. 2000). It's followed by an increasing number of juvenile self murders.

In all societies literacy is a determining factor of drop-out. While reading programmes try to form a better literacy among all students, modern media like computers, video and gaming consoles support the passive consuming habit of people instead of empowering them actively for the modern society.

Conclusions

> I remember growing up feeling like I could try school if I wanted to. But I never remember wanting to.
>
> Laurie Chancey

Traditional ways of teaching have failed in our demanding world. Nevertheless education will be the basic key to a successful live beyond poorness also in future. Therefore new ways of teaching have to be found or even better already existing and approved educational methods have to be utilized beyond fixed and traditional school walls and boundaries.

Let's discuss some actually very old and now newly awoken modern ways of education and its benefits for the students and their families.

Un-Schooling Our Kids

Home Schooling

The US Department of Education estimates that over 1 million children are home schooled and the number is on the rise. Still many countries won't allow officially to home school children like German. Often it is depending on the officers which have to make a courageous decision against traditions.

Reasons for Home Schooling *(Bielick, Chandler and Broughman, 1999).*

Table SEQ "Table" *Arabic 1: Number and Percentage of Home Schooled Students, by Reason for Homeschooling: 1999

Reasons for Homeschooling	*Number of Homeschooled Students*	*Per cent*	*s.e.*
Can give child better education at home	415,000	48.9	3.79
Religious reasons	327,000	38.4	4.44
Poor learning environment at school	218,000	25.6	3.44
Family reasons	143,000	16.8	2.79
To develop character/morality	128,000	15.1	3.39
Object to what school teaches	103,000	12.1	2.11
School does not challenge child	98,000	11.6	2.39
Other problems with available schools	98,000	11.5	2.20
Student behaviour problems at school	76,000	9.0	2.40
Child has special needs/disability	69,000	8.2	1.89
Transportation/Convenience	23,000	2.7	1.48
Child not old enough to enter schools	15,000	1.8	1.13
Want private school but cannot afford it	15,000	1.7	0.77
Parent's career	12,000	1.5	0.80
Could not get into desired school	12,000	1.5	0.99
Other reasons*	189,000	22.2	2.90

Homeschooling takes in account the individual personality and abilities of each student.

Biggest problem in homeschooling was long time the quality in teaching. Rich people were able to hire qualified teachers but poor people—often not been taught by themselves—had big problems to catch up with international standards.

Still qualified home school programmes aren't affrodable for all but more and more non profitable initiatives take care of underprivileged people and their needs. Especially for families with an internet access these financial boundaries are much more open now.

Homeschooling also empowers complete generations as teachers and students. It is often the start for a lifelong learning process which has been initiated by the student itself.

As most Home Schools doesn't interact in a fixed unchangeable time schedule they are much more flexible to follow students interests without losing track to required qualifications in our modern society.

Family Style Mixed Groups

Maria Montessori propagated at the beginning of last century family and mixed aged and even better mixed cultural learning groups. Meanwhile many schools all around the world are following her educational methods with great success. No more time boundaries or fixed curricula for an average student.

It is best for students if they can learn with their own pace and in a prepared surrounding which inspires and motivates learning. The students' absorbent mind will help to polarize and normalize them (Place, 2008).

E-Learning

The availability of internet access even in rural areas changes not only the world of living but also the way and possibilities of learning and teaching. Disabled people which are often treated like outcasts in different societies have now good chances to show their full potentials. Sick students won't miss anymore lessons if the teachers enable them to follow up via internet by putting and preparing their lessons also for and online presentation. Students in repressive political systems have an open door for unfiltered and uncensored information, to build their own mind.

E-learning provides students with a learning environment without time and location boundaries. Therefore, it is predestined to be utilized for all kind of educational purposes.

Educational Visions and Perspectives

What about a Boat, a Bus, an Open Learning Center or even a Network of Open Learning Centers all around the world which educate our children towards a global citizen.

> It appears from the surveys and from international experience that a perceived or actual lack of quality in schooling is a key factor in truancy, irregular attendance, and dropout. (UNESCO, 2005)

Combining all of the above will lead us to a new empowering way of learning and teaching.

In Cambodia the e-learning bus tours through villages to facilitate wider access to ICTs. It is reaching orphans, street children, out-of-school youth and other disadvantaged people and empowers them by using ICT equipment (Milleisea, 2005).

Self-Determined Learning

A student who is able to determine his/her own learning path and speed will benefit more as someone who has been forced to do a specific thing. It is like in real life. Things we like to do will be finished more successful than those we don't like.

Drop out prevention caused by students' attitude towards schooling has to start here (OECD, Education At A Glance 2004) (OECD, Student Engagement at School: A Sense of Belonging and Participation, 2003).

Two factors are playing a key role:

1. a sense of belonging within the school community.
2. and participation in school life.

Also Quality of Education is Very Important

Students are very often bored by the school and its "static" personal, which pull out their lesson plans hey made after they've finished their universal studies. Most likely only an individual curriculum for each student will reflect their specific needs. This requires active

teachers to fulfill this additional workload. Regular school curricula are made for an average student which causes bigger conflicts for those not been average. Also they need to be able to self-determine their complete learning process. To start a lifelong motivation for learning, learning itself must be incarnated by the student itself. It must be him/her who wants to learn and not another authority forcing them to learn.

Drop out prevention needs actually to start also in a regular school context giving students better opportunities to self-determine and self direct their own learning process.

I.e., In Montessori Schools students are learning in an prepared learning surrounding with no time or knowledge limitations. If you visit Montessori Classes you will realize, that the multi aged children in a group work on their individual theme/subject at the same time but within their own pace. The themes/subjects students' works are chosen by the student himself. The teacher isn't standing in front of the classroom but helping students individually like a coach.

Classrooms of a Montessori School don't look like sterile empty blue concrete boxes. They are filled with lots of stuff to be discovered by students of all ages. Each material in a classroom exists only once, which encourages students to interact socially with each other and it is developed as a self-learning material where students can check their own results (self-controlled material).

The Role of E-Learning

E-learning is predestined to enrich a self-determined learning environment with an open door to the global world of knowledge. It is also an ideal medium to reach people which suffer from illness, disability and even poorness.

Decentralized and mobilized IT-Learning Centers could provide rural areas and underprivileged students with an access to unlimited learning resources and qualified teachers, providing an IT-Infrastructure combined with qualified personal. Of course present lessons (e/b-learning) would help students to build up also better personal relationships to their schoolmates and teachers/coaches.

The initial cost of the IT-Infrastructure seems to be high, compared to a traditional school. Actually most of those costs can be reduces i.e. by:

1. using 1 server 20-50 thin clients.
2. Open source software.
3. Linux [Edubuntu (Ubuntu, 2008)].

Students will be able to learn from home using the internet. Dropouts don't need to be confronted with their "boring" school building or punishing teachers. 100 per cent physical abilities won't be a necessity for participating in lessons. Handicapped students could participate equally with non-handicapped using modern technology to communicate.

E-Learning will play a major role in future worlds. One small example:

LisAndi Home School provides international and Thai students with a prepared learning surrounding. Every student has access to internet using his own or a provided laptop. Students are learning in small mixed age groups, helping each other. They are using the biggest schoolbook of the world – the internet. It provides tons of multimedia lessons from all around the world. Students and their families schedule lessons individually. Often there is more intensive learning in House on rainy days, while on sunny dry day the students get scheduled for outdoor learning activities at the beaches, mangrove forest, or even sailboats. As long as students will have the possibility to access the internet or even their small private intranet of Laptops, they are able to study at any place. Wireless LAN and free hotspots as well as time boundaries aren't blocking the learning process. Several learning groups share a teacher, which means the teachers are travelling to the learning places ("schools") instead of students. This is also a big ecological factor and shows respect of natural resources.

Communicational skills get trained using IRC, Chat, VoIP and Videoconferencing with other students worldwide. Homework Assignments get is finished on time using Computers and TYPO3 as a centralized e-learning Intranet.

Each student has its own personal curriculum and he/she learns how to control the learning process and manage assignments by themselves. For several subjects LisAndi Home School is using prepared open source or freeware software solutions. But usually lessons will be designed using the material—video, flash, text, multilingual, audio ... content provided in the internet itself. It is one of the main tasks of a teacher to teach students how to use the internet for learning and providing them with qualified links.

Until now, all students were able to switch back to their normal school live in their home countries without any problems. Some even skipped one grade. Often students come to LisAndi Home School because the students had major difficulties in regular school settings.

Schools on the Go

Do we really need a school building? NO! Do we need teachers? NO! Two questions and an answer which lead to another question: Who is educating our children then? Actually our students get mostly educated outside the school, especially in high developed countries with lots of consuming potentials like TV, VSD DVD, Video-Games and other electronically toys. It is an illusion that teachers in western societies are still in control over those students. Actually they lost track. Unfortunately in many Asian systems the process seems towards the same problems like they already exist in western societies.

Schools on the Go can help to reduce lots of conflicts. A school on the Go is a temporary place of education for a specific periode of time, location and thematic. It can be anywhere. Teachers reside no more in a school building. Their offices can be anywhere, even at home. More important is, that teachers will be available for students' on-line and also for personal consultations. They need to be highly qualified in alternative educational methods (Montessori, Freinet, Summerhill, Petersen, Wild) and communicational skills. Teachers should coach their students' on their educational track.

Lessons and activities and complete lesson plans will be prepared on-line in a collaborative initiative, where students, parents and teachers work, plan and teach together. Family like integrative groups will lead students to experience cooperation and collaboration throughout generations in an early stage.

Exams and evaluations will take place individually after finishing specific tasks successfully. The goal is no more the unified student but therefore a unique student with its individual character, preparing children to live a successful life as global citizen in harmony and respect of natural resources.

Modern Communicational Technology—especially the internet—unlinks students from traditional schooling places and links them into a global worldwide learning space. From any place of the blue planet they are able to update their individual records.

Like e-learning "Schools on the Go" aren't fixed to a "hard coded" time schedule. Drop outs can easily be reintegrated into the learning process.

Project Learning

Project Learning as alternative to structured learning in subjects. Lessons will be categorized in projects. Lessons which will be organised in project units integrating multiple subjects under one theme make it much easier for drop outs to get reintegrated. They are not depending on one subject or teacher. All those lessons could be scheduled more individually.

In project-based learning, students work in teams to explore real-world problems and create presentations to share what they have learned. Drop outs can easier be reintegrated as their specific abilities can be taken in account. This learning approach has a bigger effect on students then traditional methods. They increase the self-direction and motivation of students. Deeper knowledge of the subject results improves research and problem solving skills. Students conduct research using a variety of sources, from the Internet to interviews with experts.

Project based learning prevents drop out and especially school absenteeism. Students who get actively involved in a learning process rather skip lessons or feel bored. It improves positively test scores and reduces disciplinary problems.

> Ask Seymour Papert, renowned expert on children and computing, why students are turned off by school, and he quickly offers an example:
>
> "We teach numbers, then algebra, then calculus, then physics. Wrong!" exclaims the Massachusetts Institute of Technology mathematician and pioneer in Artificial Intelligence. "Start with engineering and from that abstract out physics, and from that abstract out ideas of calculus, and eventually separate off pure mathematics. It is so much better to have the first-grade kid or kindergarten kid doing engineering and leave it to the older ones to do pure mathematics than to do it the other way around." (Curtis 2008)

> "In real life, we don't spend several hours at a time listening to authorities who know more than we do and who tell us exactly what to do and how to do it," she says. "We need to be able to ask questions of a person we're learning from. We need to be able to link what the person is telling us with what we already know. And we need to be able to bring what we already know and experiences we've had that are relevant to the topic to the front of our minds and say something about them." (Curtis 2008)

Computer Technology and e-learning combined with home-schooling and project based learning help to prevent dropout and help to reintegrate students into a lifelong learning and knowledge based society.

Mobility and new methods are asked for future educational tasks as well as open minded teachers who like to invent learning environments and empower students for the 21 Century.

REFERENCES

Bielick, Stacey, Kathryn Chandler, and Stephen P. Broughman. "Elementary and Secondary Education." *The Education Statistics Quaterly-Homeschooling in the United States,* Vol. 3 Issue 3, 1999.

Curtis, Diane. *In Start with the Pyramid: Real-World Problems Motivate Students.* 09 01, 2008. http://www.edutopia.org (accessed 09 01, 2008). div. "Vol. 21, No.1." *British Journal of Sociology of Education,* 2000.

Milleisea, Ellie. "UNESCO Bangkok Prepares for the World Information Summit." *UNESCO Bangkok.* 2005. http://www.unescobkk.org/index.php?id=3233 (accessed 09 01, 2008). OECD. *Education At a Glance.* OECD, 2004.

Pisa Studies. 2008. www.pisa.oecd.org (accessed 09 01, 2008).

OECD. *Student Engagement at School: A Sense of Belonging and Participation.* OECD, 2003.

Place, A Child's. *A Child's Place – Montessori Methode History.* 2008. http://www.a-childs-place.com/montessorimethodhistory.html (accessed 09 01, 2008).

Tomaševski, Katarina. "Globalizing What: Education as a Human Right or as a Traded Service?" *Indiana Journal of Global Legal Studies,* Winter Vol. 12(1), 2005: 2 fn.

Ubuntu. *Edubuntu.* 09 01, 2008. http://www.edubuntu.org/ (accessed 09 01, 2008).

UNICEF-ICDC. *Social Monitor Report.* p. 9, Florence: ICDC, 2004.

18

Attitude towards E-Learning among the Postgraduate Arts and Science Students

K. Thiyagu, India

Introduction

Communication is education and education is knowledge. This is an age of knowledge explosion and exploration. Rapid progress in computer technology has invaded the arena of education. Technology has had a significant effect on the education system for many years. In the classroom we have moved from the days of chalk and talk to the use of overhead projectors and more recently multimedia presentation techniques.

As we know, the teaching-learning technology has progressed from classroom lectures to seminars to videodiscs and CD-ROMS to web based training and wireless communication through various learning objects. Learning objects include CDs, electronic books, electronic journals; audiovisual aids etc. technology continues to move forward. The development in computer technology has resulted in e-learning. E-learning is considered a more effective way of teaching to a large group of students, thereby providing consistency in educational quality. Now the opportunities made available through e-learning are both significant and numerous. So that the investigator can select the topic "A study on attitude towards E-Learning among the postgraduate students of thanjavour district."

Statement of the Problem

An innovative application of computer in the teaching and learning process is e-learning. E-learning may be network-based, intranet-based or Internet-based, which includes text, video, audio, animation and virtual environments. E-learning provides faster learning at reduced costs, increased access to learning, and clear accountability for all participants in the learning process. A present study is entitled "A study on attitude towards E-Learning among the postgraduate students of thanjavour district."

Operational Definition of Key Terms

Attitude

Attitude presents individual feeling for or against something. In other words the degree of feeling of favorableness or unfavourableness towards some objects, person, groups, ideas is called attitude.

Attitude Towards E-learning

It is the attitude towards the uses of electronic material for educational and other information purposes to improve their knowledge.

Postgraduate Students

Those who are studying postgraduate course in Arts and Science colleges.

Objectives of the Study

1. To find out the level of postgraduate students' attitude towards e-learning.
2. To find out whether there is any significant difference in the mean scores of attitude towards e-learning among the postgraduate students with respect to their sex, age, subject, residence of the home and locality of the college.
3. To find out whether there is any significant difference in the mean scores of attitude towards e-learning among the postgraduate students with respect to their parents educational qualification and parents occupation.

Hypotheses of the Study

The hypotheses of the present study a formulated as follows:

1. Postgraduate students have favorable attitude towards e-learning.
2. There is no significant difference in attitude towards e-learning among the postgraduate students with respect to their sex, age, subject, residence of the home and locality of the college.

3. There is no significant difference in attitude towards e-learning among the postgraduate students with respect to their parent's educational qualification and parents occupation.

Method Selected for the Study

In the present study, the investigator employed the 'survey method'. Survey method is a method for collecting and analyzing data, obtained from large number of respondents representing a specific population collected through highly structured and detailed questionnaire or other techniques.

Selection and Construction of the Tool

The present study investigator used the self-prepared questionnaire as the tool for data collection of attitude towards e-learning as the subject content. The aim of the questionnaire that has been given is to know the attitude towards e-learning among the postgraduate students. There are totally 40 statements; each statement has been given a five-point rating scales strongly agree, agree, neutral, disagree, and strongly disagree. There is no time limit. Reliability and validity of the tool is to establish.

Population of the Study

In this study, all the postgraduate students of Arts and Science studying in at various colleges irrespective of the nature of management and other criteria but located in Thanjavour District, Tamil Nadu have been taken as the population for the study.

Sample Selected for the Study

A good sample must be a representative of the entire population. For this study, 250 samples has been collected using random sampling technique.

Limitations of the Study

- The present study was restricted to the students studying in arts and science college level at Educational District of Thanjavour alone.
- The study was restricted to students at the science, arts group only.
- Owing to the constraint of time and money only few variables could be included for this study.
- Owing to the constraint of time and money only few colleges could be included for this study.

Statistical Techniques Used

Statistical techniques serve the fundamental purpose of the description and inferential analysis. The following statistical techniques were used in the study:

- Mean
- Standard deviation.
- "T" test.

Analysis and Findings

Table-1

	N	*Mean*	*SD*
Whole Sample	250	74.35	8.6

In the above Table-1 the mean score 74.35 per cent is found to be greater than 50 per cent, and consequently, the hypothesis is to be accepted. There fore postgraduate students have favourable attitude towards e-learning.

Table-2

Variable	*Criteria*	*N*	*M*	*SD*	*SEd*	*M1~ M2*	*t*	*Remarks at 0.05*
Sex	Male	145	76.25	8.01	1.08	4.57	4.20*	Significant
	Female	105	71.61	8.76				
Age	<23	172	73.43	8.71	1.12	2.92	2.58*	Significant
	>=23	78	76.35	8.05				
Residence	Rural	188	74.86	8.75	1.19	2.08	1.73*	Not significant
	Urban	62	72.78	7.98				
Locality of the college	Urban	174	75.23	8.47	1.17	2.90	2.46*	Significant
	Rural	76	72.32	8.60				
Subject	Arts	110	75.06	8.82	1.14	1.28	1.11*	Not significant
	Science	140	73.78	7.79				
Parental educational qualification	School level	164	74.71	9.00	1.09	1.06	0.97*	Not significant
	College	86	73.65	7.78				
Parental occupation	Govt.	52	73.40	9.42	1.43	1.19	0.83*	Not significant
	Private	198	74.59	8.38				

The findings arrived from the present study are listed here under:

1. The postgraduate students have favourable attitude towards e-learning.
2. There is a significant difference between male and female students attitude towards e-learning. The male students have more favourable attitude towards e-learning than female students.
3. There is a significant difference between below 23 and above 23 age group of student's attitude towards e-learning. The above 23 age group of students have more favourable attitude towards e-learning then bellow 23 age group of students.
4. There is no significant difference between the arts and science student's attitude towards e-learning.
5. There is no significant difference between the rural and urban area students' attitude towards e-learning.
6. There is a significant difference in the attitude towards e-learning of postgraduate students' towards e-learning on the basis of the locality of the college. The urban area locality college students' have more favourable attitude towards e-learning than rural area locality college students.
7. There is no significant difference in the attitude of postgraduate students towards e-learning on the basis of their parents' educational qualifications and parental occupation.

Educational Implications of the Study

We are living in an information and knowledge-based society. The Internet has made an increasing and powerful impact upon every area and workplace like home, school, hospital, bank, research etc.; it has shown a great impact in the field of education.

Most of the teachers and teacher-educators do not have an open mind on the use of Internet in general as well as for teaching purpose. The teachers and teacher-educators should be motivated to get training in the use of Internet. It can be done with the use help of various types of workshops, which will develop in them a positive attitude towards Internet. Moreover, educational planners and administrators should be given proper orientation and practice in the use of Internet so that they can benefit from it.

One of the findings of the study shows that students have a favourable attitude towards e-learning. In this age of competition, students want to get the latest information not only in the field of academics but also in the field of jobs. So, the teachers and teacher-educators should motivate them to access different job opportunities.

Another findings show that there is no significant difference in the attitude of rural and urban area postgraduate students towards the e-learning. This finding indicates that locality of the home (rural & urban) does not have any effect on the attitudes of postgraduate students. So, more and more seminars, conferences and workshops should be arranged for the learners so that they can update their knowledge with the help of the Internet. Not only this, it will help them to happily accept the different challenges of life coming in their way. Another findings show that there is no significant difference between the students of different streams (arts and science). It indicates that students of every stream understand the importance of this modern facility, which helps them to explore various aspects in depth. In this way, the e-learning has become part and parcel of every one's life. Growth and development depends upon the frequent use of the Internet in every field.

Suggestions for Further Study

- For similar further studies can be conducted in UG college students, B.Ed teacher trainees, M.Ed teacher trainees etc.
- The present study is limited to Educational District of Thanjavour only. This can be conducted within a wider geographical area.
- This study may be extended to a large sample taking some more variables.

Conclusion

The emergence of new technological environment may revolutionize the teaching learning process. The role of the teacher will be different from the traditional classroom teaching. The teacher could be a manager, monitor, role model, counselor, facilitator and a social worker. Teaching methodology will shift from teacher-centered education to learner-centered education. Teacher's dominance will be replaced by the knowledge dominance. So students now learn through computer teacher, television teacher and Internet teacher. In future, another teacher who applies these technologies in the classrooms will replace a teacher who does not apply these technologies. The investigation end its findings will help educational experts, thinkers, teachers and all those who are interested in the field of education to focus their attention on the present problems. This findings and results are not the end of the problem, but just a beginning of the search for innovation. By applying these results, the quality of teaching learning process will improve.

REFERENCES

FERNANDO ALONSO (2005) " An Instructional Model for web-based e-learning education with a blended learning process approach", British Journal of Educational Technology, Vol. 36, No. 2, p. 217.

MOUNISSAMY, P and KALIAMMAL. A (2005) "Access of e-journals in the Institutions of Higher Technical Education through INDEST Consortium," University News, Vol. 42, No. 48, p. 13.

PREETI MAHAJAN (2004) "Technological Impact on Education: Prospects for India", University News, Vol. 42, No. 39, p. 8.

RAMES VERMA (2005) "e-learning Strategies in Teacher Education." University News, 45(18), April 2007. p. 11.

RACHNA RATHORE (2008) "Effective teaching through e-learning."
Edutracks. August 2007. Vol. 6. No. 12, p. 8.

SANJAYA MISHRA AND RAMES C. SHARMA (2005) "Development of e-learning in India," University News, Vol. 43, No. 11, p. 9.

VANDANA GUPTA (2008) "e-learning pedagogies New Approaches to Teaching and Assessment". Edu tracks. February 2008. Vol. 7, No. 6, p. 7.

BIBLIOGRAPHY

http://www.gurukulonline.com retrieved on 20.9.2007.

http://www.worldwidelearn.com retrieved on 20.10.2007.

http://www.learnframe.com retrieved on 28.10.2007.

e-learningguru.com/gloss.htm retrieved on 14.12.2007.

www.ict-waidmayr.at/e-glossary.com accessed on 8.1.2008.

www.bbk.ac.uk/ccs/elern/glossary.htm retrieved on 14.1.2007.

www.optasia.com/opguide/elearngloss.htm accessed on 24.1.2008.

19

Perception of Teachers towards the Utilization of Information and Communication Technology (ICT) in Teaching Introductory Technology in Secondary School in Delta State in Nigeria

Umunadi, E. Kennedy, Nigeria

Introduction

The present application of Information and Communication Technology (ICT) to all the activities of the world confirmed the fact that the use of ICT is becoming an indispensable tool for modern advancement in knowledge and skills. With the present day computerizations of activities in education, the focus is now on introduction of ICT in schools at all levels (Folayan and Ibrahim, 2000). The inclusion of ICT in our education and the National Policy on Education is highly necessary as we launch into the new millennium and targeting the millennium development goals. World Bank (2000) defined information technology as the integration of computer technology mainly in the form of internet and information management system. Cox (1999) pointed out that information and communication technology as well as all that is involved in gathering and processing information using modern communication technologies such as computers and other related equipment so that the services generated can reach all that desired reasonable cost and in good time to the overall benefit of mankind.

The training of youth in the schools aimed at equipping them with useful skills and at improving the knowledge in their desired areas of study at the end of training. To facilitate effective training of the youth to acquire knowledge and skills, it is the desire of the government to integrate ICT in our education systems. FRN (2004) government stated that necessary infrastructure and training for the integration of ICT in advancing knowledge and skills in Nigeria should commence immediately in our institutions. The federal

Government has set up a body known as National Information Technology Development Agency (NITDA) and the purpose according to (Enweremadu, 2001) of establishing this agency is to integrate internet into educational process, produce 500,000 professionals in the information technology network and employ the merging technology of satellite communication to provide access to the internet.

World Bank (2002) stated that when computer is properly integrated into a broader educational programme would help to improve the academic training for science and technology education and holds out the opportunity to revolutionize pedagogical methods and expand access to quality of education. There is need to brace up to the new challenges and systems of education through the development and use of ICT in junior secondary school which is at the level of acquisition of knowledge and skills in education (Okoli, 2005). Introductory technology is one of the pre-vocational subjects in the junior secondary school curriculum in Nigeria that can provide the youth with such training.

Information and Communication Technology

The following issues represent challenges to improving information and communication services:

- High cost of private provision of power.
- Lack of local manufacture or maintenance of information and telecommunication equipment and the lack of local software development capacity.
- Absence of effective and efficient postal communication.
- Inadequate human capacity and indigenous technical know how.

Policy thrust: Under NEEDS the government is committed to the following policy thrusts;

- Develop and sustain a modern information and communication technology to support private sector-driven growth and economic development and to improve the quality of life and reduce the level of poverty significantly.
- Improve access to internet connectivity, and raise the level of computer usage and literacy.
- Facilitate the development of a national multimedia super corridor, including provision of appropriate incentives for private sector involvement.

- Aggressively promote information and communications technology as an instrument of mass education, growth, and development.

Targets and strategies. NEEDS sets the following targets:

- Increase telephone density to one telephone per 25 people.
- Make telecommunication accessible to a wider range of Nigerians, regardless of where they live.
- Develop a national communications and telecommunication backbone, including a national multimedia super corridor.

NEEDS adopts the following strategies:

- Use a combination of fiscal and financial incentives to encourage private sector investment in service provision in the industry.
- Enforce intellectual property rights, and promote entrepreneurship, training, and partnerships.
- Pursue a local content policy in the manufacture of electrical and electronic equipment and communications and telecommunications equipment, including handsets, accessories, and components.
- Facilitate access to special financial support through NEXIM, the Bank of industry, SMEIES, and other institutions, for private sector-driven wireless telephone and internet connectivity development in rural areas.
- Foster an enabling environment for developing software capacity.
- Provide incentives to develop industrial parks in information communications technology.

Introductory Technology Subject in Junior Secondary School

The subject normally starts in the first year of the junior secondary courses. The introductory technology subject, which comprises of areas like woodwork, metalwork, technical drawing, electricity/ electronics and auto-mechanics, is taught in the urban and rural secondary schools in Delta State. The federal ministry of education prepared the curriculum which a solely for the teaching of the subject. While the award of certificates at the junior secondary school level in Delta State is usually carried out by the Delta State Ministry of Education. The examination is usually taken at the end of the first three years of secondary education. For effective implementation of introductory technology government shall provide necessary infrastructure and training for the integration of ICT in the school system in recognition of the role of ICT in advancing knowledge and skills in the modern world (FRN, 2004).

Statement of the Problem

The introductory technology is practical and activity oriented subject. It is because of the practical oriented activities that the subject requires integration of ICT in the teaching of the subject. The introductory technology core curriculum introduced in 1985, is implemented in secondary schools across the country disregarding the use of ICT. Okebukola (1995) pointed out that computer studies and computer-based education are now planned to be key elements in the implementation of the National Policy on Education, which started in the year 1988. It was noticed that computer based ICT education were not be integrated into the implementation programme of the secondary school in Nigeria. The success of the implementation of this curriculum will largely depend on different factors like the adequacy of equipment and effective utilization of ICT in the urban and rural secondary schools. Now there is no evidence relating to the adequacy ICT equipment and how effectively they are utilized in urban and rural secondary schools in Delta State for the successful implementation of the curriculum in this area of study.

White (1987) stated that in the past educational institutions, including secondary schools used computers only for administrative purpose such as pay roll, inventories, order forms, attendance records for the most part teachers and students' were not involved. This was because computers were very largely and far too costly to be placed in schools but now microcomputers are becoming common in the classrooms. Hence, the need arises to look at teacher perception and views towards the utilization of ICT in teaching introductory technology in secondary school.

Hypotheses

Ho_1: There is no significant difference in the mean of urban and rural junior secondary school students' with adequate information and communication technology equipment for teaching introductory subjects.

Ho_2: There is no significant difference in the utilization of urban and rural junior secondary information and communication technology equipment for teaching introductory subjects.

Research Questions

1. How adequate are the ICT equipment and facilities for teaching introductory technology subject in urban and rural secondary schools in Delta State.
2. How effective is ICT equipment utilized in teaching the introductory technology subject in urban and rural secondary schools in Delta State.

Purpose of the Study

The purpose of this study was to assess the adequacy and utilization of ICT equipment for teaching introductory technology in urban and rural secondary school in Delta state.

Specifically, the study is to:

- Verify the adequacy in terms of number of available ICT equipment in urban and rural secondary school in Delta State.
- Ascertain whether the available ICT equipment are properly utilized in teaching the introductory technology subject in the urban and rural secondary schools in Delta State.

Population

The target population for this study consists of 120 introductory technology teachers and 115 school principals in Delta State who are currently teaching and working respectively in the secondary school. There are 115 secondary schools in Delta State that are currently offering introductory technology subject, according to ministry of education, examination and standard branch, Asaba Delta State.

Sample

The researcher seeks to obtain a proportional sample that represented the schools and the staff of the chosen school. The sample of the study was selected using the stratified random sample design for the school. The proportional procedure was carried out by dividing the schools into strata of urban and rural schools then random sampling was carried out on each urban and rural stratum to select the sample size of the schools.

In this way 30 schools, 15 representing the urban and 15 representing the rural schools, was drawn proportionally from the population. In a like manner 60 introductory technology teachers,

2 teachers from each of the 30 schools and 30 principals, one principal in each of the 30 schools was randomly selected. In all the researcher have 30 secondary schools and 90 staff were involved in the study.

Validation of the Instrument

The researcher subjected items of the instrument to face validity by giving the initial pool of the instrument to research professionals and five experts in the field of industrial technical education from the department of vocational teacher education, University of Nigeria, Nsukka and three experts from the Department of Technical and Business Education, Delta State University, Abraka.

Method of Data Collection

Questionnaire was the major instrument of the study. The researcher personally administered the questionnaire to the respondents and also employed the assistance of experts in the field of industrial technical education especially introductory technology teachers to help administer the questionnaire in distance locations. Such teachers on behalf of the researcher distributed, collected and returned the completed questionnaire copies to the researcher. The reliability of instrument was established using a test retest reliability procedure. The Pearson's product-moment correlation coefficient was employed to correlate the scores. A coefficient of internal consistency (r = 55) was computed and result confirmed the questionnaire items appropriate for the study.

Method of Data Analysis

The raw scores obtained from the responses in each questionnaire items was computed and tabulated into frequency table. In analyzing the data collected the researcher used the mean, standard deviation and Z-test statistic. The mean and standard deviation was used assess the adequacy and use of ICT equipment for teaching introductory technology in schools raised in the research questions. While the Z-test statistics was used to test the hypotheses formulated for the study.

Results

Research Question 1

How adequate are the ICT equipment and facilities for teaching introductory technology subject in urban and rural secondary schools in Delta State?

Table-1
Mean Responses of Adequacy of ICT Equipment for Teaching Introductory Technology Subject in Urban and Rural Secondary Schools

Ranking of Items	*Area of Introductory Technology*	*Urban Schools* N = 42		*Rural Schools* N = 44		*Grand Mean*	*Remarks*
		XU	SDU	XR	SDR		
1.	Woodwork	2.70	0.42	2.16	0.33	2.43	Inadequate
2.	Technical drawing	2.24	0.26	2.32	0.28	2.28	Inadequate
3.	Metal work	2.18	0.31	2.02	0.28	2.10	Inadequate
4.	Electricity/ Electronics	1.98	0.12	1.81	0.22	1.89	Inadequate
5.	General workshop	1.88	0.08	1.61	0.17	1.75	Inadequate

Data presented in Table 1 shows that Woodwork received the mean score of 2.70 (urban) and 2.16 (rural). Technical drawing received the mean of 2.24 (urban) and 2.32 (rural). Metal work received the mean (X = 2.18) Urban and mean (X = 2.02) Rural. Electricity/Electronics received the mean of (1.96) urban and (1.81) rural. Then the general workshop received the mean (X = 1.88) urban and rural (1.61) . The ranking column showed the woodwork items as having the highest grand mean rating of (X = 2.43) followed closely by technical drawing items with rating of (X = 2.28) then followed by the metal workshop equipment with rating of (X = 2.10) while electricity electronics received the rating of (X = 1.89) and general workshop equipment received the lowest grand mean rating of (X = 1.75), as shown on the Table 1, none of the items has up to a grand mean rating of X = 3.50 adequacy. The remarks above are based on ranking of grand mean and cut-off point of 3.50 on a five-point scale.

Research Question 2

How effective are the available ICT equipment utilized in teaching the introductory technology subject in the urban and rural secondary schools in Delta State?

The data presented in Table 2 shows that Technical Drawing attracted the mean of 2.65 (urban) and 2.57 (rural). Woodwork equipment received the mean score of 2.76 (urban) and 2.06 (rural). Electricity/Electronics received (X = 2.25) urban and (Xr = 1.94) rural. Metalwork equipment received 2.35 and 1.82 mean of urban and rural respectively. General workshop equipment received the mean of (Xu = 2.25) in urban and the (Xr = 1.66) in rural.

Table-2
Mean Responses of Extent of Utilization of ICT Equipment for Teaching Introductory Technology Subject in Urban and Rural Secondary Schools

Ranking of Items	*Area of Introductory Technology*	*Urban Schools N = 42*		*Rural Schools N = 44*		*Grand Mean*	*Remarks*
		XU	SDU	XR	SDR		
1.	Technical drawing	2.65	0.25	2.57	0.31	2.61	Not utilized
2.	Woodwork	2.76	0.43	2.06	.28	2.41	Not utilized
3.	Electricity/ Electronics	2.25	0.21	1.94	0.71	2.10	Not utilized
4.	Metal work	2.35	0.36	1.82	0.16	2.09	Not utilized
5.	General workshop	2.25	0.32	1.66	0.14	1.96	Not utilized

The ranking column showed that the Technical Drawing equipment items as having the highest grand mean rating of (X = 2.61) followed closely by woodwork equipment items with rating of (X = 2.41) then followed by the Electricity/Electronics equipment items with rating of (X = 2.10) while metal work equipment items received the rating of (X = 2.09), as clearly shown on the Table 2, none of the equipment items has upto a grand mean rating of X = 3.50 on the rating scale. The remarks above are based on ranking of grand mean and cut-off point of 3.50 on a five-point scale.

Table-3
Summary of Z-test Analysis on Adequacy of ICT Equipment for Teaching Introductory Technology Subject

Location	*Mean X*	*SD*	*df*	*Z-test*	*Z-critical*	*Remarks*
Urban	2.19	0.32	84	3.24	1.98	Reject Ho_1
Rural	1.98	0.28				

Table 3, the figures represent mean and standard deviation of the mean responses of teachers obtained from the junior secondary schools. The calculated values fall in the rejection region. Formulated hypothesis, which states that there is no significant difference in the mean responses on the information and communication technology equipment for teaching urban and rural students' in Delta State was rejected, because the calculated value falls on the rejected region. Z-calculated = 3.24 which is greater than Z-critical = 1.96 at 0.05 level of significance with the degree of freedom *df* = 84. The statement implies that there is a significant difference in the mean responses of the urban and rural teachers on the adequacy of information and communication technology. The null hypothesis rejected and its alternative was accepted.

Table–4
Summary of Z-test Analysis on the Utilization of ICT Equipment for Teaching Introductory Technology Subject

Location	*Mean X*	*SD*	*df*	*Z-test*	*Z-critical*	*Remark*
Urban	2.45	0.24	84	6.82	1.98	Reject Ho_2.
Rural	2.01	0.35				

Table 4 represents the figures showing the mean and standard deviation of the mean responses on the utilization of information and communication technology by teachers of junior secondary schools. The calculated values fall in the rejection region. The null hypothesis is therefore rejected on the bases of the Z-calculated = 6.82 which is greater than the Z-critical = 1.98 at 0.05 level of significance with the degree of freedom of 84. The alternative hypothesis was then accepted which states that there is a significant difference in the responses of urban and rural teachers on the utilization of Information and Communication Technology (ICT) for teaching introductory technology in junior secondary school in Delta State.

Discussion of the Findings

The findings of this study were discussed in line with research questions and hypotheses formulated. The findings of the first question revealed that there is inadequate ICT equipment in terms of number required for teaching the subjects in the urban and rural secondary school in Delta State. In an effort to answer in details the research question one, the principals and introductory technology teachers were asked questions on the issues of adequacy of the ICT equipment and their responses tended more to uniformity. The teachers accepted that their schools were not supplied computers by the government.

Achuonye (2002) emphasized that ICT should be part and parcel of the teacher training programme so that the graduating teachers will in turn integrate them in their daily teaching process. It can be seen therefore that research question one which seek to ascertain whether ICT equipment in terms of number required for teaching the introductory technology subject in urban and rural secondary school has a negative responses against the adequate ICT equipment.

The findings of the research question two on how effective are the available ICT equipment for introductory technology subject are utilized in teaching the subject in urban and rural secondary schools in Delta state. The respondents pointed out that electricity light from the Power Holding Company of Nigeria (PHCN) is not always available or supplied to the urban and rural areas where it is needed for the teaching of introductory technology subject. The perception of teachers towards the utilization of ICT in teaching introductory technology subject was not encouraging, and the results shows that the teachers disagreed, most of the items were not utilized because they agreed that ICT is too cumbersome and the situation lead to the student graduates acquisition of theoretical knowledge in different areas of introductory technology subject.

Elliot (1998) stated that other part of information and communication technology is telecommunications. The technology used to bring about the communication of voice and data signals over some geographic distance. The term Information Technology (IT) assumes not only the presence of computing technology but also the organization of information systems into networks, through the application of telecommunication technology. Abindube (1999) pointed out that the use of computer requires acquisition of practical skills, which must be properly communicated to learners, and most of the teachers lack these skills and this leads to their low interest in computer utilization.

The hypothesis tested revealed that there is a significant difference in the mean responses of the urban and rural introductory technology teachers on the adequacy of information and communication technology equipment for teaching the subject. To actually make the picture clear and to address the issues, one may want to side and support the idea stated in the work that the urban schools with cyber café facilities in town has inadequate equipment than the rural schools counterpart with inadequate ICT equipment.

As rightly pointed out by the introductory technology teachers showed that effective implementation of introductory technology subject can also be made or achieved by urban and rural students' taught with adequate ICT equipment when made available. In addition, the government on the other hand is putting up workshops and installing the (ICT) equipment in various part of the country and institutions for the purpose of adequately equipping them with necessary equipment and introductory technology materials and facilities (Olorunselu, 1999).

The second hypothesis findings revealed that there is a significant difference in the mean responses on the utilization of information and communication technology equipment for the teaching of introductory technology subjects in urban and rural area in Delta State. There is a significant difference in the mean responses of urban and rural teachers on the use of ICT equipment for teaching introductory technology subject in JSS in Delta State. Ezekwe (1990) made his contribution towards the promotion of science (ICT) equipment utilization and technology management of materials in Nigeria. He stated that it is through the utilization of ICT and science materials that meaningful achievement can be attained in introductory technology subject. Agunbiade (2000) stated that practical aspect of technical skills forming has been generally ascribed to the global shortage of competent technologist in different areas. The failure of the strategies of (ICT) adopted in Nigeria to alleviate the problem is blamed on lack of equipment, computer facilities and time constraint.

Another possible reason of the discrepancy in the responses of the urban and rural introductory technology teachers is that the urban students' are exposed to private cyber café existing in towns. The respondents agreed that the (ICT) equipment were used by students' in urban and they are exposed to the use of computers in the cyber café in town than their rural school counterpart. This might account for the discrepancy between the responses of the urban and rural teachers on the utilization of ICT equipment. In this way the hypothesis (HO_2) testing and seeking to know whether there is a significant difference in the mean responses of urban and rural school teachers on the utilization for teaching introductory technology subject yielded alternative results to the stated hypothesis. In this regard, the findings revealed that there is a significant difference in the utilization of ICT equipment in urban and rural areas secondary school for teaching introductory technology subject.

Conclusion

It was the purpose of this study to find out whether there is adequate ICT equipment for teaching introductory technology and to ascertain how effective are the ICT equipment utilized in teaching the introductory technology subject in the urban and rural secondary schools in Delta State. It was as well as the purpose of this study that the findings of the research shall be used to suggest the possible solution to the Delta State Government where the (ICT) equipment are not available, inadequate and where available they are not properly and effectively utilized in teaching introductory technology in Delta State. The government from review of literature on the use of ICT for teaching introductory technology subject places high premium on this issues of the use of ICT on teaching introductory technology subject.

Among the major short falls observed from the investigation of the schools. It was discovered that there are schools where the ICT equipment are not existing at all and the teachers are not even literate in the field of ICT as a result the ICT equipment are not utilized in teaching the students' the subject in such schools. It is therefore hoped that other researchers, the government in the state as well as educational body and planners in their efforts to find out the necessary implementation problems of ICT equipment utilization for the teaching of introductory technology programme as well as to resolve such problems. The government should show enough interest and ways of providing a lasting solution to the inadequate, lack of ICT equipment for teaching introductory technology subject enumerated as the findings and utilize the findings on ICT for the growth, progress of ICT and utilization for teaching introductory technology subject.

Recommendation and Suggestions

1. The industries, non-governmental agencies and private enterprises should provide ICT, equipment, workshops, generators, steady power supply of electricity light for effective teaching and learning in secondary school in Nigeria.
2. Companies, government and other international organization should provide fund and take the responsibility of the provision of the ICT equipment and computer system programme to improve the poor state of instruction in secondary school.

3. The government should post minimum of three trained ICT experts and technical teachers to the secondary schools to enable them make effective use of the available ICT equipment and seek the advice from qualified teachers for effective implementation of the subjects.
4. Supervisors and inspectors from ministry of education should be sent to the JSS to ascertain the degree of utilization of the ICT equipment and ICT programmes and ICT provided by the government and other private organization.
5. Computers, equipment, tools gadgets provided by the government should be installed in different JSS to enable the teachers use ICT for teaching during the practical class. The rehabilitation of the secondary schools buildings and provision of ICT, equipment and facilities should be carried out to improve the learning standard.

REFERENCES

Abinbude, A. (1999). *Principles and Practice of Educational Technology.* Ibadan: International Publishers.

Achuonye K. (2000). Towards an effective integration of the information. Technology In to Teacher Education in Nigeria Eastern COESU. *Journal of Teacher Education 1*(1).

Agunbiade, W.A. (2002). Project-Venturing Technique: The key to mastering Electronic Technology. *Nigeria Association of Teachers of Technology* (NATT) pp. 209-213.

Cox, M. (1999). A world wide intellectual Network: Exploring Electronic Message for instruction. *Instruction science* 13, p. 257.

Enwermadu, G. (2001). Federal Government sets up Information Technology Development Agency. *This Day* July 29, p. 2.

Ezekwe, G.O. (1990). Press briefing by honourable minister of science and technology. *Quarterly Journal of the Federal Ministry of Education.* 3(4) 8-21

Federal Ministry of Education (1985). *Statistic of education in Nigeria: 1980-1984 statistic branch.* Lagos: NERDC limited.

Federal Republic of Nigeria (2004). *National Policy on Education* Lagos. NERDC Press.

Folayan, S.A. & Ibrahim, A.G. (2005). The relevance of computers to mathematics: Problems and Hindrances against the introduction of computers into Nigeria educational system. *13th Annual National Conference Nigeria Association of Teachers of Technology (NATT).* Technology education and the Universal Basic education in Nigeria, pp. 275-279.

Elliot, G. (1998). *Communication in Teaching in Principle and Method of Instruction in Technology Education.* Ikeja; Kitoms Academic and Industrial Publishers.

National Economic Empowerment and Development Strategy (NEEDS,2005). *National Planning Commission*. Abuja : Central Bank of Nigeria.

Okebukola, P.A. (1995). Effect of co-operative and competitive international technique in strengthening students performance in science class. *Science education Journal 61*(69) 501-508.

Okoli T.O. (2005) Perception of teachers towards the use of information and communication Technology ICT in teaching Agricultural Science in Primary Schools Nigerian *Journal of Teacher education and Teaching* 1(2) 188-194.

Olorunselu R.O. (1990). Introductory Technology: A mean toward industrialization of Nigeria. *Quarterly Journal of the Federal Ministry of Education* 3(4), 31-35.

White, C. (1987). Developing information processing skills through structure computing Research 3(1) 355.

20

Competency Requirements for Technology Enabled Teaching: A Framework

Dr. G. Venkatraman, India

Introduction

Teacher education has acquired greater importance in the 21st century in view of the rapid changes that are taking place in all walks of life. None can remain untouched by the techno-scientific explosions in communication and information dissemination (UNESCO, 1998). The challenge for the teachers is formidable and only the competent and enlightened teachers accomplish their tasks successfully in the present day context. The escalating developments in computer related technology have profound implications for the teaching profession, yet research continues to reveal a lack of appropriate competencies among groups of in-service teachers (Sharpe, 2002).

The very shape of the educational institutions and the class-rooms are changing. Computers are evolving into the present media, similar to books and note-pads and their integration and interaction in education will pose the most radical challenge to conventional formal education. The development of world wide websites and the availability of the Internet enable the user to scan and download documents in the areas of their interest thus shifting the focus from teacher-directed learning to self-motivate homemade learning. The implication of new technologies and their impact in the context of the teachers, their teaching and the preparation of teachers need to be examined carefully (Rajput and Walia, 2002).

Educational processes should take advantage of technological developments, including the application of ICT in teaching and learning, where appropriate; and train teachers to gain literacy in computer and internet uses. The Internet has enormous potential for teaching and learning and exists with huge amounts of information stored around the world. Successful integration of the Internet into teaching learning process can be accomplished gradually (Iridis).

Technology and Subject Matter Learning

According to Bansal (2007), teachers know a lot about how technology can support general pedagogy. For example, they may use:

- Grading programmes that allow students' and parents access to up-to-date information.
- Use PowerPoint or other presentation tools to provide visual supports for lectures.
- Use word processors to write texts or create handouts.

Teachers know much less about how technology can support subject matter learning and pedagogical content knowledge. Yet, it is this kind of activity that will potentially strengthen educational technology used in schools and colleges. Therefore connection between technology and subject matter and pedagogical content knowledge must be prioritized and privileged during learning experiences for teachers, which requires focused discussion of subject matter and instructional approaches to teaching that subject matter.

Issues in Teacher Training

In July 1999, Asia Pacific Economic Cooperation (APEC) conducted a workshop among nine countries in the Asia Pacific region to discuss issues and trends in ICT teacher training. The workshop discussed the following issues in Teacher Training:

- Access to technology,
- Connectivity,
- Software tools,
- Curriculum resources and teacher preparedness,
- Teachers' basic skills and knowledge in ICT, and
- Attitude towards ICT.

Initial Teacher Training Curriculum for the Use of ICT

The initial teacher training curriculum of the *Department of Education and Skills* of the United Kingdom gives a comprehensive listing of teacher competencies for ICT. These competencies are broadly categorized as follows:

- Effective teaching and assessment methods. The focus is on the methods and skills needed for the use of ICT in subject teaching. Opportunities are provided to practice the methods and skills for ICT use.
- Knowledge and understanding of, and competence with, ICT. This deals with capabilities to use the technologies. This includes the ability to handle hardware and software, and to manage technology in the classroom setting.

Competency

Simonton (2003), defines competency as any acquired skill or knowledge that constitutes an essential component for performance or achievement in a given domain. The concept recognizes that any given domain requires the acquisition of more than one component. For instance, achievement as an operatic composer presupposes competencies regarding melody, harmony, counterpoint, rhythm, form, orchestration, vocal writing, characterization, and dramatization. Accomplishments as a scientist presume competencies regarding literature search, hypothesis formation, research design, data collection, and coding, statistical or mathematical analysis, and professional communication. The acquisition of any given competency may be enhanced by both general and specific abilities, and those supportive abilities may be to a varying degree innate. A person who attains competency in all the components defining a creative domain is said to be competent in the corresponding domain. To be competent in a domain signifies a degree of skill and knowledge certainly higher than those of the novice, but not necessarily as high as a master.

Teacher Competency

Teacher competency is defined as knowledge, skill, ability, personal quality, experience or other characteristics that is applicable to the profession of teaching. A teacher is expected to possess a repertoire of competencies in order to be effective in a wide range of teacher jobs and the multifarious roles he is expected to play.

The framework for teacher competency is assumed to cover the knowledge and skills that teachers need to be effective. Performance in student teaching is assumed to be a good indicator or predictor of the ability of a prospective teacher to transfer his/her knowledge and skills into practice. According to McNamara (1992) there is a switch in emphasis from the process of teacher training to the focus upon competences.

Desired ICT Competencies for Teachers

The initial teacher training curriculum of the Department of Education, UK implies the desired ICT competencies for teachers, which could be the following:

- Positive attitude toward ICT understanding of the educational potential of ICT.
- Ability to use ICT effectively in the curriculum.
- Ability to manage ICT in the classroom.
- Ability to evaluate ICT use.
- Ability to ensure differentiation and progression.
- Technical capability.

Related Studies

IT Competencies for English Language Teachers

The article titled *"A Framework of Information Technology (IT) Competency for English Language Teachers in Malaysian Schools" by Norizan and Embi (2003)* of University Kebangsaan Malaysia (UKM), discusses the importance of English language teachers to be competent citizens, their readiness in using IT as a crucial factor in narrowing down the digital divide and information gap. The article presents a framework of IT competency for English language teachers in Malaysian schools based on a nation wide study conducted by Norizon (2003). It is proposed that this framework be referred to in preparing the new entrants to the teaching profession and as a guideline for professional development for the English language teachers in Malaysia.

The primary aim of this research is to identify the IT competencies that are important for the English language teachers in Malaysia. The identification of the competencies was done via document analysis, exploratory interview and from literature review. The identified competencies were collated and face validated by 2 educational experts and further validated for its content in a three round Delphi procedure with a panel of 15 experts.

The 98 competencies identified are summarized and classified into the following eight categories:

(i) Knowledge of computers and social impact.
(ii) Operational basics.

(iii) Basic Internet.
(iv) Computer assisted learning and teaching.
(v) Web-based learning and teaching.
(vi) Computer mediated communication.
(vii) Computer assisted management.
(viii) Assessment and evaluation.

In order to gauge the language teachers' IT competency a nationwide survey on the identified IT competencies was conducted. A total of 1123 in-service ESL teachers from 274 schools in West Malaysia responded to a self-report questionnaire.

ICT Trends in Educational Technology

Cabanatan has made a content analysis of key 1995 journals, dissertations, conferences and ERIC documents and identified trends in educational technology, as follows:

- Computers in schools.
- Networking.
- Television in the school.
- Advocacy for educational technology.
- New delivery systems for educational technology.
- Technology literacy for teachers.
- Educational technology and educational reform.

Educational Technology Trends

A 1997 study identified the following educational technology trends specific to teaching and learning:

- Tremendous increase in technology-related in-service teacher training.
- Strong trend toward the use of multimedia.
- Large numbers of professionally created multimedia titles on CD–ROM.
- Availability of powerful but user friendly authoring systems and multimedia tools.
- Students' acquiring multimedia skills earlier.
- Networking of computers for communication, research and remove collaboration.

Competencies for Technology Enabled Teaching

The author of this paper has identified the following 16 competencies based on *content analysis*. These competencies will help the teachers of all levels in the technology-enabled classroom teaching and in using the ICT tools like computers, internet etc., to enhance their subject matter knowledge.

The teachers of today will be able to:

1. Understand IT-based instructional pedagogy along with computer skills.
2. Plan and conduct a Computer Based Lesson (CBL).
3. Use ***computer as a tutor*** (This mode of instruction uses the computer to mimic the instructor in providing information, structuring learning activities, and in providing guidance and feedback).
4. Use ***computer as a cognitive tool*** or mind tool (here the computer becomes a mediating tool, facilitating the learners in the process of generating ideas and representing knowledge).
5. Use ***computer as a presentation tool.***
6. Understand and experience different roles of IT in teaching and learning.
7. Interpret new technology concepts through their professional knowledge that directs their daily teaching activities.
8. Act as 'technology integrationists' by using their general pedagogical knowledge, subject matter knowledge and pedagogical content knowledge to identify promising and innovative ways technology may be used to teach their subject area.
9. Learn about technology "in context" that is in the context of their subject mater and pedagogy.
10. Explore and identify for themselves the ways technology can serve their professional activities.
11. To choose tools appropriate for the tasks they needed to accomplish in the classroom.
12. To independently develop connections between technology and their professional knowledge.
13. To identify specific educational goals that can be supported by new technologies they have learned about in the field of teaching.
14. Work competently and independently with others in team in a technology-enabled environment.
15. Create E-learning materials using latest audio-visual equipment.

16. Use the enormous potential of the Internet for teaching and learning.

E-Learning Material Production: The Author's Experience

The author of the paper had an experience in producing E-learning material. He thinks it is worth mentioning as an instance for using such a technology-tool for material production. The author, using a machine called *Tegritycart* (product name) by Dell, recorded his presentation for a chapter of the course on 'Business Communication.' The E-learning material was produced in order to be sent as a CD to all students' of MCA programme offered by SASTRA University, Thanjavur, for the employees of Tata Consultancy Services. They are doing the course as an Off-campus programme. The CD contains Audio-Visual form of the presentations made by the teachers with the corresponding PowerPoint slides, the full text of the course material in word format and also e-books on the subject. For this type of material production the teacher has to get ready the text in word format and then make PowerPoint slides before he goes for recording.

The machine '*Tegritycart*' enables automatic capture of multimedia recordings and live webcasts from the convenience of the classroom or office, without having to use a traditional studio/ post-production process. The Tegrity WebLearner solution includes server software, instructor software and a browser-based viewing experience for students'. The Tegrity Cart can be easily set up in minutes in any room and shared among various instructors. Instructors just teach, and Tegrity® Instructor software does the rest, automatically converting natural teaching styles into effective multimedia e-learning with no production process or assistance. The incorporated Cintiq Interactive Pen Display enables the user to teach in a natural and familiar way, just like working and writing with a marker on overhead transparencies digitally.

The Significance of the Study

The study, though not a research one, is significant in the sense it talks about a very relevant issue in teacher training and education. Any tradesman or professional needs a set of competencies to perform his/her job to the expected level. A teacher of a present day environment is in a compulsion to use technology in the classroom. The Tamil Nadu Government is going to supply a TV and a VCD player shortly for all the Primary Schools in the state under the

Sarva Skisha Abiyan (SSA) Scheme. The schools will be supplied English Language Learning CDs meant for primary classes. The primary teachers are expected to use electronic equipment to play the CDs and are expected to tap the E-learning tool to teach the communication skills of the primary students'. This requires additional competencies. If such is the case even in the Government primary schools, one can imagine the use of technology in the secondary and higher educational level.

The author of this article believes that the set of 16 competencies given above which are identified by him based on the content analysis of the available literature on this field, will help acquire the necessary competencies for the teachers of today to perform better in the technology-enabled classroom situation. This topic has the potential of being taken up as a research study. The identified competencies are only a framework and are generic in nature. As a research study, specific competencies according to the subject and level of teaching can be identified and validated.

Conclusion

There is so much that a teacher has to learn to become competent in the use of ICT for teaching tasks. There is also the prospect of having to keep up with developments in technology. ICT teacher training should therefore be considered as a continuing process, with the need for continuing support. The initial training may take place as part of pre-service training, or it could be part of in-service training (Iridis).

Teachers must believe that the benefits of ICT for student improvement and teacher fulfillment have been proven through academically justified studies. The teacher training agencies must concentrate on providing competency-based training to the teachers to enable them in acquiring the technology competencies.

REFERENCES

1. Bansal, Harish. 2007. *Teacher Training Concepts*. New Delhi: APH Publishing Corporation.
2. Cabanatan, G. Priscilla. ICT Trends in Teacher Training Curricula: An Asia-Pacific Perspective. SEMEO INNOTECH.
3. Idris, Noraini. Comparative Studies on ICT Among Australia, Vietnam, India, Indonesia, and Malaysia. Malaysia: Faculty of Education, University of Malaya.

4. Rajput, J.S. and K. Walia. 2002. *Teacher Education in India.* New Delhi: Sterling Publishers Private Ltd.
5. Sharpe, D.B. 2002. *Optional Strategies for Developing Teacher Technology Competencies.* Computers in Education. Issue 3-6 December 2002.
6. Venkatraman, G. 2007. "Developing a Set of Competencies for Teachers of English in Engineering Colleges" (Unpublished Ph.D. thesis). Thanjavur: SASTRA University.

21

The Use of Computer Assisted Instruction (CAI) in Arabic Language Learning in Islamic Sciences University of Malaysia (USIM)

Waidah Ismail, Malaysia
Lubna Abd Rahman, Malaysia
Wan Azura Wan Ahmad, Malaysia

Introduction

ICT is one of the tools that are being used to support teaching and learning activities. The use of ICT in education in Malaysia has been increased due the support by the Ministry of Education. At present, the Malaysian Government has built many computers laboratories in primary and secondary schools to educate the students' from their young ages the importance of using ICT in learning process. The government also provided the same facilities to the university students' in this country. The use of ICT in Malaysian education today is not only limited to the sciences and engineering courses, but it also plays a role in other courses as well such as in language teaching and learning. Using ICT in language teaching and learning can change a dull learning situation to become more interesting, attractive and easier.

ICT in Malaysia

In Malaysia, the government has been emphasizing the importance of this technology since 1990's. In this country, the demand for ICT use has been increased from year to year as shown in the Table 2 below. It is clearly shown that there is improvement in terms of buying computers as personal computers among Malaysians from 1995 to 2001. Besides that, the use of internet among Malaysians has also increased tremendously from 1995 to 2001. This indicates that Malaysians are aware of the importance of ICT in their lives.

The growth of ICT users in this country has also increased over 50 per cent if compared to the last few years. This indicates that Malaysia is moving forward to utilize this new technology in all walks of

Table-1
The Use of Computers and Internet in Malaysia
([1] N.A. [2007] "ICT at a Glance Malaysia")[2]

Computers and the Internet	*1995*	*2001*	*2001*	*2001*
Personal computers per 1,000 people	37.3	126.1	19.1	84.7
Installed in education (thousands)	31.4	121.9	–	–
Internet				
Users (thousands)	40.0	6,500.0	50,901.8	27,607.4
Monthly off-peak access charges				
Service provider charge ($)	–	5.3	21.8	21.6
Telephone usage change ($)	–	0.24	0.24	0.42

lives, for example in business, communication, education and so forth. Malaysians are also aware of the ICT wide application and its contributions to their country. The use of ICT is indispensable in this era which is known as the era of globalization, the era that brings a competitive way of life; in politics, economics, education and others.

The application of ICT is very important in education. The Malaysian government, for example, has concentrated its effort to enhance the use of ICT in learning institutions including schools, colleges and universities. The Government of Malaysia views ICT as a tool to revolutionise learning, produce richer curricula, enhance pedagogy, empower learners and many more (Tian Belawati. n.d. "Malaysia: ICT use in education"). Thus, the government has introduced various initiatives to facilitate greater integration of ICT in order to enhance the effectiveness of education and training programmes. Schools with ICT enabled named "Smart schools" were established to introduce technology and deliver education in a better way. Now, most schools, including in the rural area, have been provided with computers. Besides that, campaigns like "*Celik IT*" (IT Literacy) were also carried out all over the country to expose the young generation on the importance of ICT in their lives, especially in education.

This shows that the Malaysian education system has been developed in line with the growth of ICT in this country. In order to achieve Vision 2020 as announced by the former Prime Minister, Tun Dr. Mahathir Mohammad, Malaysia is looking forward to produce experts in ICT and create new generation who are adept with new technologies.

Using CAI in Language Learning

Computer Assisted Instruction (CAI) id defined as the use of computer to provide course content instruction in the form of drill and practice, tutorials and simulations It is also known as Computer-Based Instruction (CBI) or Computer-Based Education (CBE) in the United States, or Computer-Assisted Learning (CAL) (A. Chambers J & W. Sprecher J, 1983). CAI is used especially to improve learning skills.

In Malaysia, the use of this technology in teaching second languages has been increasing from year to year especially in English language learning. As a matter of fact, technology is becoming a bigger part of in-class study when the use of CAI and other technologies are being supplemented in the learning process.

On the other hand, CAI in Arabic language learning is not being use widely. It is probably because it is difficult to find Arabic software related to education . In order to improve the learning of Arabic language in Islamic Sciences University of Malaysia (USIM), the students' are encouraged to serve the internet to search for relevant information in order to widen their knowledge and increase their Arabic vocabularies. Besides that, Arabic language lecturers have put their efforts to design curriculum that would relate Arabic language learning with the use of computer as tool of instruction in the class. Thus, they provide the students' some materials in form of CDs which contain Arabic texts and also books that contain questions related to the texts to be applied in the class. This new curriculum has been applied for one semester and the role of this paper is to investigate whether or not this curriculum is effective. In order to get the feedback from those students' regarding the application of CAI, questionnaires have been distributed to some of them. Below is the data analysis from the questionnaires.

Result

This research focused on four faculties which in second semester students' in USIM. There are around 100 respondents for this research. The outcomes of this study are as follow:

(a) Gender

The population on the gender of the male is 74 per cent and 26 per cent are female on the distribution of the questionnaire.

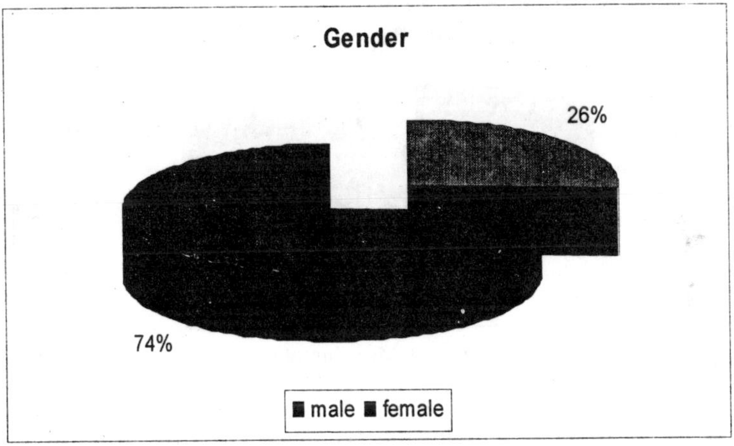

Figure 1: Gender

(b) Faculties

There are four faculties involved in answering the questionnaire which are Faculty Syariah and Law (31.8%), Faculty of Leadership and Management (5.9%), Faculty Economic and Muamalat (36.5%) and lastly Faculty of Major Languages Studies (25.9%).

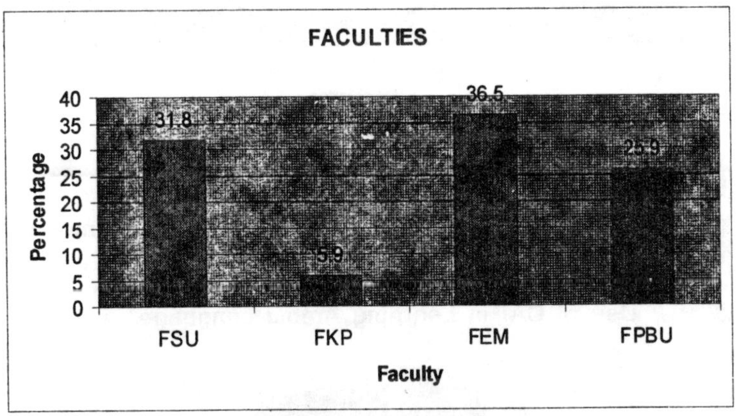

Figure 2: Faculties

(c) Meaning of CAI

Most of the students understand the meaning of CAI which is 79 per cent and 21 per cent did not understand the meaning of CAI.

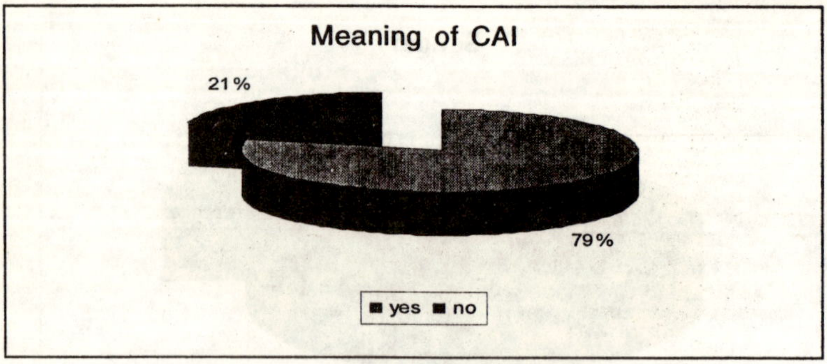

Figure 3: Meaning of CAI

(d) Source of knowing meaning of CAI

78.8 per cent students' knowing the meaning of CAI from the lecturer follows by friends which are 12.9 per cent and books (7.1%) and lastly internet which is 1.2 per cent.

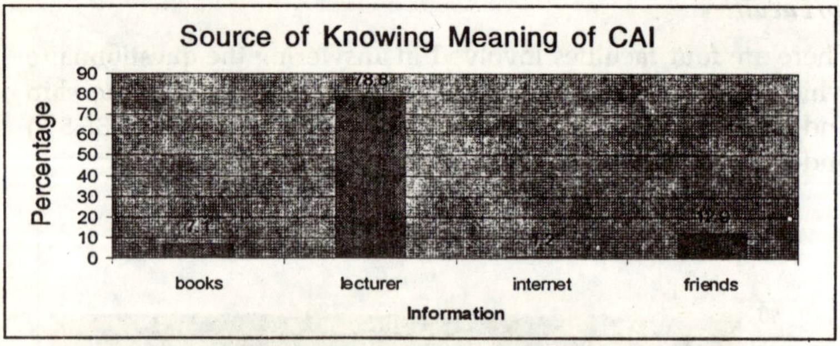

Figure 4: Source of Knowing Meaning cf CAI

(e) Use of CAI in learning Arabic language

94 per cent students' agreed in the use of CAI in the learning of Arabic language and 6 per cent disagree.

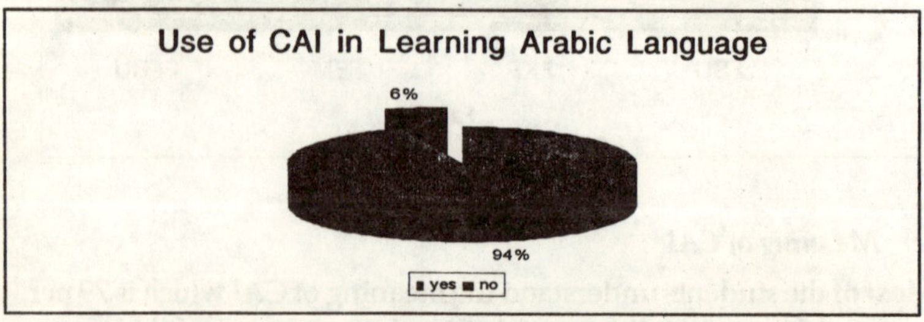

Figure 5: Use of CAI in Learning Arabic Language

(f) Interest in using CAI

96 per cent students have interest in using the CAI and others did not have interest at all.

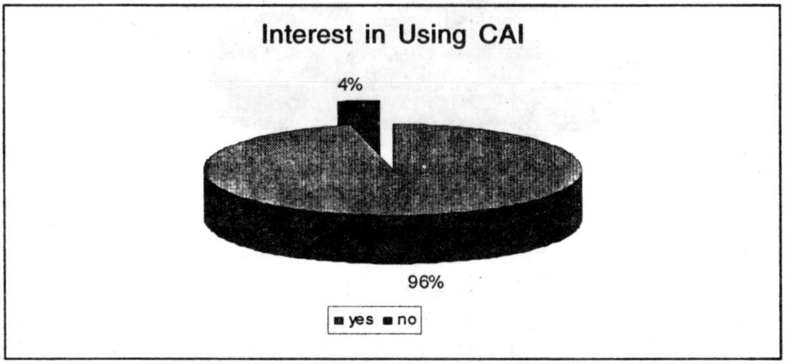

Figure 6: Interest in Using CAI

(g) Agree CAI can improve understanding Arabic language

96 per cent students' agree by using CAI can improve the understanding of Arabic language.

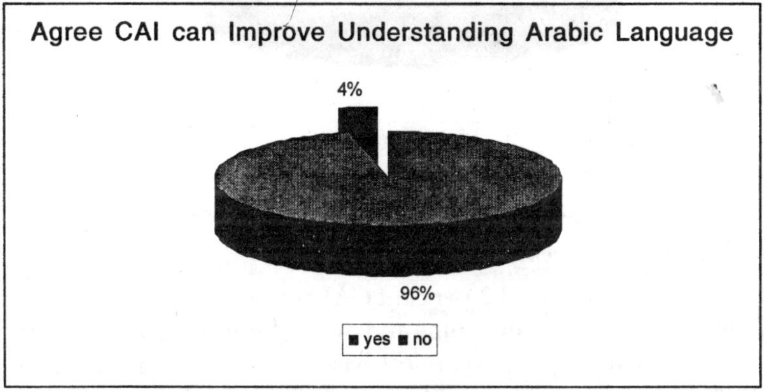

Figure 7: Agree CAI can Improve Understanding Arabic Language

(h) Using CAI develop increase skills

94 per cent students' agreed that using CAI can develop and increase the skills but only 6 per cent disagree.

(i) CAI enhance of independence

88 per cent students' prefer CAI can enhance study of the independence but 12 per cent students' disagree.

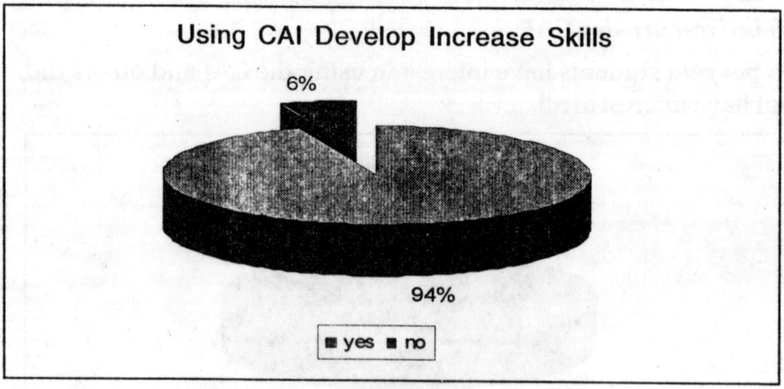

Figure 8: Using CAI Develop Increase Skills

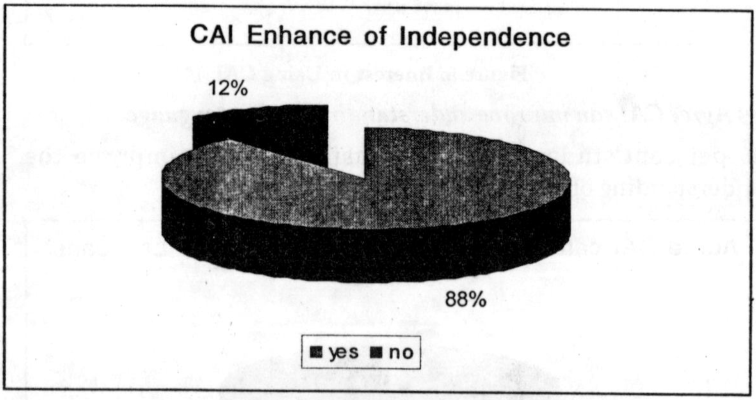

Figure 9: CAI Enhance of Independence

(j) Reason CAI is benefit to students

Students' agreed that 48.2 per cent CAI can be benefit due to they can learn at a distance, own time and own pace and also allow more practical, collaboration and project-based work than many form of classroom teaching. Secondly student (20%) facilities real-time communication with peers and tutors traditional correspondence course and lastly 15.3 per cent students' choose to form communication regardless of location.

(k) Preference of Studying Arabic

Most of the students' 75.3 per cent are preference studying Arabic language using ICT and only 24.7 per cent still preferred in traditional approach.

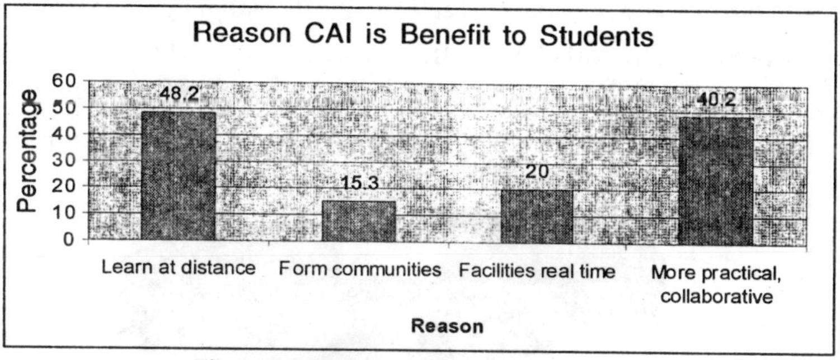

Figure 10: Reason CAI is Benefit to Students

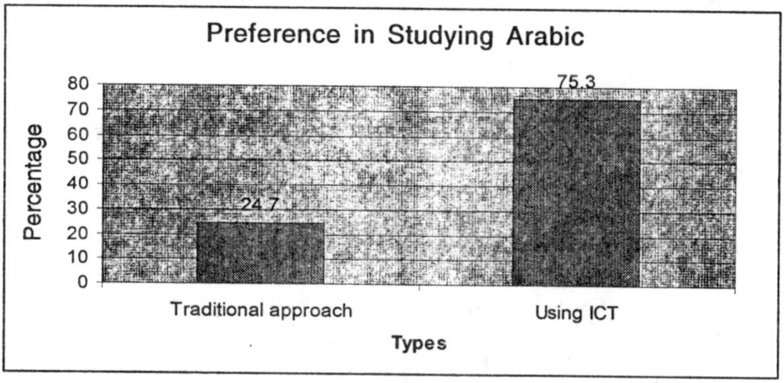

Figure 11: Preference in Studying Arabic

(l) Difficulties in using CAI at general

83 per cent students find difficulties in using CAI at general and 17 per cent disagree.

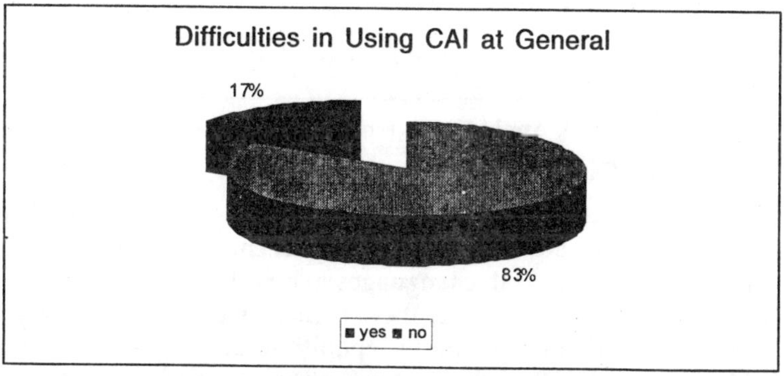

Figure 12: Difficulties in Using CAI at General

(m) Difficulties in using CAI to learn Arabic language in USIM

71 per cent students have difficulties in using CAI to learn Arabic language in USIM and 29 per cent disagree with the agreement.

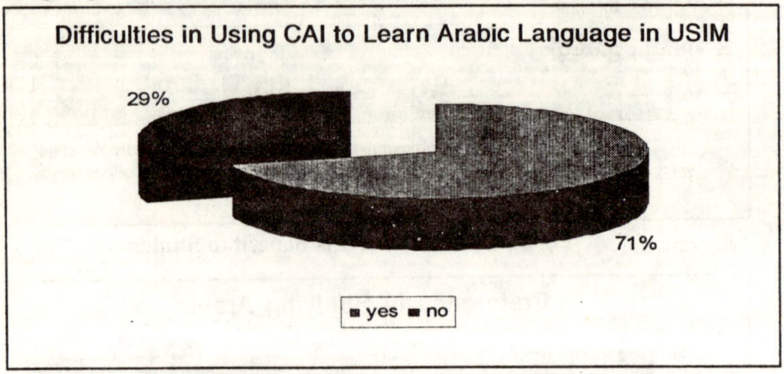

Figure 13: Difficulties in Using CAI to Learn Arabic Language in USIM

(n) Apply CAI in other Arabic subjects in USIM

Almost 96 per cent agree on applying CAI in other Arabic subjects in USIM and only 4 per cent disagree.

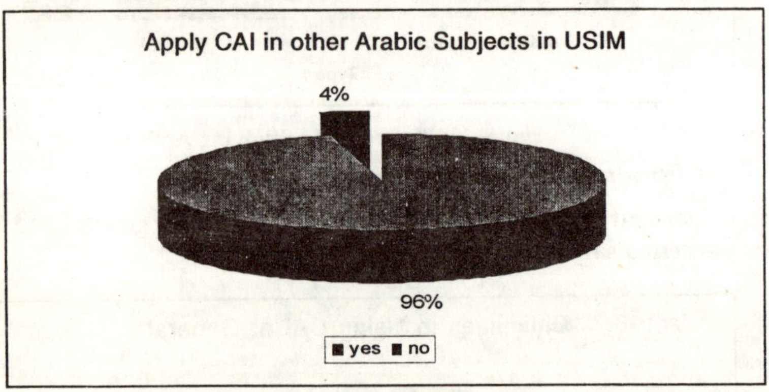

Figure 14: Apply CAI in other Arabic Subjects in USIM

Result and Discussion

Most of the respondets who took Arabic languages in the second semester are mostly female which 74 per cent. This show female has been dominating Arabic languages in USIM. We only choose four out of eight faculties because they are mainl y uses Arabic languages as their communication and preparation for their working in the Middle East. And the four selected faculties which are Faculty Syariah and Law (31.8%), Faculty of Leadership and Management (5.9%), Faculty Economic and Mualamat (38.5%) and Faculty of Major Languages Studies (25.9%).

79 per cent of students' understand the meaning of CAI and their main source are from their lecturers (78.8%). The students' understand the meaning of CAI based on the explanation from the lecturers during their subjects in the Arabic language using CAI. Other students' also have the initiative asking their friends (12%), books (7.1%) and also internet (1.2%). Only 21 per cent students' did not understand the meaning of CAI. But overall students' USIM understand the meaning of CAI.

94 per cent students' agreed in the use of CAI in the learning of Arabic language. Only 6 per cent disagree, this is because they are preferred using the traditional way which are face to face communication with their lecturers. And also the students' are not too anxious to explore the software tools provided by the lecturers. 96 per cent of students' have interested in using CAI, believe that they can improve their understanding of Arabic language and also develop their skills in communications. By using CAI will provide additional advantages in enhance their skills in confidents in speaking and understanding Arabic languages and also align with the ICT.

88 per cent agreed that CAI can enhance their study in the independences. The students' agreed (48.2%) that they can learn at a distance have their own time and own pace as long they have computers. And also they can have more practical, collaborative and project-based work between their friends rather than teaching from the lecturers. 12 per cent disagree on CAI of study independences, they stills need lectures or tutor to guide them if they have difficulties.

When we mention of CAI, students' will be using ICT as their learning tools. And 75.3 per cent agreed using ICT but 24.7 per cent agreed in the traditional approach. The reasons if they have difficulties they will ask their lecturers during the classes. But in USIM, we are teaching them traditional way as CAI is as additional tools to improve themselves.

83 per cent students' find difficulties in using CAI at general because they still not familiar with the software. This because their first time using the software and they did not have computer background. But 17 per cent disagreed that they have difficulties. 71

per cent students' have difficulties using CAI as learning Arabic languages in USIM because the software are too complicated and some of them did not understand the pronunciation in the software. USIM should consider to evaluate the use of Arabic software that can align with the students' needs and future requirement.

However, it is found that 29 per cent of the respondents did not have difficulties using CAI. They found it easier because they can repeat the sentence or the scene if they did not understand. They preferred exploring and learning by themselves. In fact, most respondents (96%) agreed that CAI should be implemented in other subjects in USIM as well .

From the above result, this research concluded that the use of CAI in Arabic language learning is better because it enhance positive attitudes among the students', besides improving their learning styles. The universities should set up some Arabic materials using this technology in order to improve teaching and learning process in the future.

Conclusion

The use of CAI in teaching and learning is a necessary nowadays. The traditional approach is the most famous technique used by many lecturers in teaching Arabic language in Malaysia. However, it is found that by using CAI, they can achieve the effectiveness in the language teaching because it can enhance the teaching activities, develop skills and improve students' understanding towards the subjects. In order to make sure that the use of CAI achieves the target in the Arabic language teaching and learning, USIM should restructure its module and provide software that could be utilised by the students'. Moreover, the university should also encourage the lecturers to use CAI in their teaching because it is one of the best ways to improve the students' skills.

REFERENCES

N.A. [2007] "ICT at a glance Malaysia" http://www.msc.com.my/xtras/fact_figures/Facts&Figures2.pdf . [Access Online : 23-02-2007]

A. Chambers J and W. Sprecher J. 1983. *Computer-Assisted Instruction: Its use in the classroom.* New Jersey: Prentice-Hall, Inc.

N.A. 2007 "ICT at a glance - Malaysia" ≤http://www.msc.com.my/xtras/fact_figures/Facts&Figures2.pdf≥

Tian Belawati. (n.d). "Malaysia: ICT use in education" <http://www.unescobkk.org/fileadmin/user_upload/ict/Metasurvey/MALAYSIA.PDF>

Contributors

Adebanjo, Adetayo Adekunle completed his M.Ed in 2000 in Educational Technology with computer-education at the University of Ibadan. Nigeria. He is currently a lecturer in Department of Curriculum Studies and Instructional Technology, Olabisi Onabanjo University, Ago-Iwoye, Ogun-State, Nigeria. He is also Doctoral Degree Student at University of Ibadan, Nigeria. He has a sizeable number of publications in learned journals both local and international with main research focus on ICT and education.

Andreas Becker received his 1st and 2nd State Exam. in Education, Geography, Music and Technology from Ph Ludwigsburg/ Germany in 1992 and in Mediation with emphasis on Family, School and Victim—Offender Mediations from University Hagen/Germany in 2003. Presently he is writing on his Masters Thesis in Mediation and working as a CEO/CIO Consultant for LisAndi Co. Ltd. Phuket/Thailand. He is Innovator and Visionaire and likes to solve problems others have already given up. Nothing is impossible! As Educator and Teacher developing new individual learning methods and learning materials for all age groups from Baby to Seniors is his favourite task. He is also creator of T3Pack Packages (t3pack.com) based on TYPO3 and other Open Source Solutions like to webempower people and institutions with an easy way to get their businesses and activities presented online. International Conferences like to listen to his unconventional talks about Global Classroom, Home-schooling, eLearning and education for All beside TYPO3 which is his major technical interest. As TYPO3 web developer he is setting up UNESCO Bangkok Website.

Dr. Austin Njiribeako Nosike is a leading scholar, editor and Senior Research Fellow at The Granada Management Institute. Since

1996, Dr. Nosike has been President of Development Africa Consortium (DAC) and Editor of African Journal of Development Studies. He is also a Visiting Fellow at Centre for Applied Development and Public Policy and maintains consulting status with the United Nations Economic Commission for Africa, Afro-Euro Centre for Development Studies and many other institutions. Dr Nosike has been a Consultant on human capacity building to the African Union Commission, Addis Ababa-Ethiopia. He has over 100 publications to his credit and received several awards, honours, grants as well as contributed to many research projects.

Arjun Das is currently pursuing his research as JRF under North Bengal University, West Bengal. He has done M.A. in English and Journalism & Mass Communication and also done PG Diploma in Public Relations Management. Recently he has visited Philippines to present his paper in International Conference organized by the Asian Congress for Media and Communication. He has in his credit several article published in book, magazine and newspapers and presented a good number of papers in International and National Conference and Seminars. He has more than six years work experience with print media.

Ayesha Mariam is a Lecturer in the faculty of Physics, Khadir Mohideen College, Adirampattinam, Thanjavur District, Tamil Nadu. She obtained her M.Sc., M.Phil in Alagappa University, Karaikkudi, B.Ed in Madurai Kamaraj University, Madurai and PGDCA in Madura College, Madurai and pursuing her Part-Time Ph.D. in Alagappa University Karaikkudi. She has been teaching Physics in Khadir Mohideen College for more than 8 years. Her field of specialization is *Preparation of Nano-materials for the applications of Gas Sensors.*

S.R. Balasundaram National Institute of Technology, Tiruchirappalli, India.

B. Ramadoss National Institute of Technology, Tiruchirappalli, India.

Dr. Cheng Chi Keung is currently an Assistant Professor in the School Partnership and Field Experience Office of the Hong Kong Institute of Education. He has received his B.Sc. degree in computer science from University of Portsmouth, M.A. degree in administration from Australia Catholic University, M.Ed. degree from Open University of Hong Kong, MSSc. in social science from the Chinese University of Hong Kong and EdD degree in education management from the University of Leicester. His research interests include educational management, lesson study, knowledge management and organizational learning in education. He has worked as a teacher trainer in many school development projects in Hong Kong.

Chrisantha Silva is B.Sc. Graduate from University of Sri Lanka. He also has Post-Graduate Diploma in Management. He obtained his professional qualifications in IT from the British Computer Society and he is a Chartered Member (CITP) of the British Computer Society. Chrisantha has more than 25 years experience in Information Technology in the areas of Software Development, IT Project Management and IT Consultancy. He is currently employed as Manager IT Business Systems at Sri Lankan Airlines the National carrier of Sri Lanka. He has published papers in IT magazines and has presented papers at several National and International IT Conferences.

Neeran Gautham is an M.B.A. in International Business having a doctorate in Marketing from Holland. He has rich and vast 26 years of experience in corporate and academics. He has been at apex positions in companies and is in academics for the last 12 years. He has specialised in marketing strategy and logistics. He is a member on International Form on Disaster Management, Netherlands and a fellow member in Institute of Futurology and Holistic Sciences, U.S.A. He has been associated with top B-Schools in Northern India. He has published many papers in National and International Journals. He has also presented papers in the international forum in Germany, Holland, Netherland, Poland and U.S.A.

H. Chittoo is Associate Professor in Development Management in the School of Public Sector Policy and Management. He has more than 15 years experience of lecturing, research and consultancy. He is member of several boards nationally. Dr. Chittoo has advised governments internationally on development issues and public sector reforms and has provided consultancy services to several international organizations. He is presently Head of School for the School of Public Sector Policy and Management in the University of Technology, Mauritius.

Rakesh Ramchurn, is a doctorate student at the University of Technology, he has done his M.Sc. Ebusiness at the University of Mauritius and BA (Hons) in Economics with management at Napier University. He has fourteen years experience in teaching businees studies in mauritius state colleges. He is a medal winner in manegerial economics.

Bhissum Nowbutsing is an academic at the University of Technology Mauritius since January 2005. He has previously served as Economist at the Ministry of Finance and Economic Development (Mauritius). Mr. Nowbutsing is registered for a Ph.D. jointly supervised by Prof. Oliver Morrissey (University of Nottingham) and Dr. H.B. Chittoo, the title of his Ph.D. is "FDI Impacts and FDI Incentives." His research interest includes: Public policy, poverty and poverty alleviation, development financing (i.e., foreign aid, FDI).

Mohun Prasadsing Odit is a lecturer at the University of Technology, Mauritius. His research interests are in Financial Leverage, Corporate Investment, and Earnings Management. He finished his bachelor degree of commerce in 1998 at the University of Pune, India. Furthermore he holds an MBA. Mr. Odit is member of several boards, for instance, he is a member on the accreditation programmes by the Tertiary Education Commission in Mauritius. At the University of Technology he acts as Programme Director for B.Sc. in Public Sector Financial Management, Master in Banking and Finance and also he is a Member of the School Board (SOPSPAM, UTM).

Sareetah Devi Motee is a research assistant working with Dr. H.B. Chittoo. She has completed her bachelor degree in Information Technology Enabled Services (ITES) and is now pursuing her postgraduate degree in Banking and Finance at the University of Technology Mauritius. She has written a paper "Training Needs Analysis in the BPO Sector in Mauritius" which was presented at the 6th IIDS Conference 2008.

A. Felix is a doctoral ICSSR Project Fellow at Periyar University, Salem. He was a principal in Thiagarajar College of Education, Valappady, Salem (Dt). He has completed M.Sc in Zoology with a specialization in Biotechnolgy from Loyola College,

Chennai, M.Phil in Zoology and a B.Ed at Achariya College of Education, Pondicherry, M.Ed and M.Phil at Educational Technology Department, Bharathidasan University, Trichy. He has presented more than 25 research papers in both National and International Conferences.

Jackie Yeoh Lay Kean, graduated with a degree in Bachelor of Education (TESL), Bachelor of Jurisprudence and Masters in English (MESL) conferred by the University of Malaya. She is an experienced trainer with more than six years of hands-on experience in the field of human resources specializing in training & development as well as in HR management. During her five and a half years tenure in Taylor's College, she has taught the South Australian Matriculation (SAM) programme, Cambridge A-Levels Programme, MUET, English proficiency courses for foreign students and various English for Specific courses, ESP for Law, ESP for Bio-Medical, ESP for Engineering and ESP for Hotel & Tourism, to name a few.

Malaya Kumar Nayak is an IT Manager at Optimity Ltd., London and Director of U-Com Software (P) Ltd., Orissa, India. He has over 12 years of IT management and IT infrastructure design experience, with a focus on networking and security systems. He has received his B.Sc. degree from Utkal University, Orissa and M.Sc. degree in Information and Communication Technology from Assumption University of Thailand. He has also a Professional Diploma in Network-Centered Computing. He is currently a Senior Member of the IEEE and IEEE Computer Society, USA and Senior Member of Computer Society of India. He is also a Chartered Member (CITP) of the British Computer Society, UK. He got awarded Chartered Engineer (CEng) from Engineering Council, UK and Certified IT Project Manager (CITPM) from IDA and Singapore Computer Society. He has published papers at several National and International IT/Management Conferences. His current research interests include project management and risk management.

Dr. Meenu Agrawal, specializes in the areas of Women Empowerment, Consumer Behaviour, Rural Development and Poverty Alleviation Related Issues. She has more than 25 years of teaching experience of UG and 17 years of PG classes and

18 years of research experience. She obtained Ph.D. Degree in Economics from Ch. Charan Singh University, Meerut in 1991. She has authored 1 book, co-authored 3 books and edited 6 books. She has conducted 5 National Seminars, sponsored by U.G.C. and I.C.S.S.R. Her over 35 research articles have been published in reputed Indian Magazines, Journals and Books. She has contributed and presented more than 52 papers in the different areas in National and International Seminars. Presently, Dr. Agrawal is Major Research Project Director, (Sponsored by University Grants Commission, New Delhi and Indian Institute of Public Administration, New Delhi), Reader and Head, Department of Economics, GDM Girls PG College, Modinagar.

Dr. Nadia Yusuf is the Programme Director and a faculty of Business Administration, at Millennium Institute of Technology and Management, Jeddah, Saudi Arabia, Associated to Lambton College, Canada. Her doctoral work is on *role* of Lead Bank in Financing Agricultural Sector in India, with Reference to Aligarh District. She has presented many papers in International Conferences and has published few papers and articles in journals and newspapers.

P.C. Okwelle, is a Lecturer, Faculty of Science and Technical Education, Rivers State University of Science and Technology, Port Harcourt, Nigeria.

Dr. Paul TJ James is a Senior Lecturer/Reader in the Graduate School, Bangkok University, Thailand. He holds a Ph.D. in Quality Management (Education) from Lincoln University, UK, and has four Masters degrees (M.Phil., MBA, M.Sc. and an MEng./BEng.) from various universities including Cambridge University. He has written 9 books on quality management and ICT in Education and also 3 children's books; and produced a variety of academic articles. His current research interests involve e-learning in universities in Thailand, ICT in Asian Schools and quality management in Asia.

Sachidanand Menon is currently employed as a Subject Matter Expert in the e-learning and publishing micro-vertical of HCL. He has worked as a journalist for over 6 years with leading publishing brands in the Indian publishing industry—The Times Group, The Hindu, The Indian Express and Deccan

Chronicle. This exposure has given him a chance to closely examine and understand social issues—education being an area of interest among them. With a Bachelors degree in computer science, he also has an appreciation for the role technology plays in the e-learning space. Taking a break from journalism he pursued a full-time management degree in marketing communications. Sachidanand did his Bachelors in Science (Computers) and also holds an MBA in marketing communications.

Swaraj Chakraborty received his Bachelors in Engineering (Electrical) from the University of Burdwan, West Bengal, India in the year 2004 and his MBA in 'Marketing' from the West Bengal University of Technology, West Bengal, India in the year 2007. Presently he is working as a Business Analyst in the e-learning and publishing micro-vertical of HCL Technologies. e-learning being his key area of work, he understands the processes and technologies in this area in a holistic way and is researching in this area to develop better solutions around the e-learning space.

Dr. Shobana Nelasco, is a reader in Economics of Fatima College, Maryland, Madurai, India, working for twenty years, is a recipient of *Best Teacher in Economics Award* from Malcolm Adiseshiah Trust, *Young Economist Award* form Association of Economist of Tamil Nadu and *Lion's International Award.* She has done researches in the area of 'External debt of Asian Developing Countries', 'Women Empowerment' and in issues of developing countries. Her academic background includes M.A., M.B.A., M.Phil. with distinction, Diploma in Computer Application and Doctorate in Economics. At present pursuing Post-Doctoral work and guiding doctoral scholars in Management and Economics. As the Head of U.G. Economics Department, Fatima College (2005-06), she introduced drastic changes in teaching, learning and evaluation practices. She has conducted 11 workshops and training programmes. She has published many papers in International Journals and in National Journals. She has presented papers in 18 International Conferences and in 30 National Conferences. (www.shobananelasco.wetpaint.com)

K. Thiyagu is a lecturer in mathematics education at the Dr. Sivanthi Aditanar College of Education. At present he is preparing his

Ph.D thesis in Educational Technology, at Bharathidasan University, Tamil Nadu, India. His research is related with e-learning modules. He had begun his professional career in 2005, and he has experience in the teaching and in research. His main interest is in educational technology and in the application of new methodologies in teaching – learning the mathematics.

Umunadi E. Kennedy is a Lecturer in Vocational and Technical Education at the Faculty of Education, Delta State University, Abraka, Nigeria.

Dr. G. Venkatraman is working for SASTRA University, Thanjavur, India as Assistant Professor of English in the School of Humanities and Sciences. He has got more than two decades of experience in English language teaching. He is handling courses like Technical Communication, Business Communication and HR Skills for B.E./B.Tech., M.B.A., and M.C.A. Programmes. He has worked on "*Developing a Set of Competencies for Teachers of English in Engineering Colleges*" for his Ph.D. programme. He has 4 Journal Articles and 20 Conference Presentations to his credit, one of which was at an International Conference in Malaysia in November 2005. He has acted as resource person for many teacher training programmes. He is the member of the editorial board of *ITIHAS* – the quarterly Newsletter of SASTRA University. His areas of interest include English Language Teaching, Technical Communication, Teacher Competency, Indian Culture and Ethics. He is currently authoring a book titled "A Monograph on Teacher Competency."

Waidah Ismail is a lecturer in the Faculty of Sciences and Technology, Islamic Sciences University of Malaysia (USIM), Bandar Baru Nilai, Negeri Sembilan, West Malaysia. At present, She is pursuing her Ph.D in University of Brunel, United Kingdom. She finished her bachelor in IT in Liverpool. She received her diploma and master degrees in the same field from MARA Institute of Technology.

Lubna Abd Rahman is a lecturer in Islamic Sciences University of Malaysia (USIM). She is currently teaching Arabic courses in the Faculty of Major Languages. She has bachelor and master degrees from International Islamic University Malaysia (IIUM) in Arabic linguistics. Her current area of research interests includes Arabic syntax, linguistics, translation and Arabic for Special Purposes (ASP).

Wan Azura Wan Ahmad has a bachelor degree from University of Al al-Bayt, Jordan and a master degree in Arabic language and literature from Universiti Kebangsaan Malaysia (UKM). Her research interests include teaching Arabic as second language and translation. She is currently a lecturer in Islamic Sciences University of Malaysia (USIM), teaching Arabic courses in the Faculty of Major Languages.

Index